Whitley Stokes

Remarks on the Celtic additions to Curtius' Greek Etymology

Whitley Stokes

Remarks on the Celtic additions to Curtius' Greek Etymology

ISBN/EAN: 9783337125158

Printed in Europe, USA, Canada, Australia, Japan

Cover: Foto ©ninafisch / pixelio.de

More available books at **www.hansebooks.com**

REMARKS

ON

THE CELTIC ADDITIONS

TO

CURTIUS' *GREEK ETYMOLOGY,*

AND ON

THE CELTIC COMPARISONS

IN

BOPP'S *COMPARATIVE GRAMMAR,*

WITH NOTES ON SOME RECENT IRISH PUBLICATIONS.

BY

WHITLEY STOKES.

"Why, the healthy progress of science depends on antagonism: it is by the flails of disputation that the truth is threshed out."
The Ibis, July 1874, p. 270.

CALCUTTA : 1875.

REMARKS

ON

THE CELTIC ADDITIONS

TO

CURTIUS' *GREEK ETYMOLOGY*,

AND ON

THE CELTIC COMPARISONS

IN

BOPP'S *COMPARATIVE GRAMMAR*,

WITH NOTES ON SOME RECENT IRISH PUBLICATIONS.

BY

WHITLEY STOKES.

"Why, the healthy progress of science depends on antagonism: it is by the flails of disputation that the truth is threshed out."
The Ibis, July 1874, p. 276.

CALCUTTA : 1875.

CONTENTS.

	Page.
On the Celtic Additions to Curtius' *Greek Etymology*	1
Preliminary	1
Corrigenda	2—5
Addenda	6—42
Notanda	42—46
On the Celtic Comparisons in Bopp's *Comparative Grammar*	47—53
Appendix A.—Mr. Crowe's publications	54—62
Appendix B.—Facsimiles of Neo-Celtic Texts	62—64
Appendix C.—Mr. Hennessy's paper on the Irish Goddess of War	65—66
Appendix D.—*Goidelica*, second edition	67—72
Appendix E.—Additional Old-British Glosses	72
Appendix F.—Corrigenda to the Old-British Glosses published by Zeuss	72—73
Appendix G.—Irish Glosses in Parker, No. 279	73
Appendix H.—O'Curry's *Manners and Customs of the Ancient Irish*	73—75
Mr. Sullivan's Glossarial Index	76—82
Addenda	82—85
Index	86
Indices Verborum	90—97

LIST OF ABBREVIATIONS.

A.S. Anglo-Saxon.
Beitr. *Beiträge zur vergleichenden sprachforschung*, vols. i—viii.
B.M. *Beunans Meriasek*, a Cornish Drama, London, 1872.
Br. Breton.
Brocc. h. *Broccán's hymn*, printed in *Goidelica*, pp. 137—140.
Cath. *The Catholicon of Lagadeuc*, ed. Le Men.
Colm. h. *Colmán's hymn*, printed in *Goidelica*, pp. 121—123.
Corm. *Cormac's Glossary*, printed in *Three Irish Glossaries*, London, 1862.
Corm. Tr. *Cormac's Glossary*, translated by O'Donovan, Calcutta, 1868.
Fél. *Félire Oengusso*, in *Lebar Brecc*, pp. 75—106.
Fiacc's h. *Fiacc's hymn*, printed in *Goidelica*, pp. 126—128.
Fick. *Vergleichendes Wörterbuch der indogermanischen sprachen*, 1870.
Glück KN. Glück's *Die bei Caius Julius Cæsar vorkommenden keltischen namen*, München, 1857.
Goidel. *Goidelica*, London, Trübner & Co., 1872.
H. 2. 16.
H. 3. 18. } MSS. in the library of Trinity College, Dublin.
Ir. Gl. *Irish Glosses*, Dublin, 1860.
Juv. *Codex Juvenci Cantabrigiensis*, Beitr. iv. 385, vii. 410.
LB. *Lebar Brecc*, a 15th century MS. in the library of the Royal Irish Academy.
LH. *Liber Hymnorum*, an 11th century MS. in the library of Trinity College, Dublin.
Lhuyd AB. Lhuyd's *Archæologia Britannica*, 1707.
Lib. Arm. *Liber Armachanus*, a 9th century MS. in the library of Trinity College, Dublin.
Lith. Lithuanian.
LL. *Book of Leinster*, a 12th century MS. in the library of Trinity College, Dublin.
LU. *Lebar na huidre*, a 12th century MS. in the library of the Royal Irish Academy.
M.Br. Middle-Breton.
Ml. *Codex Mediolanensis*, Bibl. Ambros., C. 301.
NHG. Modern High German.
O'Cl. *O'Clery's Glossary*, Louvain, 1643.
O'Dav. *O'Davoren's Glossary*, printed in *Three Irish Glossaries*, pp. 47—121.
O'Don. Gr. O'Donovan's *Grammar of the Irish Language*, Dublin, 1845.
O'Don. Supp. O'Donovan's *Supplement to O'Reilly's Dictionary*.
OHG. Old High German. O.Ir. Old-Irish. O.N. Old-Norse.
O'R. O'Reilly's *Irish-English Dictionary*, 1821.
O.Sax. Old-Saxon. O.W. Old-Welsh.
P. *The Passion*, a Middle-Cornish poem, Asher, Berlin, 1862.
Rel. Celt. *Relique Celtiche*, ed. Nigra, 1872.
Rev. Celt. *Revue Celtique*, ed. Gaidoz.
Sg. *Prisciani Codex Sancti Galli*, in Z. and Rel. Celt.
SM. *Senchas Mór*, vol. i, Dublin, 1865; vol. ii, Dublin, 1869; vol. iii, Dublin, 1873.
South. The Southampton Psalter, *Goidelica*, pp. 58—60.
Tur. *The Turin Glosses*, Goidel., pp. 3—13.
W. Welsh.
Z. Zeuss' *Grammatica Celtica*, ed. Ebel, 1871.

I.

ON THE CELTIC ADDITIONS TO CURTIUS' GREEK ETYMOLOGY*.

WHILE reading the additions made by Professor Windisch to Curtius' famous book, Plato's epigram has often sounded through my brain:—

Ἀστὴρ πρὶν μὲν ἔλαμπες ἐνὶ ζωοῖσιν Ἑῷος,
Νῦν δὲ θανὼν λάμπεις Ἕσπερος ἐν φθιμένοις.

For here the young scholar, already renowned as an Orientalist, has left the East for a time, and re-appeared, a veritable Hesperos, among the dead or dying languages of the Celt. Only, thank God, the 'θανὼν' is inapplicable, for Windisch has a long life of happy and useful activity before him. Curtius is indeed to be congratulated on having secured the aid of a linguist who has not only been trained in the best school of the new philology, but having also mastered the Grammatica Celtica, has worked at the Dublin MSS., and thus gained a considerable knowledge of Old-Irish,—the Gothic (as Schleicher called it) of the Celtic family of speech. How excellent a recruit the little band of Celtic scholars has obtained in Windisch may be seen from his review of Fick's Wörterbuch in Kuhn's Zeitschrift xxi, from his recent article in the Beiträge viii. on the loss and upgrowth of p in Irish and Welsh, from his comparisons in Curtius' book of Ir. *cruaid, comdiu, dia* for *dés* = δείξει, *fual, máo*, and *olann*, and from the caution and judgment which his work almost invariably displays. It is to be regretted that Windisch has not yet made thorough studies of the British languages; for in the preservation of initial y, and the treatment of the combinations tn, nt, ks, sv, they stand on a higher level than the very oldest Irish; while their regular mode of dealing with the diphthongs ai and oi, with vowel-flanked c, g, t, and d in anlaut and inlaut, with cc, tt, and pp, with the combination sp in anlaut and the combinations dv, rv, lv in auslaut, often throws valuable lights on the primeval form of Celtic words. Had Windisch, for instance, remembered the British forms corresponding with the Irish *teg* (τέγος), *tech*, he would never have doubted (Grundzüge No. 155) that the *ch* of *tech* (τέγος) is the representative (*vertreter*) of infected g. Had he borne in mind that Modern Welsh *dd* invariably represents an Old-Celtic D, that Modern Welsh *d* between vowels invariably represents a primeval T, he would not have confused, as he has done at No. 635, the derivatives from an Old-Celtic root ending in D (BAD ex GVADH, whence Ir. *bádud* 'mergere,' W. *boddi*, i. e. *bodhi*, Bret. *beuziff*) with those from a root ending in T,—BHAT (Ir. *báth* 'sea,' *baithis* 'baptism,' O.W. *betid* now *bedydd*, Br. *badez*: cf. O.N. *bath*, A.S. *bädh*, Eng. *bath*),—and then added to these Celtic vocables the loanword

---

* Grundzüge der Griechischen Etymologie von Georg Curtius. Vierte durch vergleichungen aus den keltischen sprachen von Ernst Windisch erweiterte auflage. Leipzig, 1873.

baitsim (from *baptizo*), O.Ir. *baitzimm* (*baitzis-i* 'baptizavit eum,' Goidel^c. 87).
Had he, lastly, been familiar with the following Welsh words:—
  pall 'defectus': cf. OHG. *fal*, gen. *falles*, Lith. *pùlti* 'to fall':
  pelechi (gl. clavæ): cf. Gr. πέλεκκον, Skr. *paraçu :*
  pell 'procul,' 'remotus': cf. περαῖος, Skr. *para :*
  pêr, peraidd 'dulcis': cf. Lat. *pirum :*
  perchu 'venerari,' *perchenog* 'possessor': cf. Lith. *perkù* '1 buy,' *prēkis* 'price':^a
  poues 'quies': cf. παύω, παύομαι, Z. 1053:
  prid 'carus': cf. Skr. *prt* (priṇâmi), Goth. *frijôn :*
  pryder 'cura': cf. Lith. *prota-s*, Goth. *frathi* νόημα :
  prydu 'canere': cf. Lat. *inter-pretor :*
  picyo 'ferire': cf. παίω, Lat. *pavio :* to which add—
  Corn. *pals*, Br. *paot* 'beaucoup,' 'plusieurs': root PAR, No. 375,
he would hardly have formed, much less published, his theory (Grundzüge, x) that Indo-Germanic *p* has never been kept in Celtic.

What I have here to say may be conveniently arranged under three heads. First, I shall point out the few other errors into which (as seems to me) Windisch has fallen. Secondly, I shall mention certain words and forms which he appears to have overlooked, and which may with advantage be placed under one or other of the 664 Numbers into which the bulk of Curtius' work is now divided. Lastly, I shall notice a few of the Greek words which Curtius has omitted, but which have their cognates in the Celtic languages, and may, therefore, deserve to be dealt with in a book intended not merely for classical students, but also for all comparative philologists.

I.—CORRIGENDA.

First of all, on behalf of sound philology, I must protest against the use of O'Reilly's dictionary for scientific purposes. The book is quite untrustworthy: it swarms with forgeries and blunders; and its only value lies in the extracts which it contains from O'Clery and other old glossarists, whose explanations O'Reilly often misunderstands. Yet from this polluted source Windisch takes at No. 8 *art*[b] 'bear'; at No. 54 *capat* 'head'; at No. 258 *duad* 'toil'; at No. 302 *aidhe* 'house' (a blunder for *aicde*); at No. 411 *bar* 'getreide'; at No. 543 *leon, leoghan* 'lion.' It is to be hoped that these figments will be expunged from the next edition of Curtius' book. So, at No. 68 Windisch should not have cited Mr. Crowe's *celt* 'hair.' Windisch was long enough in Ireland to learn that certain self-styled Irish scholars are like some of the Paṇḍits here in India, able to produce any word for any meaning, and any meaning for any word[c]. *Celt* (anglicised *kilt*) means 'vestis' according to Cormac (so O'Clery: *cealt* .i. *édach*), and belongs to *celare* and other words noticed at No. 30. In the passage referred to by Mr. Crowe (*issed ētach fil impu celt asas tréu,*

---
[a] Cf. A.S. *weordhan* 'revereri' from *weordh* 'pretium.'
[b] Forged in imitation of the Welsh *arth*, just as O'Reilly has *sciberneog* 'barc' and *cae* 'hedge,' counterfeits of Welsh *ysgyfarnog* and *cae*.
[c] See Appendix A.

LU. 95b, the author uses *celt* to denote 'hair' just as Lucretius v. 672, uses *vestis* to denote the beard as the *covering* of the chin.

At Nos. 129 and 443 Windisch's trustfulness in a dangerous guide has again misled him. At No. 129 he cites as cognate with γέρανος, *grus*, etc. 'altir. (*grén?*), gen. *griúin*,' and refers to a quotation from Lebar na huidre, describing Cúchulainn's seven fingers, *con-gabáil ingne sebaic, co-forgabail ingne griúin*, which Mr. Crowe (seduced by the accidental similarity in sound of O.Ir. *grén* to Mod. Eng. *crane*, A.S. *cran*) translates 'with the catch of the talons of a hawk, with the detention of the talons of a crane'; but which means, I think, 'with the grasp of a hawk's talons, with the clutch of a falcon's (?) claws.' Whatever *griúin* may mean [a], it cannot be 'crane,' for a crane has blunt-nailed toes, which have no power of grasping or 'detention.' At No. 443, Windisch renders *ro-snaidet* by 'sie schwimmen stark.' This is a literal rendering of Mr. Crowe's absurd 'they strong-swim'; but *ro-snaidet* is a preterite formed by prefixing the particle *ro* (= pro) to the present (Beitr. vii. 3) and simply means 'they swam.'

At No. 166 Windisch has been misled by Zeuss: *ocht* (leg. *ócht*) means 'frigus,' not 'angustia.' It occurs, spelt *uacht*, in Fiacc's hymn, l. 27, spelt *úacht* in LU. 40a, and is now *f-uacht* with prosthetic *f*. In Z. 1006 *ócht* is misrendered by 'necessitate' and *ocht* (leg. *ócht*) by 'angustia.' In the former case substitute 'frigore,' in the latter 'frigus.' The Irish cognate of *angustia*, άχος, etc. is *ochte*, a feminine *yā*-stem, which occurs in Z. 68.

No. 190. Windisch puts Irish *géd* (W. *gwydd* f., Corn. *guith*, Br. *goaz*) with χήν from χένς; he has not, however, explained how this is possible, nor would he find it easy to do so. *Géd* and the British words above quoted come from **gēdā, *gēndā, gendā* (the Teutonic *ganta* [b]), just as W. *ysgwydd* 'shoulder' f., Corn. *scuid*, Br. *scoaz*, come from **scēdā,* scēndā, *scendā* (the Skr. *skandha*), and as Ir. *gruad* (gl. mala) Z. 22, W. *grudd* 'cheek' come from **gronda* = Skr. gaṇḍa[c] : cf. the Latin *mētior, vēsica* (from *mentior, vensica*), the Gr. μήδεα, ἥσομαι, and other examples cited by Schmidt, *Zur geschichte des indogerm. vocalismus*, 118, 120.

No. 194. There is no such Irish word as *gaim* 'winter,' although this form is found in the place whence Windisch takes it. It is a scribe's mistake for *gam*, O'Clery's *gamh .i. geimhreadh*. The British forms have a diphthong, like χειμών : O.W. *gaem*, Z. 104, Corn. *goyf*, Br. *gouaff*.

No. 205. ἀστήρ. The Cymric '*stirenn*' (here cited from Ebel's Zeuss, p. 120) is non-existent. The MS. (which, by-the-way, is Old-Cornish, not Cymric) has *scirenn* (W. *ysgyren*), Z. 1063, and the mediæval Latin *stella*, which it glosses, does not mean 'star,' but 'splint,' the French '*estelle* de bois.' *Scirenn*, M.-Corn. *skyrenn* (pl. *skyrennou*, B.M. 3403), M.Br. *squezrenn* (leg.

---

[a] I take *grén* to come from **grebno*, as *nél* from **neblo*. Root *grabh*, Fick 66. Cf. ἅρπη, Il. 19, 350, cognate with *rapio*, Curtius No. 331.

[b] (Anseres) e Germaniā laudatissimi. Candidi ibi, verum minores *gantæ* vocantur, Plin. 10, 22, 27, cited by Diefenbach *Origg. Eur.* 347. Cf. OHG. *ganzo*, A.S. *gandra*, Eug. *gander*, A.S. *ganot, ganet*, Eng. *gannet* 'fulica.'

[c] Here the lingual *n* is, as usual, due to a lost *r*. May we not follow Bühler in connecting Lat. *grandis*, (Etrusc. *clant·l*, Corssen, 155), A S. *greát*?

— 4 —

squerenn [a]), appear connected with σκόλοψ, *qui-squiliæ*, Curtius No. 114. So perhaps Ir. *scol-b* (*scolb tige*, gl. tegulus, Ir. Gl. No. 446).

No. 238. Here is a strange mistake. The Ir. *tair* 'come' has nothing to do with the root TAR. It is the 2d sg. *s*-conjunctive (here used as an imperative) of a verb of which *tairic* (= *do-air-IC*) .i. *tig* 'venit,' O'Cl., is the 3d sg. present. No pure Irish word can end in *rs* [b], and *tair* stands for *tairs, *do-air-s, *do-air-IC-s*, just as *coméir*, Fél. Aug. 26, the 2d sg. *s*-conj. of *comérgim*, stands for *coméirs; but the *s* is found in the 3rd pl. *tairset* (*do-air-IC-sent*) 'veniant,' Colm. h. 45, and the 1st pl. *comairsem* (*com-air*-IC-*semm*) 'attingemus,' Z. 467. The *s* is also lost in the 3rd sg. *do-mm-air* 'veniat mihi,' *con-om-thair* 'ut mihi veniat,' *ni-m-thair* 'ne mihi veniat,' Z. 466. The root is ANK, and *tair* belongs to No. 424, not to No. 238.

No. 267b. 'Ir. *druim*,' says Windisch, 'geht auf *drosomi wie *tírim* auf *tarsimi.' But these hypothetical forms would have given *dróimh and *tírimh, whereas the *m* in *druim* and *tírim* is hard [c]. *Druim* (better *druimm*), moreover, is a stem in *men* (acc. pl. *tocraid forn-drommand fri fraigid uli* 'put your backs, all of you, to the wall!' Mesca Ulad, LU. 19a). Read therefore '*druimm* (gen. *drommo*, acc. pl. *drommann*) geht auf *drosmen für *dors-men.' As to *tírim* it is probably from *tírimbi-s, *tarsimbi-s.

No. 275. Here Windisch says that *daur* (gl. quercus) is for *daru*; but it is a stem in *c* not *u* (*cnu na darach* 'nux quercus,' Z. 260, *hi tech ndarach* LU. 19a), and stands for **dair(ic)*, *daric. The Old-Irish genitives *daro*, *dara* (like *Temro*, Lib. Arm. 10, a. 2, regularly *Temrach*, the gen. of *Temair*) are only instances of momentary deviation into the *i*-declension. As to the *au* in *daur*, before *r* or an infected dental, *au* is frequently written for *ai* (the infected *a*). See Zeuss 7.

No. 326. Windisch here refers to the root BHADH (πενθ, *bandh*, *band*) three Irish words, *cobeden*, *cobodlas* (not '*con-bodlas*'), *coibdelach*, compounded with the preposition *con*. But this would have given *combeden, *combodlas, *coimbdelach. The fact is (as Ebel has seen, Z. 871) that these words stand for *con-feden*, *con-fodlas*, *con-fedelach*, that the root is VADH 'to bind' Fick [2] 179, and that the *b* is here, as in many other cases, the graphic representative of a *v=f* infected by the *n* of *con*.

No. 342. Here Windisch, misled by a printer's error in Ebel's edition of the Gr. Celtica, says '*niae* bedeutet auch soror.' The passage cited in support of this—'*im orba mic niath*'—means 'circa hereditatem filii filii sororis.' What seems a fuller form of the same word, *gnia* .i. *mac seathar* 'filius sororis,' is given by O'Clery, and belongs to No. 128.

No. 375. Here (following Ebel) Windisch states *il* to be an *i*-stem. But that it is an *u*-stem, identical in form and meaning with Goth. *filu* πολύς, appears from the following: *togæthfaid sochaide. soifid iliu hé* 'he will wound a multitude, he will turn many,' LL. 77a. 2, *ciaboen fri iliu* 'though he was one

---

[a] *zl*, *er*, for *l*, *r* are often found in M.Bret.: cf. *louhazl* 'securis,' *bouclezr* 'bouclier,' etc.
[b] *fers*, Z. 993, is of course borrowed from the Latin *versus*.
[c] So in *trum*, the Modern Welsh representative of *druimm*. For Modern Welsh *tr* = Ir. *dr*, see Rhys, Revue Celtique, i. 363.

against many,' ib. 78b. 2. Had *il* been an *i*-stem its derivative *ilar* 'multitude (ex **ilu-āra*, as *ginán*, Z. 12, ex **ginu-āna*) would have been **iler* or **elar*.

No. 429. Here (following Z². 223) Ir. *formet*, oftener *format*, is rendered by 'memoria.' But it means 'invidia': it is identical with the W. *gorfynt*, Br. *gourvenn*, and is radically connected with O.N. *for-muna* 'invidere.' The Irish words for 'memory' are *cuimne* and *foraithmet*, Z.² 998, where *format* is rightly explained.

No. 446. The Old-Irish *ainm* 'nomen' is for **anme*, **anmen*, not, as Windisch writes, *anmi*. So at No. 517 *sruaim*, another stem in *men* (dat. pl. *sruamannaib*, O'Dav. Gl. 117) is for **srōmen* = in form Lat. *rūmen*, in meaning *Rumo*, Στρύμων.

No. 474. Root μιγ, μίσγω. The Old-Irish *cummasc* 'mixtio' (not 'commutatio'), whence *cummascthai* 'promiscua,' Z. 182, stands for **cum-mesc*, the vocalic sequence *u-e* regularly becoming *u-a*: cf. *asluat*, *druad*, *Samual*, *toddiusgat* from **asluet*, **drued*, *Samuel*, **toddiusget*, and the *Succat* 'deus belli' of the scholiast on Fiacc's hymn from the *Succetus* of Lib. Arm. 9 a. 2. There is therefore no ground for Windisch's conjecture '*cummasc* ...... scheint des Vocals wegen abzuliegen.'

No. 492. *Ara*, gen. *arad* 'charioteer' cannot ever have been, as Windisch here asserts, a participle present active. Had it been a participle, its gen. sg. would have been **arat*, ex **arantos*. A similar mistake is made under No. 415, in dealing with the ant-stem *tipra*.

No. 518. *Sreth* never means 'strues,' though Zeuss 992 seems to think it does. The Irish word for 'strues' is *sreith*, and comes under No. 215.

At p. 572 a serious error has been committed. The Old-Irish *tarb*, *delb*, *fedb* are cited as examples of the hardening of *v* to *b*. Nothing can be more certain than that here, as in *Ioib*, *breib* and *barn* 'vester,' Z. 339, as in *cobeden*, *cobodlas*, *coibdelach* No. 326, as in the Hiberno-Latin *bobes* (Z. 54) *corbus*, *fabonius* (Reeves' Columba xviii), the *b* is a mere graphic representative of *v*. If the *b* in *tarb* were really a *b*, we should certainly have sometimes found the word written as *tarp* or *tarbb* (see Z. 60); but it is always *tarb* or *tarbh* in mediæval Irish MSS.[a]; and we should have had *tarb* in the modern language instead of the actual *tarbh*, pronounced *tarv*, with an 'irrational vowel' between *r* and *v*. The Ganlish and Welsh forms *tarvos*, *tarw*, also speak unmistakeably for our theory.

It will have been seen that most of these errors [b] are due to Windisch's belief in his predecessors. *Oportet discentem credere*. But Windisch is now a teacher, not a learner, and in no department of philology is the apostolic precept *Omnia probate* more needed than in the Celtic, with its forged words, inaccurate texts, deceptive facsimiles [c], unfaithful translations, and (at least in the case of Irish) ignorant and reckless native scholars [d].

---

[a] In the *Crith Gablach*, as printed in the third volume of O'Curry's Manners and Customs of the Ancient Irish, p. 486, l. 16, it is true that we find *tarbb*; but in the MS. (H. 3. 18, p. 254), of which I have a photograph before me, the word in question is distinctly *tarbh*.

[b] One or two others will be more conveniently noticed *infra* at Nos. 62, 76, 158, 204, 270, 279, 326, 360, 366 and 474.

[c] See Appendix B.   [d] See Appendix C.

II.—ADDENDA.

Let us now proceed with the second division of this Paper, namely, the further additions which, I venture to think, may be made to Curtius' work:—

No. 1. Root ἀγκ. To the root AK belong the Mid.-Br. *iguenn* 'hamus,' Cath., and the Old-Irish *ánne* 'ring' (now *f-áinne* with prosthetic *f*), Corm., which stands for *acn-nio*, as the cognate Lat. *ānus* for *acnus*. To the nasalised form of this root, ANK, belongs the O.Ir. *écath* for *écath* (gl. hamus) Z. 1009 = *ecad* .i. *saith ecca* .i. *biad necca* ('cibus mortis') .i. *pisci*, O'Mulc. Gl. H. 2. 16, col. 101. Rhys (Rev. Celt. ii. 188) adds the Welsh *ach* 'stemma,' *ach-fen* 'scham-bug.' The Ir. *aic-mae* 'genus,' Z. 770, may also be added.

No. 2. Root ἀκ. Add the Old-Welsh *auc* (= ācus, ὠκύς) in *di-auc* (gl. segnem), Juv. 93, Br. *di-ec* 'segnis,' 'piger: 'the Welsh *egr* 'acer'= O.Ir. *aicher*: the Old-Welsh *cem-ec-id* (gl. lapidaria), Z. 1061, = Mod.-W. *cyf-eg-ydd* 'pickaxe': the O.Ir. verb *do-r-acráid* (gl. exacerbavit), Z. 462, *do-accradi* (gl. exasperat), Ml. 28a, Br. *di-egraff* 'exacerbare,' Cath. To the extended root AKS (whence ὀξύς) the Old-Welsh *och*, Beitr. vii. 412, now *awch* 'edge,' appears to belong.

No. 4. ἀκχός. Windisch (*Vorrede*, p. x) has put *asil* (gl. artus) to this Number: (cf. *inn-asill*, Brocc. h., gl. 100). He might also add the diminutive *aislean* (gl. articulo), Goidel². 23, and the M.Br. *asquell* 'āla' (for *axla).

No. 7. Root ἀλκ, ἀρκ. Add O.Ir. *timm-urc* 'coarcto,' Z. 979; *du-imm-airethe* (gl. artabatur), Z. 884; *tess-urc* 'defendo,' 'servo'; *du-m-es-urc-sa*, Z. 881, 949, 953n; *do-nn-es-aircfe* 'nos servabit,' Goidel². 133.

No. 13. To the root DARK 'to see' the Ir. *con-darc-ell* 'conivens,' *con-darc-ille* 'coniventia,' Z. 870, the Ir. *drech*, W. *drych* 'aspectus,' 'visus' = Br. *derch* and W. *drem* 'visus oculorum,' Br. *drem* 'vultus' (ex *drec-m*) should be referred. Siegfried's ingenious explanation of Lat. *larva* ex *dar(c)va* (as *laurus* ex *daurus*, *lacryma* ex *dacruma*) is also deserving of notice.

No. 14. Root ζικ. O.Ir. *adéos* .i. *sloinnfed no inneosad* 'I will declare,' (or 'I will relate,') O'Cl., is for *ad-décsú*, where *décsú* = δείξω. The same root is also in *con-daig* 'quærit,' Z. 870, *cuin-dch-id* 'petere,' Z. 484.

No. 15. The Irish *doich*, *doig* 'verisimilis,' Z. 74, 305, compar. *dochu*, Z. 276, certainly goes with ἐοικέω. Glück (Neue Jahrbücher für Philologie, 1864, s. 602) connected the Old-Celtic names *Decangi*, *Decanti*, *Decetia* with *decus*, *decor*. With these also goes the Irish adjective *dech*, *deg* used as a superlative to *maith* 'good' (*deach* .i. *fearr*, O'Cl.), *innaní as-deg rochreitset hier.* (gl. electorum dei), i. e. 'of those who best believed in Christ,' Z. 611, where it is wrongly explained by Zeuss.

No. 28. κάκκη. Add W. *cach* m., where *ch* is from *cc*, Z. 151.

No. 29b. Ir. *cailech* (gl. gallus), LH. 8a, (= *calico-s) belongs to καλέω and the other words here cited. The Ir. *caol* .i. *cail* .i. *gairm* 'clamor,' O'Cl., and perhaps the W. *ceiliog*[a] 'gallus,' come from a by-form of the root, KIL: cf. O.N. *hjal*, OHG. *hël* (in *gi-hël*, etc.), NHG. *hell*, Fick 725.

---

[a] The Old-Breton *kelihuc* (Rev. Celt. ii. 208) shews no trace of a diphthong.

— 7 —

No. 30. With the root καλ, Lat. *celare*, OHG. *hëlan*, the Welsh *celu* ' to hide,' ' to conceal,' is connected. In Irish the root is found not only in *cel-t* ' vestis,' but in the verb *fo-n-ro-chled* [a] ' occlusi sumus,' Z. 483, and the substantive *cleith* .i. *ceilt* ' concealment,' O'Cl., whence the adverb *fochleith* ' clam,' O'Don. Gr. 267, *cleth* (gl. laterna) Sg. 51b, and the following words cited by Nigra (Reliquie Celtiche i. 36n.), *clithith* (gl. latex), *inna cletha* (gl. latebras), *á-chlid* (gl. latibulum suum), *nu-da-chelat* (gl. latentes), *con-ai-celt* (gl. desimulavit), *in-chlide* (reconditæ).

The Irish *cell* is a loan from *cella*, here cited, and *caille* (whence *caillech* ' nun '), which Ebel, Beitr. ii. 169, connects with *celo*, etc., is certainly (like W. *pall*) a loan from *pallium*. ' Ich kann mir nicht denke,' says Windisch (Beitr. viii. 18), ' dass die nonne das pallium getragen habe und danach benannt worden sei.' But this only proves that an excellent scholar may be unfamiliar with the barbarous Latin from which the Irish took most of their loanwords. Let Windisch look at Henschel's Ducange, tom. v. p. 34, col. 3, and he will find ' Pallium, Velum sanctimonialium .... Collectio Canonum Hibern. lib. 43, cap. 10 : Virgines palliatæ, id est, velatæ.'

The Gaulish *celicnon* (whence Goth. *kelikn*) might be added to this Number.

No. 31. The Ir. *cêl*, W. *coil*, *coel* ' augurium ' are connected by Fick with καλός, the Celtic and Northern-European forms resting on **kaila*. The Ir. *cêlmaine druad* 7 *methmerchurdacht*, LB. 137a, *an-ceoil* .i. *uile orra* ' evils on them !' O'Cl., *celini* ' auguras,' ' portendis,' Sg. 66a, and the W. *coelfain* ' glad tidings,' may also be here cited.

No. 32. W. *can*, *caniad* ' song,' Corn. *can*, pl. *canow*, Br. *canaff* ' chanter,' Cath., are cognate with *cano*, κανάζω. The Irish *cainte* ' satirist,' Corm. Tr. 31, SM. i. 86, *ban-chainte* ' female satirist,' [b] *caint* ' speech,' may also be cognate, though the hard *t* is not easily explained.

No. 37. The Gaulish *gabro-s* (in *Gabro-sentum*, *Gabro-magus*, Glück, KN. 43), Ir. *gabar*, W. *gafr*, Corn. *gavar*, Br. *gaffr* ' cheure,' Cath., can hardly be separated from κάπρος, *caper*, etc. We must assume in these Celtic words an abnormal sinking of the tenues, which we also find in Ir. *gabáil* = ' capere,' κώπη No. 34, Ir. *goirt* ' bitter ' = Lith. *kartus*, Skr. *kaṭu*, ' sharp,' ' pungent,' and possibly in Ir. *no-déitnaigtis* (gl. stridebant) Ml. 54a : cf. Lat. *tintino*.

No. 41. O. Ir. *crip*, for **cirp*, which O'Davoren 63 and O'Clery explain by *luath* ' swift,' is almost certainly cognate with καρπ-άλιμος and κραιπνός. See further Corm. Tr. 143.

No. 42b. Ir. *cloch* ' stone ' f. is = κρόκη here cited : *cora* ' stones.' Corm. Tr. 87, *cert-fuine* ' the flag on which bread is kneaded or baked,' O'Don. Supp.,

---

[a] Fiacc's hymn, line 15 : ' Robo-chobair dond-érinn tichtu patr*aice* fo-ro-chlad' should, I now see, be rendered ' Patrick's coming was a help to Ireland, which had been shut up. The allusion is to Galatians iii. 23 (Vulgate) : ' Antequam autem venisset fides, sub lege custodiebamur, conclusi ad fidem quæ patefacienda erat.' Correct accordingly my Goidelica [*] 130. Other blunders in the same book are corrected in Appendix D.

[b] Not ' dieneriu,' as Windisch (Beitr. viii. 246) seems to think. Another Irish word for ' satirist ' is *cáinh* .i. *cainte* II. 3. 18, p. 66, col. 2. Hence probably the name *Lebar-cham*.

also belong to this Number. Rhys, Revue Celtique i. 364, also puts W. *corwg*, Irish *curach* 'a little boat' (cf. Lat. *carina*) and W. *caregl* with Skr. *karaka* 'coconnut-shell' here cited. The Irish *curach* is from **curoch* = *curuca* (which actually occurs in Adamnán's Life of Columba, ed. Reeves, pp. 176,177), the sequence *u-o* becoming *u-a* as in *pudar* from *putor*, *sdupar* from *stupor*, Corm. Tr. 157.

No. 45. The Low-Latin *cayum* 'domus' (= a Gaulish *caion*), Ir. *cae* .i. *tech*, O'Curry's transcript of Brehon Laws, p. 100, *cerdd-chae* (gl. officina, 'fabri domus'), Z. 60, is surely cognate with κοί-τη, *quies*, *hei-va* (domus) and the other words here cited. The W. *cae* = *kae* 'sæpimentum,' Z. 285, pl. *caiou* (gl. munimenta), Br. *quae* 'haye d'espine,' 'seps,' Cath., is a different word, and has perhaps lost a vowel-flanked *g*: cf. O.N. *hagi*, NHG. *ge-hege*.

No. 45b. Ir. *scian* 'knife,' W. *ysgïen*, are certainly cognate with *de-sci-scere*, (σ)κείω. So M.Bret. *squeiaff* 'coupper,' 'amputare,' Cath. = W. *ysgiaw*. Curtius' ingenious argument, Grundz. p. 109, for connecting *scio* with *de-sci-scere* is supported by the Irish *sliucht* 'cognitio,' Z. 878, which comes from the root SLAK, whence O.Ir. *ro-se(s)laig* 'cecīdit' and Goth. *slahan*.

No. 47. O.Ir. *céle* 'socius,' 'maritus,' Z. 229, W. *celydd*, seems cognate with κέλευθος, *callis*, just as O.Ir. *sétche* 'wife' with *sét* 'via,' and Goth. *ga-sinthja*, NHG. *ge-sinde*, with *sinth-s*.

No. 48. O.Ir. *céle* 'servus' (*sóir-chele*, gl. libertus, Z. 365; *céle dé*, Trip. Eg. 13b, 1) is cognate with κίλης, *celer*, *colo*: Ir. *bua-chail*, W. *bu-gail* = βου-κόλος.

No. 49. The Irish preposition *cen* 'sine,' Z. 655, the adjective *cenathe* (gl. absens) and the adverb *in-chenadid* (gl. absque) Z. 6, seem cognate with κενεός, çūnya. No relations in the British languages except possibly *kyn* in the Corn. *kyn-byk* 'a wether-goat,' Lhuyd A.B. 65c.

No. 50. κέρας. The Old-Celtic forms κάρνον (σάλπιγγα) and κάρνυξ are well established (see Diefenbach *Origg*. 280) and should here be cited.

No. 53. Ir. *ceart* .i. *beag* 'little,' O'Cl., is in form identical with *curtus*. Ir. *ir-chre* 'interitus' (*er-chrae* gl. eclipsin ; *er-chru* gl. defectu, Z. 183, 868, whence *irchride* 'irritus,') reminds one of Κήρ, κηραίνω, which Curtius places under this Number. The Br. *di-scar* 'obruere,' like Ir. *co-scéra* 'destruet,' and Ir. *scrissid* 'rasorium,' Z. 657, ex **scrad-tati*, **scard-tati* (ON. *skerdha*, *skardhr* 'beschnitten' Fick² 900) tends to show that κείρω, etc. have lost initial *s*.

No. 55. κῆλον, çalya. Add W. *col* 'peak,' 'sting,' Ir. *cuil* (gl. culex 'stachelbegabt,' Schmidt *die Wurzel AK*, 52) Goidel¹. 57, W. *cylion* 'gnats.'

No. 57. The Corn. *ke* 'i,' pl. *kewgh* 'ite,' the M.Br. *quæ*, now *ké*, pl. *kit*, come certainly from the root KI, whence κίω, *cio*, etc. The Irish cognates seem to be *cái* .i. *slighe no conair* 'road or path,' O'Cl., *cian* 'remotus,' *cein* 'time,' *cach 'la céin...in-céin n-aili* 'modo...modo,' Z. 360: cf. the Teutonic *tíd*, *zeit*, *tími*, *tíma* from the root *dī*, in Skr. *diyate*, *dedīya*, δίεμαι.

No. 59. Welsh *clo* 'lock,' *cloig* 'hasp,' should be put with *clavis* and the other words here cited.

No. 60. O.Ir. *cloen, clóin* 'iniquus,' Z. 31, *clóine* 'iniquitas,' Z. 1007, is cognate with *clino*, κλίνω and other derivatives from the root KLI.

No. 62. Ir. *cloth* = κλυτός and W. *clod* 'praise' might also be added: '*la cluaissn*' (sic !),—cited here from Mr. Crowe's inaccurate[a] edition of the Táin bó Fráich—is in the MS. *lacludiss* ngléssa, the *n* of the accusative appearing only in the anlaut of the following word. This *n*, when found after neuter *i*-stems, *u*-stems and *s*-stems, is due to false analogy, and it is an unscholarly mistake to deviate from the MSS. and to write (as Mr. Crowe would write) *mindn apstalacte, muirn Icht, techn darach, glendn gáibthech*. In fact, in Old-Irish, after the acc. sg., the transported *n* had merely a syntactical value. This is amusingly shewn in the Félire, Oct. 4, where we actually find *áil Marcellum n-epscop*. Even Mr. Crowe would hardly, I suppose, write *Marcellumn epscop*.

No. 63. The river-name *Clōta*, now the *Clyde*, Ir. *Cluad*, gen. *cluade* in *Ail-Cluade* 'rupes Clotæ,' (gl. on Fiacc's hymn, 1), now Dumbarton, is certainly connected with *cluere*, κλύ-ζω, *hlu-tr-s*. So *Glana* (pura, clara) is the name of many Celtic rivers, Glück, KN. 187n.

No. 64. In Kuhn's Zeitschrift xxi. 429, Windisch puts Corn. *scouarn* (gl. auris) with the Hesychian (σ)κόᾳ ἀκούει. The *f* (= infected *b*) in Modern Welsh *ysgyfarn* is curious. The Old-Celtic form may have been *scobrand, *scovrand, *scov-arnā* : cf. *Sabrina* infra.

The Old-Ir. adj. *con* has been equated with the Goth. *skau-n-s, schön*, here cited, just as the synonymous *cáin*[b] is certainly = O.S. *ski-n*, Eng. *sheen*. But the only equivalent of *con* is καινός, *καν-jος.

Glück, KN. 68, puts the Irish *conn, cunn* 'sense,' 'understanding,' with κοννέω from κοϝνέω here noticed; but *cunn* (ex *cug-no*) is rather to be connected with Goth. *hug-s* νοῦς. Other examples of Neo-Celtic *nn* from *gn* are :—

 Ir. *buinne* (gl. tibia) Z. 67, Lith. *búgnas* 'trommel':
 W. *rhynn* 'algor,' '*rigor*' (Davies):
 Ir. *tinne* 'bar,' 'beam,' dat. pl. *tinnib*, 1 SM. 188, Lat. *tignum*:
 Mod. Ir. *dorinne* 'fecit' = O.Ir. *dorigni*.

No. 65. Welsh *cwch* m. 'boat' seems cognate with κόγκος, cankha. So *truch* (gl. truncate), Beitr. iv. 423, Br. *trouch*, Corn. *trogh* with *truncus* : W. *llech* 'tabula saxea' with *planca*; and W. *trochi* 'to immerse' (Ir. *fothrucad*, Br. *gouzronquet* 'balneari') with ἀ-τρεγκ-τος· ἄβροχος. See also Rhys, Rev. Celt. ii. 188.

No. 66. Ir. *cuach*, W. *cóg*, Br. *coc* 'cuculus,' are all cognate with κόκκυξ, *cucūlus*.

No. 69. The *crú* in *crú-fechta* 'corvus prœlii'[c] certainly goes with *corvus* and κόραξ. See Corm. Tr. 39, and add the following glosses : *is crú* (.i. *badb*) *fecta modcernæ*, LU. 109a, *crú* .i. *bodb, fechta* .i. *cath*, H. 3, 18, p. 61a.

---

[a] This is too indulgent an epithet. Consider the samples (*pauca de plurimis*) given *infra* in Appendix A.

[b] *Con-róiter* .i. *cain* ro(*fh*)*itir*, LU. Crowe's *Amra* p. 38. *Con-fig figleastair* .i. *cain no taitnemach cach figell 7 cach sleachtain roficheastair* .i. *rofuachtnaig* .i. *fria cholaiun*, H. 2. 16, col. 698.

[c] Cf. Dan. *ral-ravn*, OHG. *wala-hraban* 'corvus stragis,' Grimm, DM. 949.

No. 71. Curtius doubtfully places κόρδαξ with κραδάω, Skr. kūrd, kūrdana. Fick 205 also adds σκόρδαξ from Mnesimachus. The root seems to occur in Celtic: Ir. ceird .i. ceimniugud no cing 'a stepping or going,' O'Dav. 64: mairg misceird [a] .i. mairg dia ceimniter (leg. céimnigther) in ceird sin 'woe to him for whom that journey is travelled,' ib. O.W. (Br. ?) credam (gl. vado) Z. 1053, for cerdam, Mod. W. cerddaf: Corn. kerd (gl. iter), M.Br. querzet 'cheminer, aler.'
With Lat. gladius (for *cladius), Slav. korŭda here cited, the Irish claid-eb, clainn (= *cla-n-d-i-s), cloinn Corm. 'sword,' clainneb 'cleaver,' dat. sg. clainniub, T. B. Fr. 142, are certainly connected.

No. 72. Root KAR. Besides the Ir. cer-d 'faber' cuir-im 'pono' here cited, the Ir. créis 'crevit' (súi slan créis crist 'sapiens sanus qui crevit in Christo,' Amra Chol. 72, Goid²., p. 166) and cor 'manus' (acc. sg. coir .i. laim, Fél. Dec. 12, Franciscan copy) in ten-chor πυρολαβίς, Z. 84 = Skr. kara, and the W. peri 'facere' seem to come from this root.

No. 74. κρίας, caro. The Irish carna .i. feoil 'flesh' and cairin .i. feoil gan tsaill 'flesh without fat,' O'Cl., and the W. crau 'gore' should be added. The Ir. crí (rogab crist crí, LB. 143) is = the Goth. hraiv here cited, the A.S. hrā, hrāv 1. 'corpus hominis vivi,' 2. 'cadaver' (Grein).

No. 76. Root κρι in κρίνω, etc. Many British words belong to this Number. O.W. cruitr (gl. pala) Juvencus, p. 14, Corn. croider (gl. cribrum), whence kroddre 'to sift,' D. 882, Br. croerz (leg. croezr?), and the O.W. cri-p 'pecten,' Z. 1059, now crib, Br. crib 'paingne' Cath. The following Irish words may also be added:—

cír (gl. pecten), mar(c)-cir (gl. strigilis) Z. 23:
crích 'limes,' 'finis,' Z. 21:
craeth in the phrase rath craeth .i. rath n-eicsi 'rotam scientiæ,'[b] LH. 34a 1; creth, Corm. s.v. Caill crinmon:
int-in-crechad ἡ κριτική, LH. 11a, LU. 14a: ro-inchrech 'reprehendit,' LH. 13a:
r-er-choil 'decrevit,' Ml. 46c, er-choiliud 'decretum,' Z. 8.

The ground-form of the Irish críathar is crētra (not as Windisch says, misled by me, crētara), Z². 166: the second a is an 'irrational' vowel.

No. 77. κρύος. Add Corn. kriv (ex *crūmo-), W. cri 'raw.'

No. 77b. O.Ir. cin 'delictum,' a t-stem, Z. 258, may have lost initial s and be cognate with A.S. scinn-o, scin 'dæmon,' 'nocivus,' Fick 201, Gr. κτείνω, καίνω from *σκινjω, *σκανjω.

No. 79. Ir. cuach (gl. scyfum) South. 25a = caucus, Skr. koça 'fass, kufe, eimer,' Gr. κύαθος, belongs to the root κυ.

No. 80. Glück, KN. 28, compares Gaulish cumba 'convallis,' W. cwmm, Old-French combe with κύμβη, κύμβος.

No. 81. Root κυρ, κυλ. W. cor-wynt 'turbo' = Br. cor-uent 'tourbillon,' and W. crych 'crispus' (ex *crinca, Rhys), O.N. hríngr 'circulus.' Besides

---

[a] i. e. mis-ceird. So mis-imirt .i. droich-imirt, O'Clery, mis-cuis 'odium,' Z. 864, (cuis = W. eas, Eng. hate). Mis- is of course = Goth. missa. Mi (aspirating) is perhaps = Skr. mithu.
[b] cf. ἐγκύκλιος παιδεία.

the Irish words which Windisch puts with κυλίω, κίρκος, etc., there are Ir. *cul* 'chariot,' Corm. Tr. 39, and fo-*chrid*-igedar (gl. accingit), from the extended root CRID, whence also *cris* 'girdle' (ex *crid-tu*) Z^e. 954 and M.Br. *crisaff* 'succingere,' Cath. So O.Ir. *cruind* (**cur-indo-s*), Z. 15, W. *crwnn* 'rotundus,' Br. *crenn*. So also O.Ir. *cromb* (**curumbo-s*), W. *crom*, whence Ir. *cromman*, W. *crymman* 'falx,' 'secula.' The O.Ir. verb ro-das-*cload* 'eos vertisset,' Br. 53, may also belong to this root.

No. 84b. W. *cŷn* 'wedge,' if not borrowed from *cuneus*, is cognate with that word and κῶνος. The Ir. *cath* 'a sage' (*don cath* .i. *don shtruith*, Br. 19) is = *catus* here cited.

No 85. Root λακ, ἔ-λακον. In O.Ir. *at-luchur*, *dutt-luchur*, Z. 438, the -*luchur* is identical in root and meaning with Lat. *loquor*. The root-vowel *a* appears in the conjunctive *tod-laiger-sa* (gl. postolem), Ml. 38c, and in the preterites *do-r-oth-laig*, *ro-thoth-laigestar*, Goid^c. 137, 141.

No. 86. From the root LAK (whence λάκος, *lacer*) a reduplicated form occurs in LU. 57b, viz. *lelgatar* (= **le-lach-atar*) .i. *lomraiset* 'totonderunt.' With the same root Nigra, Rev. Celtique i. 153, puts O.Ir. *du-rig* (gl. nudat) and other examples, to which add *di-rgetar* (gl. exuantur) Ml. 136b, *du-n-dat-re-siu* (gl. quæ possit te ... exuere) Ml. 133a, *in-de-rachtae l. huare narbu de-rachtae* (gl. successu prospero destitutum) Ml. 18d, *ni con-de-rae-rachtatar* (gl. nunquam ... destituerint) Ml. 57d, *ro-de-racht* (nudatum, exutum est) Corm. B. s.v. *Disert*. These Irish words, like ῥάκος (Æol. βράκος), may all have lost *v* in anlaut.

No. 89. λύκος, vŗka. The Irish *brech* 'wolf,' now written *breach* (*breach* .i. *cú alluid*, O'Cl., *Breach-mhagh* 'wolf-field,' *Four Masters* ed. O'Don. 753, 1260) is = Skr. vŗka, the *vr* becoming *br* as in the following instances :—

braig 'chain,' *braga* 'prisoner,' root VARG, infra No. 142 :
bran 'raven,' Slav. *vranŭ*, Lith. *várnas*, *varna* (Ebel) :
brat 'pallium,' root VAR, No. 496 :
briathar 'verbum,' = (*F*)ρήτρα, No. 493 :
broen 'pluvia,' cf. (*v*)*rigo*, (*v*)*rign* infra No. 166b :
brogais 'crevit,' root VRAG, VARG, No. 152 :
sabrann a river-name, *Savara*, root SU, No. 604 :
drebraing, *rodrebrainy* (= *ro-do-vre-vrai-n-g*) Fél. Ap. 2, 17, Aug. 26, root VARG, Skr. *valg* 'to go by leaps.'

No. 90. Ir. *moaichfid* 'magnificabit,' SM. iii. 30, (*oa* = *â*, Goidel^2. 55), Ir. *mocht* .i. *mór* 'magnus,' O'Cl., *mochtae* 'magnified,' 'glorified' = W. *maith* 'ample' (*cyn-faith*, *gor-faith*, *mawr-faith*) are cognate with the Lat. *macte* and the other words here noticed. And as metathesis of *r* is frequent, the Ir. *morc* (.i. *mór* 'magnus,' O'Cl.) may be = μακρό-ς.

No. 92. To the root MUK, whence μυκ-τήρ, *mungo*, etc., the Ir. *mugart* 'a fat pig,' Br. 59, *mucc* 'pig' (dat. pl. *muccib*, Tir. 6), W. *moch* 'swine' (ex **mu-n-câ*, v. supra No. 65), certainly belong.

No. 93. νέκυς. From a root ANK = NAK come Ir. *écaib*, *éc* 'death,' Corn., and Br. *ancou*, W. *angeu*.

No. 98. The Old-Welsh *pelechi* (gl. clavæ) Juv. 94, is, I think, cognate with πέλεκκον (*ch* ex *cc* as usual). It can hardly be a loan.

No. 99. πεύκη. O.Ir. *bí* (gl. pix), Z. 21, *bíde* 'piccus,' Z. 792, W. *pyg*, Br. *peo*, are all loans. For the sinking of *p* to *b* in anlaut cf. *brolach* from *prologus*, W. *prol* (Davies), and *bóc* (gl. osculum) Z. 28 from *pāc(em)*, W. *poc*, Corn. *im-poc, poccuil*. 'Pacem dare, osculari : osculum enim pacis est symbolum et concordiæ.' (Ducange.)

No. 100. Root πικ. O.Ir. *oech* 'enemy,' Corm, (with loss of initial *p*) is = A.S. *fāh*, Eng. *foe*, and (in form) Lith. *paika-s* 'unnütz, dumm' and is cognate with the OHG. *fēhjan* and other words here cited.

No. 102. Stem πλακ. Ir. *lecc* 'flagstone,' whence *lecán* (gl. lapillus) Z. 273, W. *llech* 'tabula saxea' seems = *planca* (see No. 65 supra). The Ir. *liae*, gen. *liace*, dat. *liice*, a dissyllabic stem in *nc*, comes from a quite different root.

No. 103. Add W. *plygu* 'plicare,' *pleth* = πλίκτη and *hy-blyg* = εὐπλεκής, unless they be loans.

No. 106. The Irish *cerp* seems to belong to this Number. It is glossed by *teascad* 'a cutting,' O'Dav. 63, but rather means 'sharp' : *gorm claidemh cerp cinntech or derg ima dorncur* 'a blue sharp sword, red gold (is) settled (to be) around its hilt,' *conchend catha ceirp* 'a wolfshead of keen battle,' LU. 47b, and is = O.N. *skarp-r*, OHG. *skarph*.

No. 107. Root SKAND. Add Ir. *ascnam* (.i. *ath-ascnam*) Br. 12, *asgnam* .i. *imthecht*, O'Dav. 50, *do-da-ascansat* 'cam adierunt,' Br. 31.

No. 110. Stem σκαρπ. The W. *ysgarth* 'offscouring,' *ysgarthu* 'to purge out,' Ir. *ascartach* 'stuppa,' W. *carth*, belong either to this Number or to No. 53.

No. 111. Root SPAK, σκεπ. W. *paith* 'a glance,' 'a prospect,' 'a scene' (Spurrell) = Lat. *-spectus* in *conspectus, adspectus, prospectus*, should be added. For loss of initial *s* cf.—

pâr 'hasta' = *sparus*, A.S. *spër* :

peilliaid 'pollen,' for *spollen, Curtius, No. 389 :

peuo 'anhelare,' root SPU, Curtius, No. 652 :

poer 'sputum,' root SPU, Fick[2], 415 :

prwst 'hurry,' 'bustle' ex *sprud-ta*, Goth. *sprauto* ταχέως.

No. 112. Ir. *sciath* 'shield,' W. *ysgwyd*, O.Br. *scoet*, certainly go with σκιά, σκιάς. From the root SKA come not only Old.Irish *scáth, scáterc* 'mirror' = *scáth-derc*, but Corn. *scod*, Br. *squeut* 'ombre.' The Irish *cathair*, a *c*-stem, W. *caer*, cannot be separated from *castrum* (ex *scad-trum*), the combination *str* losing *s* in Irish, *st* in Welsh, here as in Ir. *sethar-*, Z. 855, W. *chwaer* pl. *chwïor-ydd* = *svistr-*, Goth. *svistar* (Ebel. Beitr. ii. 156) and in Ir. *fethal* (gl. ephoth) Tur. 87 = Skr. *vastra-m*, Gr. γέστρα (= Ϝεστρα στολή, Hesych.

No. 116. ἄγος. See infra, at No. 120.

No. 117. To the root AG belong Ir. *ágh* .i. *cur* 'pone,' *ághaid* .i. *cuirid* 'ponunt,' O'Cl., the simplex of the forms cited by Windisch : and the compound verb *do-sn-ach-t* .i. *ro-s-immaig* 'he drove them away,' LU. 34b. 1. Also the nouns *aige* .i. *graifne ech* 'horse-race,' Corm. Tr. 115, s.v. *mag, ágh* 'contest' (ἀγών, Lat. *ind-agon-*) .i. *cath*, O'Cl., gen. *dga* (*déca a rígu rem n-aga*, LU. 47b.: *indlema ind áya ernbais*, Rev. Celt. i. 37) : *âr*, W. *aer*

— 13 —

(ex *agro), 'battle,' 'slaughter,' and Ir. ám (gl. manus 'a body of persons'), Z. 268, a neuter stem in men, identical in every respect with agmen, (ex-)ámen. In the British languages g disappears between vowels. We find accordingly W. af, yd-a-f 'ibo,' Z. 579, = Corn. yth-af, 580, Br. aff, 581, Cymr. aet ('eat'), Z. 585, = Lat. 3d sg. imper. agito.

No. 120. aïξ. With Skr. aja 'buck,' ex *aga, Rhys puts W. ewig 'doc,' Corn. euhic gl. cerva (ex *agīk·a); as with ἄγος, No. 116, he puts the Welsh adj. ew-og 'guilty' (ex *agáka). The Ir. agh f., which O'Clery explains by bó 'cow,' occurs in the Senchas Mór ii. 238, 254, meaning 'a bullock-calf,' and is probably cognate with ajá. The acc. pl. aige (cf. litre, Z. 246) means 'deer' in the Táin bó Fráich : dosennat na .uii. naige do ráith chruachan 'they drive the seven deer to Rathcroghan.' So in LH. 19b. (Goid². 149) comtis aige alta.

No. 121. Root arg. W. ariant = argentum should be quoted as preserving the n, which in the Irish arget is lost before t.

No. 122. Ir. guaire .i. uasal, Corm. Tr.,p. 91, is surely cognate with γαῦρος.

No. 123. γάλα. With the Skr. jala-m 'water' here cited cf. Ir. gil .i. uisge 'water,' O'Cl.

No. 128. The original a of the root GAN appears in Ir. ad-gainemmar-ni 'renascimur,' Ml. 66b, and in W. ganedig 'natus' (geni 'nasci'), Br. ganet 'ortus' (guenell 'nasci'). To the Irish words here cited should also be added in-gen 'filia,' gean .i. bean 'mulier,' O'Cl., gean .i. inghean, O'Cl., and gnia .i. mac seathar 'filius sororis,' O'Cl.

Windisch (Beitr. viii. 41) has proved that there is no relation between the words treated under this Number and the numerous Celtic derivatives which seem to come from a root CAN, KV-AN—the Irish cana 'cub,' W. cenaw (cf. Gaulish Canaus, Canavilus?); cenêl 'tribe' = W. cenedl f. γένεθλον, γενέθλη, Ir. cinis 'orta est,' Brocc. h. 4, 3rd pl. ro-chinset, rochinnset ª, Z². 464, ciniud iar tuistiu 'bringing forth after begetting,' SM. i. 256, cuiniu 'woman,' Corm. s.v. arg.

No. 129. γέρανος. The Welsh garan, the Gaulish tri-garanus, should have been quoted in preference to the doubtful grên (ex *grebno, root GRABH?).

No. 130. γέρων. May we not put the Ir. n-stem bró, gen. broon (gl. molac) Lib. Arm. 10a 2, W. breuan 'molendinum,' with the Skr. grāvan 'stein zum auspressen des Soma, 'press-stein,' Grassmann 419, and the Hesychian γραῖα 'kneading-trough' here cited? The O.Ir. verbs bruid 'contundit,' LU. 47b, and bronnaim (ni bronna 'non deterit,' Fiacc's h. 8) may also belong to this Number.

No. 133. γῆρυς. The Irish gáir 'cry' = W. gawr 'clamor' and Ir. grith 'cry' = W. gryd should have been cited here. Also the O.Ir. adgaur ᵇ (gl. convenio 'I accost,' 'I sue'), Z. 428, whence ad-ro-gar-t, etc., Z. 455, at-gairith, Z. 994. The Ir. for-gall, Colm. 49, also belongs to this Number.

ª Liquids in position are often doubled, Z. 41. Thus innsib, Fiacc's h. 10. Forgetting this, Windisch (Beitr. viii. 43) erroneously treats ro-chinnset (= rochinset LU. 39b), as if it were connected with Ir. cenn and W. penn 'head.'

ᵇ Wrongly connected (Kuhn's Zeitschrift, xxi. 430) with ἀγείρω. See Z. 1024, ad-gaur 1. duttluchur.

— 14 —

No. 133b. Ir. *glicc*, compar. *gliccu* 'sapientior,' Z. 276, *isin-glicci* 'in astutia', Z. 248, seems cognate with Goth. *glaggvus* and Gr. γλαυκός. The primeval Celtic form may have been *gla-n-c-vo*, *a* becoming *i* as in *ingor = ancora*, Z. 5. The W. *gloiu, gloyw* 'limpidus,' 'lucidus,' like Ir. *glé*, Colm. 37, seems cognate with A.S. *gleáw* 'splendidus.'

No. 134a. γλύφω, Lat. *glūbo* ex *glu-m-bo*. The Ir. *lomm* (gl. nudus) Z. 959 = W. *llwmm* 'glaber,' *lu-m-bo*, belong to this Number—initial *g* being lost as in *lestar, llestr*, No. 544, Fr. *loir = glirem*, and Eng. *liquorice* γλυκύρριζα. The Ir. verb *lom-r-aimm* is formed like the Lat. *glab-r-o*, No. 134.

No. 135. Root γνω. Add *in-gnaidi* 'intellectus,' Ml. 63a, *in-gnae* 'intelligentia,' Ml. 44d, *co asa-gnoither nand sechmadachte* ('that it may be known that it is not a preterite'), Z. 743, *etar-gne* 'cognitio,' *etar-geuin* 'agnovit,' *itar-gninim* 'sapio prudentia.' The O.Ir. *gnáth*[a] ('solitus,' 'consuetus'), Z. 16, and W. *gnawd* are identical with γνωτός, *(g)notus*, and should be here cited, as preserving (like Lat. *gnā-ru-s*) the original vowel.

Ir. *gnó* .i. *oirdeirc* 'conspicuus,' O'Cl., is = the Lat. *gnāvu-s*, whence *gnávare, návare* 'to shew,' 'to exhibit.' With the other Latin *gnāvus* 'active,' the Irish *gnó* 'business,' *gnó(th)ach* 'busy,' are cognate.

In the following Irish words from O'Clery's Glossary the *g* is lost, *nós* 'custom,' *noudh cearda* .i. *oirdhearcaighim ealadha* (*noud* = Lat. *noto:* cf. *noadh* .i. *urdarcughadh, nuithear* .i. *oirdearcaigther*, O'Don. Supp.), *nois* .i. *oirdheirc, do-noisigh* 'notavit,' *noitheach* .i. *oirdheirc*.

The O.Ir. *cia do-gnia* .i. *cia do aithéonta*, O'Cl., seems the 2d pers. sg. of a reduplicated future from the root *gnâ* 'to know.' Hence, too, the O.W. *am-gnau-bot* 'conscientia,' Z. 1056.

No. 141. Root *Fεργ, ἔργον*. Not only O.W. *guerg* (gl. efficax), but the Gaulish *vergo-bretus* and the O.Ir. *ferg* .i. *laech* 'hero,' Corm. Tr. 80, O'Dav. 84, should be added. So, too, *com-orgair* 'help,' O'R., if the word be genuine.

No. 142. Root *Fεργ, εἴργνυμι*. O.Ir. *braig* 'chain,' SM. i. 6, *braga* (gen. *bragat*) 'prisoner,' Corm. Tr. 24, go with ἐ(F)έργω, etc. Here *br* is from *vr* as in the cases mentioned at No. 89 *supra*.

And as *rg* often becomes *rc* (Z². 61), we may also compare the O.Ir. verb *do-farcai* 'cingit' in the St. Gall verses (Z². 953):—

Domfarcai fidbaidæ[b] *fál* Me cingit dumeti sepes :
fomchain lóid luin luad nad cél mihi sonat merulæ cantus celer quem
           non celabo :

---

[a] Hence *gnás* 'consuetudo,' Z. 25.

[b] See Nigra, Reliquie Celtiche i. 23, and note that *fidbaidae* is the gen. sg. of *fidbad* governed by the subsequent *fál* (Z. 915): that the verb *fo-chain* means 'sonat': *im chloe focain cethra* ('for a bell which cattle sound'), Senchus Mór i. 126, 142: that the adjective *luad* (better *lúath*) agrees with *lóid*, not with *luin*, the gen. sg. of *lon*: that *medair* is O'Clery's *meadhair* .i. *caint no urlabhra*, and means neither 'metri' (= Ir. *metir*, Z. 915) nor 'hilaris' (Rev. Celt. i. 479): that *brot* is the dat. sg. of *brat* 'pallium,' and does not mean 'cespite': that *debrath* is explained (?) by *délabrath* (*Debrath ebraice brath* .i. *loquella, debrath din délabrath*, H. 2. 16, col. 99): that *cóima* is the gen. sg. of *cóim* 'a feast,' O'Reilly's *caomh:* and that *coimmdiu cóima* is to be compared with *fiadu firén na fledæ* 'deus justus dapis,' (scil. eucharistiæ) Rumanu in Laud 610, fo. 10. a. r. In the last line *oid* may possibly be the acc. sg. of *oid* (*oidh* .i. *ceol, odh* .i. *ceol*, O'Cl.) Fél. June 1. O'Curry's rendering of these verses, in his Manners and Customs, etc., ii. 387, is a curiosity.

huas molebrán indlínech
fomchain trírech inna nén.
Fommchain cói menn medair mass
himbrot glass de dindgnaib doss.
debrath nomchoimmdiu cóima
cáin scribaimm foroid (n-óibda).

super meo libello interscripto
mihi sonat melodia avium,
Mihi sonat cuculi loquela clara,
pulcra,
in pallio glauco e summitatibus
arbustorum,
debrath (?) e meo Domino epuli,
bene scribo ad symphoniam amœnam.

No. 143. If ἐρεύγω, *ructo* are for εϝρευγω, (v)*ructo*, we may connect Ir. *bruchtaim*, W. *brytheirio*, with the usual change of *vr* to *br*. No. 89.

No. 144. Root ζυγ, Skr. *yuj*. Pictet (Nouvel Essai, p. 40) puts with this the O.Ir. *iúg* in *iúg*-shuide (gl. tribunal) Z. 183 and the Gaulish *Ver-iugodumnus*, which he renders 'valde-iustitia-magnus.'

No. 146. The Ir. *lesc* (gl. piger) for **lecs* (as *losc* for **locs* = λοξός), n. pl. *leiscc*, Z. 67, Br. *lausq*, is identical in form and meaning with Lat. *laxus*, and should be here cited. Why (may I venture to ask) does not Curtius connect with λήγω here noticed the O.Sax. *slac* 'hebes,' Eng. *slack*, OHG. *slah?* As Aufrecht points out (Trans. Philolog. Soc., 1867, p. 20), the Homeric ἄλληκτος, ἀπο-λλῆξαι shew that λήγω has lost an initial consonant. So in the cognate Ir. *logmait* 'dimittimus,' *loghdha* .i. *lagsaine* 'slackness,' O'Cl., and in *lag*, O.Ir. **lac*, ex *la-n-ga*, to be compared with *la-n-guidus*.

No. 150. Root μελγ. Add O.Ir. *tomlacht* (= *do-fo-mlacht*) .i. *bleghan no crudh* 'milk or curd,' O'Cl.

No. 152. The Ir. *ferg* 'anger' (= ὀργή) is from VARG. The Irish forms *broghadh* .i. *biseach* 'increase,' *broghdha* .i. *iomarcach*[a], *broghain* .i. *iomarcaigh no eccoir* 'excess,' O'Cl., *brogais* 'crevit,' O'Don. Supp., come from VRAG, with the regular change of *vr* to *br*. And as *g* before *t* becomes *c*, *ch*, we may also place here Ir. *bracht* 'fat' Corm. Tr. 6, O'Dav. 56, whence the adjective *brachtach* (gen. sg. f. *curadmir ferba brachtchi* 'a champion's portion of a fat cow,' LU. 109a) and its opposite *anbrachtach* 'consumptive' (gen. sg. f. *anbrachtaige*, LB. 60b).

No. 153. ὀρέγω. In *Rigid a laim seacha cotuc meis combind doib* 'he stretches his hand across her and brought them a dish with food,' Tochmarc Bec-fola, H. 2. 16, col. 767, the Irish cognate means 'porrigit.' Ir. *rogh* .i. *geis* 'prohibition,' O'Cl., and *recht* = W. *rhaith* belong to this Number.

No. 154. O.Ir. *lig* (leg. *líg?*) .i. *dath* ' colour': *mesir liga asa saoire 7 asa suthaine* 'thou shalt estimate colours by their nobleness and by their lastingness,' O'Dav. 103, seems cognate with ῥηγεύς.

No. 155. Root στεγ. The Old-Welsh *tig* (in *bou-tig* 'stabulum') now *ty*, pl. *tai*, Corn. *ti*, later *chy*, Br. *ty* 'maison' shew that the root to which the Celtic words are referrible ends in *g*, not *c*. In *con-u-taing* 'protegit,' LL. 204b. 2, *co-ta-u-taing* 'eam protegit,' Ml. 36b., we seem to have a nasalised form of this root, to be compared with στεγνόω.

---

[a] Cf. *ba fer borb brogda*, LU. 82b.

No. 156. σφάραγος. Corn. *fráu* 'crow,' Br. *frau* 'choe,' 'monedula' point to a root SPRAG (= Skr. *sphurj*). Examples of birds' names suggested by the sound of their voices, are *graculus, gallus* (root GAR), Ir. *cailech* (root KAL), *ci-conia, lus-cinia*, κύ-κνος (root KAN), OHG. *swan-a* (root SVAN), to which Corssen (*über die sprache der Etrusker* i. 312) adds Etr. *tus-na* 'swan,' root TUS. From the root SPRAG comes also the W. *ffraeth* 'eloquent' ex *sprakta, *sprag-ta (so *maeth* 'nutritio' ex *mak-ta, Z. 102, *llaeth* 'lac' ex *mlakta, *chwaeth* 'sapor,' ex *svakta) : cf. A.S. *sprëcan*, NHG. *sprechen*. Other instances of British *F* from *SP* are—

Br. *faez* 'vaincu' ex SPAC-TA, Corn. *fethe*, like Zend ςpaς 'unterdrücken,' Justi : cognate with σφίγγω, *spa-n-ge*, etc. No. 157 :

Br. *felch* 'rate,' 'splen,' Ir. *selg*, ex *spelga, σπλήν, No. 390 :

Corn *felja* 'to split,' Br. *faut* 'fissura' ex *SPALT, with *spalten :*

W. *ffion* 'rosa,' pl. *fionou*, Mart. Cap. 9, b, b, Br. *foeonn-enn* 'ligustrum,' Ir. *sion* 'digitalis' : cf. παιωνία ex *σπαιωνία(?) :

W. *ffon* 'baculus,' 'hasta,' Ir. *sonn* 'stake,'[a] ex *spu-n-d-a : root SPUD : cf. O.N. *spjöt* 'spiess,' *spýta* 'riegel' :

W. *ffothell* = Lat. *(s)pustula :* root SPU, No. 652 :

W. *ffraw* 'state of motion' (ex *spraga), *ffrawdd* 'tumult' : cf. σπέρχομαι, No. 176b :

W. *ffroen* 'nostril,' Ir. *srón* (gl. nasus), Z. 23, ex *sprogna, cognate with *spargere :*

W. *ffrwst* 'haste' ex *sprud-to, cognate with Goth. *sprauto* ταχέως :

W. *ffûn* 'breath' ex *spuna, root SPU, No. 652.

No. 158. With ὑγρός Siegfried equated the Ir. *úr* 'fresh,' 'new,' 'green' (*húrda* gl. viridarium, *hurdae* gl. viridia, *úrdatu* gl. virore, *n-uraigedar* gl. cui virere). Cf. W. *ir* 'juicy,' 'fresh,' 'green.'

The Ir. *oss* (gen. *oiss : iricht oiss allaid*, LU. 15, b, *ois*, SM. i. 272) deer' (whence *oissín* 'fawn'), a masc. *a*-stem = Skr. *vasta* 'goat,' can have nothing to do with the Welsh *n*-stem *ych* 'bos,' pl. *ychain*, which Windisch places under this Number. The Irish *ess* 'ox' (Corm. s. v. *Essem*) is the cognate word, and both may be referred to the root VAGH, No. 169.

No. 165. O.Ir. *arg* 'hero,' Corm. Tr. 2, O'Dav. 48 (gen. sg. *airg*, Corm. s. v. *Lorg*, dat. pl. *argaib*, Scirgl. Conc.) is certainly = ἀρχός : cf. also the following specimen of native etymology : *arg* .i. *fiann* 'champion' .i. *tiachar* ('it comes') ab Arg(iv)is .i. *o grecaib* ('from the Greeks') *ar febus an occ* 'because of their warriors' excellence,' O'Mulc. 57, H. 2. 16, col. 89.

No. 166. Root ἀχ, ἀγχ. Add *ochte* 'angustia,' Z. 68, *tachtæ* (*do-achtæ*) gl. angustus, Sg. 60b, *tachtad* (gl. aggens), Sg. 14b., *no-m-thachtar* (gl. angor) *cumcai*, Z. 656, (W. *cyf-yng-der*), whence *cumcigim* (*cum-uc-igim), gl. ango, Z. 435.

The Gaulish *octo-* in *Octodurus* 'arx in angustia sita,' Glück, KN. 133, is also probably cognate. For the change of *ng* to *c* we may compare the Gaulish patronymics in *i-cnos* from *-ingnos, i-gnos*.

---

[a] Hence *ro-sonnta* 'palo infixi sunt,' Fél. Prol. 33, and *sonnach* 'vallum,' 'sepimentum,' LU. 23b, O'Don. Gr. 277, *sonnach farn*, LU. 114b, (*sonnach* .i. *labhun* 'a bawn,' O'Cl.).

— 17 —

No. 166b. Ebel, Beitr. ii. 174, puts O.Ir. *bróen* 'pluvia,' Z. 31, with βρέχω, *rigo*, Goth. *rign*. Here, as in *bran*, etc., No. 89, *br* is from *vr*.

No. 167. To the root *dhragh* here postulated I refer the Irish nasalised forms *imm-drang* (O'Clery's *iomdhrang* .i. *comtharraing*) 'circumtrahere' and *tri-an-drong* .i. *tri deocha* 'tres haustus,' three *draughts*.

No. 168. Fick² 391 connects ἐλέγχω, ἔλεγχος, here cited, with Ir. *lingim* 'salio.' The Ir. *locht* 'crimen,' Z. 1040, *no-lochtaigtis* 'criminabant,' Ml. 74c, *loigthiu* (gl. perpetrato) Ml. 48c, would have been more in point. The Ir. *lingim* 'salio,' *léim* 'saltus' ex *léngven*, O.W. *lammam* 'salio' ex *langvāmi*, seem at first sight cognate with Skr. *langh* 'to jump over,' 'to disregard,' 'to violate.' But as the O.Ir. reduplicated preterite of *lingim* is *ro-leblaing* (for *ro-vlevlaing*), the root is more probably VLA-N-G ex VALG, with the loss of initial *v* noticed infra No. 589.

No. 169. Glück (Neue Jahrbücher, 1864, p. 599) connects with *vah*, ὄχος, *veho*, the Gaulish *co-vinnus* (ex *covignos*, vide supra No. 64, and the Welsh *cy-wain* 'vehere,' *ar-wain* 'ducere,' *am-wain* 'circumducere.' To this Number may also belong the Irish *ess* 'ox' = W. *ych* (pl. *ychen* = Corn. *ohan*) ex *vexan* (see infra, at No. 589), Goth. *auhsa* (as the beast of draught), and Lat. *uxor*, *voxor* (as she who is led home : cf. *uxorem ducere*). And, as *c* may come from *ng* not only in the Irish but the British languages (see No. 166), we may also cite the root UC (ex *ung = va-n-gh*) in Ir. *ro-h-ucad*, W. *d-wc*, Corn. *d-ok*, Br. *d-ouc*, Z. 477, 586, 588.

No. 172. ἔχις, ἔγκελυς, *anguis*. Add O.Ir. *ongu* in *esc-ongu* (gen. *escongan*, LU. 74a, acc. *escongain*, ib. 76b.) or *esc-ongon*, LU. 76b, 'eel,' lit. 'water-snake.' In Welsh, *ag* often becomes *eu* (Rhys, Rev. Celt. ii. 193) : we find accordingly the plurals *eu-od* 'lumbrici lati in hepato ovium' (Davies) and *eu-on* 'bots,' 'worms in horses' entrails.'

No. 173. Root λεχ. Add O.Ir. *laigid in gerran occo andsin* 'decumbit caballus ibi secum,' LU. 39b. *no-laiged isinganium* 'decumbebat in arenâ,' LH. 34b. 2 (Goid. 161), *nach laighfedh* .i. *nach cuirfedh*, H. 3, 18, p. 210, and the expressions *laigid for* 'superiacet,' 'anteponitur,' *ni laig for* 'non superiacet,' O'Don. Supp. The cognate noun is *laige* 'concubitus' (*oc laige la mnái*, Corm. s. v. Orc tréith. In Ir. *con-lé* .i. *cob-lige* 'coitus,' Corm. Tr. 49, the *g* seems lost between vowels (Z². 63, 1083).

No. 174. Root λιχ. Add Ir. *ligur* 'tongue,' Corm., W. *llio* (Rhys) and *llyaw* 'to lick,' Br. *leat*. So probably Ir. *liagh* 'ladle,' O'Don. Supp. (gen. sg. *na leighe*, acc. *leig*, SM. iii., 212 = W. *llwy* 'spoon,' Br. *loa* 'cullier,' 'cochlear'), which is certainly cognate with the Latin *ligula*, *lingula* 'spoon,' 'ladle,' 'skimmer.'

No. 176b. The W. *ffraw* (from SPRAG) 'state of motion,' *ffraw-dd*, 'tumult,' etc., seem cognate with σπέρχομαι. For *ff* ex *sp* see No. 156. For *aw* from *ag* see Rhys, Rev. Celt. ii. 193.

No. 178. Root τρεχ. The Old-Celtic *ver-tragos* 'a swift dog' is quite authentic, and should have been here cited. See Glück, Neue Jahrbücher 1864, p. 597. So also W. *tro* = τρόχος (Br. *tro* 'tour'), O.W. *traet* 'pedes' = Ir. *traigid*, Br. *troat* 'pes.'

The Irish *tach* in *an-tach* (gl. otiosa, gl. quieta) LH. 11b, 14b, Goid. 67, 71, is = ταχύς for τακυς, Skr. *taku* here cited.

No. 189. The Irish *gil* .i. *lám* 'hand' (O'Curry's transcript of the Brehon Laws, p. 1446) is identical with χείρ and the Old-Latin *hir*. So *gillae* 'servus' is to be compared in root and meaning with χείριος, ὑπο-χείριος, in meaning with Lat. *man-cipium*. *Geilsine* .i. *munteras* 'famulatio,' LU. 13a, is also connected; the suffix *sine* (ex *-s-tan-iâ*) is also in *coceilsine* 'societas,' and *fáithsine* 'prophetia,' Z. 77. The Brehon-law *geil-fine*, the junior division of the Irish family, perhaps meant originally the father and those of his sons who were still *in mancipio ejus*. The root is *ghar* 'rapere,' whence also Lat. *hirudo*, Ir. *gil* 'leech' (Corm. Tr. 83), and W. *gel*, Corn. *ghel* (gl. sanguissuga), unless (as Rhys thinks) we should compare Skr. *jalūkā*. Corn. *ghel* is (wrongly, I think) connected by Ebel (Beitr. ii. 175) with OHG. *egala, ecala*.

The resemblance of Ir. *cron* in *dio-chron* .i. *gan aimsir* 'without time,' O'Cl., to χρόνος here cited, is accidental. Fick 73 connects with χρόνος the O.N. *grann* 'gray.' This adjective seems identical with the Ir. *grant* .i. *liath* Corm. s.v. Crointile.

No. 193. The Celtic words for '*yes-terday*' are possibly cognate with *heri* (*hesi*, *hjesi*), Ir. (*ind*)*hê* Z. 609, W. *doe*, Corn. *doy*, Z. 617, 618 (ex *djai*, *jasi?*), Br. *dech*, Z. 618, ex *djehi* as *pelloch*, Z. 298, ex acc. sg. *peljôhen*, *peljôsen*.

No. 197. Here Ir. *gel* 'white' is put with χλωρός, *haris, helvus*. I would rather connect it with χαλ-κός, No. 182. Curtius' theory, here stated, that the *f* in *flâvus* comes from *gh*, is rendered at least questionable by the Irish *bla* (leg. *blá*) .i. *buidhe* 'yellow,' O'Dav. 56 and O'Cl., whence the dissyllabic man's-name *Bládán*, Fél. Aug. 10. See too Fick's Wörterbuch[2] 381. 'An. *blâ-r*, ahd. *blâ* heisst auch *flavus* (nach Schade).'

No. 200b. The O.Ir. *gromma* 'satire,' *gromfa* 'he will satirize,' Corm. Tr. 86, *grim* .i. *cogadh*, O'Cl., *gruaim* 'morositas,' *gruamda* (gl. acer), Ir. Gl. 1065, W. *grwm* 'a murmur,' 'a growl,' all seem to belong to the root GHRAM, whence χρεμίζω, χρόμη, *fren-dere*, etc.

No. 201. χρίω, χρῖμα. O.Ir. *gert*[a] .i. *lacht* 'milk,' O'Dav. 94, was equated by Siegfried with Skr. *ghṛta* 'ghee'; and certainly belongs to the root GHAR 'to sprinkle.'

No. 204. Here, following Glück KN. 24, and Ebel, Beitr. ii, 184, the Gaulish particle *ande*, the Irish *ind, inn*, are equated with ἀντί, Skr. *anti*, Lat. *ante*, etc. But, first, the Irish form (we know nothing certain of the meaning of the Gaulish *ande*) not only implies motion to or against (*ind-rid* 'incursus'), but also motion from something (cf. *ind-arpae* 'ablatio' *ent-erben*) and, secondly, the tenuis in the combination NT is always (so far as I know) preserved in Gaulish[b]. In Irish (except in loanwords like *cland* = planta,

---

[a] *Cen gert ferbba* (sine lacte vaccarum) LU., cited in Corm. Tr. 37.
[b] Cf. *argento-, carpento-, Nantuates, Commontorios*, etc. *Candetum* for *canteton*, if genuine, is an exception.

*talland*ᵃ = τάλαντον, *andoóit*, Tir. 10, = antas γερουσία, Ducange) the dental is kept, while the nasal disappears, often lengthening the preceding vowel, as in *cét, tét, dét* = W. *cant, tant, dant*. We should accordingly expect the Irish cognate of ἀντί, etc. to begin with *ét*-, and this actually occurs in *étan* 'forehead' (dat. sg. *étun: atracht in lúan láith asa-étun* 'the hero's light ᵇ rose out of his forehead,' Táin bó Cúalnge LU. 80), which I unhesitatingly put with the Latin *antiæ* 'forelock,' and the OHG. *endi* 'forehead,' Fick 425. The British cognate of ἀντί is (as might be expected) the Br. *ent*, Z. 616. The Latin cognate of *ande-, ind-, inn-* seems *ind-* in *ind-igeo, ind-ustria, ind-ulgeo, ind-āgo, ind-uo*.

No. 206. ἄστυ, *vāstu*. The Welsh cognate is *gosam* (in *guor-cosam*, Z. 963, Rev. Celt. ii. 279) = Ir. *fosaimm* 'maneo.' As to Irish, add *feiss* (*do feiss aidche hi linnib*, Fiacc's h. 27), and for *i-fhus, i-fhos* read *i-fus, i-fos*. Windisch should have noted here that in the Lebar Brecc and in Codex A of Cormac's Glossary (from which he cites these forms) the dotted *f* is used not only to express the *f* infected by flanking vowels, but also the *f* changed to *v* by the influence of a preceding nasal.

No. 208. The Ir. *saith* (.i. *ionnmhas* 'treasure,' O'Cl.) ex **sati* and the synonymous *sét* (n. pl. *seuit*, Tir. 6, acc. pl. *seotu*, LU. 74a) ex **sant-o* are cognate with ἐτεός, *satya*, and A.S. *sóth* ex **santh-s*.

No. 209. O.W. *at-, et-*, Z. 900, Corn. *as-*, Br. *az-, at-*, and (as I conjecture) the Gaulish *eti-c* should be added to ἔτι, etc.

No. 211. Ϝιταλός. With *vatsa* Siegfried equated the Mediæval Latin (Gaulish?) *vassus*, W. *gwas* 'servus,' 'famulus,': cf. O.Ir. *ainder* (W. *anner* 'bucula') 'heifer,' 'young woman.'

No. 214. Root PAT, πέτομαι, πίπτω, *fintha*. O.Ir. *étar* 'impetratur,' Z. 504, should have been placed with Goth. *fintha*. The Old-Welsh *ataned*ᶜ 'wings,' *atanocion* (gl. alligeris) Rev. Celt. i. 360 (cf. Ir. *ethaite*, O'Don. Supp.) and Ir. *aithed* 'elopement,' LU. 42a, preserve the *a*-vowel of the root. So the O.Ir. *áith* (gl. pinna) = **pāti-, deáith* (gl. bipennis), which Zeuss, Gr. C. 30, wrongly puts among the examples of the diphthong *ái*. They should be transferred to p. 17.

The O.Ir. *iall* 'a flight' (acc. pl. *ialla*, Brocc. h. 91) is from **petla*, as *ciall* 'intellectus' from **cetla*, cognate with Skr. *cetar* 'wahrnehmer, aufmerker,' Beitr. viii. 39.

With πίτνημι (a clerical error for πιτνέω) and πίπτω Windisch (Beitr. viii. 3) connects the Ir. *tuitim* 'cadere' (=**do-fo-pint-imbi*). To this verb

---

ᵃ In the Old-Irish glossary inserted in Schleicher's Indogermanische Chrestomathie, Ebel seems to regard *talland* as a genuine Celtic word. But it occurs with the meaning of a definite weight (.*uii. cét talland argait*, LU. 114b), as well as with that of 'faculty,' and is borrowed from τάλαντον, the double *ll* being due to the accent. In like manner, I should explain the double *n* in *crann* = **queráno-s* (not **quarn-* Beitr. viii. 39).

ᵇ I venture to connect *lúan* (from **lucno-*) with Lat. *lūna, lūmen* (for **lucna, *lucmen*) and Gr. λύχνος from λυκνος.

ᶜ 'Illa recondit (.i. *renovat*) opus (.i. *hi hetaned*),' gloss recently found by Mr. Bradshaw in the Oxford copy of Ovid's Ars Amatoria. See Appendix E.

belong the reduplicated *s*-forms *taithis*, LU. 74a., *tocthsat, to-thoethsat*, Beitr. vii. 49.

No. 216. Root στα. The British cognates of ί-στημι, *sto*, etc., come from an extended root STA-M, losing the *t* as usual : W. *sefyll, safiad*, etc., Br. *seuell* 'surgere.' The W. *ystof*, Br. *steuffenn* are loans from *stämen*. To the Irish words here cited add *samaigimm* 'pono' (*samaiges* 'posuit,' Fiacc's h. 55) and O'Clery's *seise* .i. *sesamh*. In his *stá* .i. *seas* (= siste),—'*stá a athaigh ar Conall*,'—the *t* is kept.

No. 221. With στερέω cf. *serbh* 'theft' (O.-Celtic *stervā), *fo-serba bega* .i. *mingata* 'petty thefts,' O'Dav. 117 : *searbhaidh* .i. *goid* 'theft,' O'Cl., *siorbhai* .i. *gadaigheacht* 'thieving,' O'Cl.

No. 222. στερεός. With this are connected not only Ir. *seirt* .i. *neart* 'strength,' O'Cl., *ro-n-sert*, Fél. Ep. 11, *seiric* .i. *laidir* 'strong,' O'Cl., but also O.Ir. *us-sarb* ' death,' Corm. : 'gewiss,' says Curtius, 'heisst sterben eigentlich erstarren .... Die Begriffe starr, fest, stark berühren sich hier vielfach.'

No. 226. Root στιγ, στίγμα. O.W. *tigom* (gl. nevi), Windisch, Beitr. viii. 252.

No. 227. Add to the derivatives from the root STAR the O.Ir. *có-sair* .i. *leabaidh* 'lectus,' O'Cl., *sreith* (gl. strues) Z. 992, (gl. pratum) Sg. 20., W. *sarn* 'stratum,' 'pavimentum,' *sarnu* 'to strew' and O.Ir. *fo-sernair* 'is spread abroad' (*fosernair senfocal* 'vulgatur proverbium,' O'Dav. 54. To the by-form STRU (whence Goth. *strauja*) we may refer W. *y-strewi, trewi* 'sternutare,' Br. *struyaff*, and Ir. *sreod* 'sneezing,' 'the omen drawn from sneezing.'

No. 230. Some important Celtic derivatives from the roots TAN, TAM-P should be added—O.Ir. *tana* (*is-gann membrumm, is-tana an-dub* 'parchment is scanty : thin is the ink,' Z. præf. xii) = W. *teneu*, Br. *tanau* : the Ir. verb *ro-thinsat* 'extenuati sunt,' LH. 6b., the noun *tinu* 'tenuitas,' Amra Chol. 101, Goid[2]. 168 : the O.Ir. *tonach* .i. *léine* 'indusium' .i. *brat* 'pallium,' O'Cl.[a] ; and, lastly, the O.Ir. *timpán* 'a small stringed instrument (Corm. Tr. 163, *tet* .i. *tiompán*, O'Cl.) played with a bow ' (O'Curry's Manners and Customs iii. 362), which has nothing to do with *tympánum*[b], but is connected with the Lithuanian *timpa* 'sinew,' the O.N. *thömb* 'bowstring,' and perhaps also with the Latin *tempus, templum* and *temptare*. The Ir. *tan* 'time,' *in-tain* 'when,' Z. 708, also belong to this Number.

No. 231. *Tám* .i. *bas*, O'Dav. 121, (*tám roselaig dáini* 'pestilentia quæ occīdit homines,' Corm. 45), *tamh* .i. *plaigh*, O'Cl. and its derivative *taimthiu*, Fél. July 2, etc., seem, like *tābes*, to come from the root TAK. Hence, too, O.Ir. *ro-tachatar* (fugerunt, *ro-the-thachatar), Ml. 44a ; *arateget* (quia fugiunt), Ml. 48d ; *in-tech* 'path,' Goidel[2]. 155.

No. 234. The Ir. *tummud* 'a dipping' (n. pl. tri *tuimthea* gléso in letraim dídenach, Lib. Arm. 78 a. 2), *tumud na cainnell*, SM. ii. 252,

---

[a] *Tuinech* .i. *cochall*, O'Dav. 120, is a loan from *tunica*.
[b] Hence is borrowed Ir. *timpan* (with a short *a*), gen. sg. *timpain* : 7 si oc *senmaimm thimpain* 7 oc *cantain chiúil* 'and she, Miriam, sounding a timbrel and singing music,' LB. 118b, referring to Exodus xv. 20.

is for *tumbuth, *tungvātu, Lat. tinguere, just as the neuter n-stem imm, imb [a] 'butter' is = Lat. unguen. In the root-vowel the Irish form agrees with OHG. thuncon, duncon. Other instances of hard m (mb) from ngv are :—
Ir. remmad 'to distort,' Corm. s. v. reimm, = *(v)rengvátu, ῥέμβειν, A.S. vringan, O.N. rangr :
Ir. léimm 'leap,' Z. 1053, ex *vlēngven, léim ro-leblaing-seom, LU. 111a (root VLA-N-G, Skr. valy 'salire') :
Ir. cruim .i. toirneach 'thunder,' O'Cl., ex *crongvi, O.N. hrang 'strepitus' :
Ir. dram .i. iomad 'multitude,' O'Cl., ex *dra-n-gva: cf. dru-n-gus 'a force,' Ir. drong, O.Lat. forc-tus.

With these examples compare the Sardinian limba, imbena, sámbene, ambidda = lingua, inguen, sanguinem, anguilla, Ascoli, Corsi i. 132.

No. 235. Root τεκ. The Ir. tuag 'bow,' Z. 22, and tál 'adze,' Ir. Gl. No. 252, Goidel. 59, like τόξον, and the Slav. tesla 'axe,' belong to this Number. The O.Ir. techtaim 'habeo' may be compared in form with τίκτω, in meaning with OHG. digju. The infinitive conutecht (*con-od-tech-t, Ml. 130c, Goidel[2]. 29) seems to belong to this root.

No. 236. Root τελ, ταλ, Skr. and Lat. tul. From tul we have (according to Rhys), in the compound maur-dluith-ruim (gl. magno vecte) Juv. 90, the O.W. tluith, now llwyth = Ir. lucht 'a weight,' 'a charge,' Brocc. h. 47. In Ir. ro-lomur 'audeo,' Z[2]. 438 (ni lamad cor de 'he durst not stir,' LU. 10a.) compared with τολμάω, we again find loss of the first element of the combination tl.

W. tlawd 'poor,' needy' is = τλητός : cf. Ir. tlaith ; and with τέλος, meaning 'tax,' 'duty,' 'toll,' the Ir. taile (gl. salarium), Ir. Gl. No. 739, tuarastal (= *do-fo-ar-as-tala) 'hire,' 'wages,' and W. tal 'payment,' tal 'persolve' = Ir. tale (MS. talle) Goid[2]. 157 are certainly coguate.

With Lat. tollo I would put Ir. ro-n-tolomar ('let us upraise ourselves' ?) Colm. 35, tall .i. goid 'theft,' O'Cl., tallsad .i. dogoidsead 'they stole,' ib., teallsadar (.i. dogoidsead, ib.) = O.Ir. *tellsatar.

In the c-stem teol 'thief,' O'Cl., (n. pl. (bain)teolaigh 'she-thieves ') an Old-Celtic *teulax, we have the enhancement found in Skr. tālayāmi.

The Ir. tlás or tlus .i. dirnéis no spréidh (= prǣda) 'cattle,' O'Cl., and tletid 'tollunt,' O'Don. Supp., should also be added.

No. 237. The Irish tét .i. sligi 'road' from *tem-ta, Goidel[2]. 171, may belong to the root τεμ. So sét (O'Clery's séd .i. samhail) 'likeness,' Fól. June 16, is from sim-ta : (cf. Lat. simitu, simul), létenach (gl. audax, Z. 18) ex *lam-tanach (No. 236), and cétach 'mantle,' acc. sg. cétaig, Tir. 6, ex *cam-tacā cognate with camisia, OHG. hamo, hemidi.

No. 239. Root τερ, τείρω. The O.W. tarater, Corn. tardar, Br. tarazr 'terebrum ' should be added.

---

[a] Wrongly placed by Ebel (Gr. Celt[2]. 234) among the masc. i-stems. The dat. imim (better imbimm) occurs in SM. ii. 254 : the acc. sg. (la cét-im 'with first butter') in Brocc. h. 25, Goid[2]. 143, where it is wrongly rendered. The Welsh ymen-yn, emen-yn, as usual, shews the stem.

No. 241. τέρσο-μαι. In the Irish *tair, terad* 'dry weather' [*ba-tair* (.i. *ba-terad*) *coidchi innagort* 'there was dry weather till night in her field,' Brocc. h. 30] no trace of the *s* of TARS is discoverable ; this *s* may therefore be regarded as a determinative, Fick 1013.

No. 242. The Old-Ir. *tethra* agrees in declension with τέτραξ. Its gen. sg. *tethrach* is glossed by *badb* 'scallcrow' in LU. 50a, top margin— Mac Lonan *dixit :—*

Mian mná tethrach[a] *atenid*[b]　'The she-scallcrow's longing is her fires[b],
slaide sethnach[c] *iarsodain*　Slashing of sides thereafter,
suba[d] *luba*[e] *folubaib*[f]　Blood, body under bodies,
ugail[g] *tróga*[h] *dir drogain*[i]　Eyes, heads (?), a meet word !'

So O'Clery : *teathra* .i. *badhb no feanog.*

No. 243. W. *tat* now *tâd*, Corn. *tâs*, Br. *tat* 'pater' are identical with *tata*, τέττα. Such words are unlikely to have been borrowed.

No. 247. τύ-λος, τύ-λη. Add O.Ir. *túithlae* (= *tū-tal-ia), gl. gibbus, Z. 767 : *túare* 'cibus,' Z. 247, may also come from the root TU. So also the adj. *tol* (*ic toi tol-rig* .i. *ic ardd-rig toi,* 'with Tay's high king,' Amra Chol. 119, and the noun *tul* 'umbo' (*tul n-óir*, LU. 129a). The Welsh *tyfu* ' crescere,' *twf, tyfiad, tyfiant* 'incrementum' may also be added.

No. 251. Ir. *dub* 'dark' is either cognate with Goth. *daubs* 'deaf,' *du-m-b-s* 'dumb,' and τυφλός for *θυφλός, or (if *b* = *gv*) with O.N. *dökkr* 'dunkel' (Rhys).

No. 252. The Gaulish SVADV-RIX on the Besançon bronze knife (Rev. Celt. ii. 112) and the Irish name *Sadb* i. e. *Sadv*, all probably go with *sua(d)vis*, ἡδύς, *svādu.*

No. 255c. δα, δέδαεν. Add Ir. *dán* 'ars,' 'ingenium,' 'facultas,' 'scientia,' Z². 238, 776, 998, dat. pl. *danaib* Sg. 156b. an *u*- stem, and, I think, a different word from *dán = donum*, No. 270.

No. 260. O.W. *or dometic* (gl. domito), Z. 1057, *ardomaul* 'docilis,' Mart. Cap. 9. a. b., *ni-cein-guo-demisauch*[j] (gl. non bene passa, estis), Z. 1057, Br. *dauat* 'brebis,' might be here added to the derivatives from the root DAM.

No. 262. Ir. *dair* 'inire vaccam vel ovem,' gen. *dara*, SM. i. 144, ii. 45, *darmna*, Book of Aicill 230, O'Dav. 79, *con-da-ro-dar-t* 'eam, scilicet vaccam, inivit,' Rev. Celt. i. 44, seems cognate with δαρθάνω and *dor-m-io :* cf. the use of the Germ. *be-schlafen.*

No. 265. Root δεμ. Ir. *daimh* .i. *teagh* ' domus,' O'Cl., should be added.

No. 266. δεξιός. In W. *deheu* 'right,' 'south,' Br. *deho*, the suffix resembles that of Goth. *taihs-va.*

No. 267. Root ἑερ. Br. *darn* 'pars,' W. *darn* ' a piece or patch ' (whence the English verb *to darn*) should be added.

---

[a] .i. *badb* 'scallcrow,' (Rev. Celt. i. 33), the *corvus cornix* or hooded crow.
[b] .i. *gle 7 arm* ' battle and arms.'
[c] .i. *táeb* ' side.'
[d] .i. *fuil* ' blood.'
[e] .i. *corp* ' body ' (so O'Clery, *lubha* .i. *corp*).
[f] .i. *fo feraib* ' under men.'
[g] .i. *súli* ' eyes.'
[h] .i. *cend* ' head.'
[i] .i. *fúach* ' word.'
[j] Printed *deimisauch*, Z. 2057. Other corrigenda in these glosses are mentioned infra in Appendix F.

No. 268. δίεσθαι. Add O.Ir. *do-n-con-diath* 'hath sped (or fled?) from us,' Amra Chol. LU. 8a.

No. 269. The instructive Old-Welsh *duiutit* (*-tit* = Lat. *-tūtem*) 'divinitas' should have been cited, as well as the O.Ir. *doi* (*doi-duine* ,i. *day-duine* Corm.) = *divus* δῖος, and *tré-denus* 'triduum,' Z. 302.

No. 270. Root δο. Add *dan* (leg. *dán?*) *airgid* .i. *maoin no aisgidh airgid*, O'Cl., *dathadh* .i. *tiodhlacadh* 'a giving,' ib. This *dan* (*dán?*) = *donum* seems quite a different word from the *u*-stem *dán* 'ars,' No. 255c, though Windisch treats them as one and the same. From *dan* = *donum* we have the verb *dánigur* and the nouns *danán* (gl. munusculum) and *danigud* 'largitio,' Z. 998.

No. 279. Root ἰδ. Ir. *ithim* 'mando,' Z. 429, here cited, seems rather connected with *ith*, W. *yd* 'corn,' an *u*-stem = *pitu*. But O.W. *esicc* in *leu-esicc* (gl. cariantem) 'louse-eaten,' Beitr. vii. 388, now *ysig* 'corroding,' is almost certainly from **ed-ticio*.

No. 280. Root ἱδ, *sedeo, sita*. The O.Ir. *sadb*, Corm., W. *haddef* 'a dwelling' certainly (like Skr. *sadman*) belongs to this Number, though the suffix is obscure. So *assoith* 'resedit,' Fiacc's h. 58, 59. In *con-sádu* 'I set together,' Fél. Jan. 23, *ad-suidet, ar-said*, SM. iii. 10, we have a causal meaning.

In *adh* .i. *dligheadh* '*ge-setz*,' O'Cl., (whence *adha*, *com-adas*, etc.) the initial *s* seems lost, as in *amal* 'instar,' *uaim* = seam, the article *ind* = (*s*)*ind*, and the negative prefix *an-* = *sēmi*.

No. 281. Root ἰδ, Skr. *sad, á-sad* 'adire,' 'accedere.' With *sedulus* here cited I would connect the O.Ir. adverb *for-sidit*, Fél. Ap. 16, which is glossed by the Latin *cito* in LB., by the Ir. *forrith no colluath* in Laud 610.

No. 282. Root Fιδ. O.Ir. *fiad* 'coram,' Z. 643, W. *yn-gwydd* 'in praesentiâ,' 'coram,' and Ir. *fetar* (= **ved-da-r*) 'scio.'

No. 284. κήδω, κήδομαι. Fick 30 refers κέκαδον, κεκαδόμην, with Lat. *cado, cēdo*, to a root *kad* 'gehen,' 'weichen,' 'fallen.' To this I would refer W. *cwyddo* 'to fall,' in *dy-gwyddo, tram-gwyddo, cwyddol* 'falling,' and Ir. *casair* .i. *cioth* 'a rainfall,' 'a shower,' O'Cl., ex **cad-tric*.

No. 286. Root μεδ. W. *meddwl* 'thought,' 'mind' belongs to this Number. Very beautiful is Windisch's explanation of *coimdiu* 'dominus' as **con-midiu*. Compare *dia már midedar cach ní* ('a great God who judges everything') *Aided Echach maic Máireda*, LU. 40a, and the Old-Norse name for 'gods,' *rögn*, as μέδοντες.

No. 298. ὕδω. With ἀ(F)οιδή (root VID) the Irish *faed*[a] 'cry,' W. *gwaedd* 'clamor,' 'ejulatio' are identical. From the root VAD (Skr. *vadāmi* 'dico') I would derive the Ir. *fuidhir* .i. *briathar* 'word,' O'Cl. So the O.Ir. *odh* .i. *ceol* 'music,' *oidh* .i. *ceol*, O'Cl.

In the Irish *fonn* (from **fo-n-d*) 'a tune,' 'a song,' the root is nasalised as in Skr. *va-n-dē* 'celebro,' to which Rhys (Rev. Celt. ii. 190) refers O.W. *guetid* 'dicere.'

---

[a] Dat. sg. *faeid*, Corm. s. v. bachall.

In Ir. *uissiu* 'lark' (now *f-uiseóg* with prosthetic *f*), O.Ir. *ús* (ex **ud-tu*, **vad-tu*) .i. *slonnadh no aisneis*, O'Cl., *im-thús* (= *imm-do-ús*) 'history,' *imthúsa* ' tidings,' we have the common dissimilation exemplified in Greek by ᾀστέον from ᾀδ-τεον. In *fusc* (*ex *vadco*) 'nuntiatio,' SM. i. 258, we have the assibilation of the dental found in Ir. *basc, mesc, trosc* and *uisce*, and in the Latin *es-ca* from **ed-ca*.

No. 300. ὕδ-ωρ. Add *os* (= **ud-ta*) in *os-bretha* 'water-judgments,' SM. i. 182. The nasalised form *fa-n-d* ('ainm na dére') occurs in LU. 45a with the meaning 'tear.' It also seems to occur in *di-unnach* 'capitolavium,' Corm., *diunnach* .i. *glanadh o pheacadh* 'cleansing from sin,' O'Cl., and in *foinsi* .i. *tiobrada no toibre* ' wells,' O'Cl.

No. 301. ἄ-εθ-λον, *va(d)s*, Goth. *vadi*. With these, I think, goes the Ir. gen. sg. *ois* (= **vad-ti*) in the phrase *cáin óis, cáin éra*,[a] *cáin airlic[th]e* ' a law of bail, a law of refusal (to lend without security), a law of pledge', LU. 46b, which O'Curry renders 'a law of lending, a law of extortion, a law of pawn.'

No. 302. Stem *aiϑ*. W. *aidd* ' calor,' ' studium,' Br. *oaz*, should be added. The O.Ir. *ésce, ésca*, ' moon,' Z. 229 (ex **êd-cio*, as *usce* 'water' ex **ud-cio*) seems, like Lat. *eidus, idus*, Skr. *i-n-du*, referrible to a root ID.

No. 303. Root δλϑ. To this Number surely belong Lat. *arduus*, Gaulish *ardvo-s* (in *Ardu-enna*), Ir. *ard*.

No. 306. Root ἐρυϑ. W. *rhudd* 'ruddy,' Br. *ruz*, should be added.

No. 307. Root θα, θη. Add O.Ir. *did, τίτθος (ba did do bochtaib)*, Amra Chol. 85.

No. 309. Root θε. Add O.Ir. *dan* .i. *obair* 'work,' Leb. Lec. Vocab. No. 446, *in-denim* (gl. debilitatum), Parker 115[b], pl. *indenmi* (gl. imbecilles), Z. 860.

No. 312. Fick 99 puts the Gaulish *dunum (dūnon)* with *dhanu*, θίς.

No. 313. With θέω, θοός, has been compared the Ir. *dó* in the common phrases *dó duit dotig* 'go thou [c] to thy house,' LU. 45b. ; *do duit uaim* ' go thou from me,' ib. 47a ; *dó dúib iarom dia-saichthin* ' go you then to her,' ib. 110a. But, like *dothar* .i. *abann* ' river,' *duithir na hoidche* .i. *maidin* ' morning,' O'Cl., it rather seems cognate with δύω, δύνω, OHG. *zūwen*, Fick[2]. 95.

The verb θήγω 'I sharpen,' here mentioned, is compared by Fick 772 with O.N. *dengja*, A.S. *dencgan* 'to hammer.' Whether he is right or wrong, these Teutonic verbs seem cognate with the Irish *de-daig* 'compressit,' Goidel[2]. 133, *lase for-ru-de-dgatar* (gl. obprimendo), Ml. 63a., and the nasalised forms *for-dengat* (gl. opprimentes), Ml. 29a, *fordingit* ' opprimunt,' LB. 39a, *for-dengar* (gl. deprimitur), Ml. 57d. The *s*-futures *for-diastar* 'opprimetur,' O'Dav. 77, 85, *for-n-diassatar* (gl. opprimi), Ml. 39b, may also be mentioned.

No. 315. θρασύς. Glück (Neue Jahrb. 1864, p. 600) connects 'Ανδράστη, the name of a British goddess of victory, with Skr. *dhṛsh* ' vincere,' and translates 'die unüberwindliche.'

---

[a] Cf. *era* .i. *ni tugais ní do neoch gen bai* ' thou gavest nought to any one without cows,' O'Mulc. Gl. H. 2, 16, col. 104.
[b] For other glosses in this MS. see Appendix G.
[c] Lit. 'a going to thee.'

No. 316. θρᾶ, θρήσασθαι. The Ir. *dír* 'debitus,' 'justus,' *díre* 'merces,' 'pœna,' = W. *dir* 'certus,' 'necessarius,' *dirwy* 'mulcta,' 'pœna pecuniaria' are connected in meaning, as well as identical in root, with Skr. *dharma* here cited. And the Ir. *del-b*, W. *del-w* ex (**del-vâ*, **dhar-vâ*) 'forma,' Ir. *dolbh* .i. *druidheacht* 'magice,' O'Cl., *dolbud* 'figmentum,' ro-*dolbi* 'finxit,' *doilbthid* 'figulus,' Z. 10, may be put with Skr. *dhar-iman*, Lat. *for-ma*.

No. 317. Root θρε. To this, I think, belong two Celtic words: Ir. *drogain*, which is glossed by *fúach* 'word' supra No. 242, and *dord* 'susurrus,' Corm. s.v. adann, = W. *dwrdd*, whence O.Ir. *dordaid dam* 'mugit cervus,' LU. 11b, *fo-dordchu* (gl. susurratores) Z. 73. With *drog(ain)* cf. (τον)θορυγίω. In the O.Ir. neut. *men*-stem *deil-m* 'sound,' 'thunder,' the *r* has become *l*.

No. 319. θύρα. The Gaulish acc. pl. *dvorico* (Inscription of Guéret) should be cited as showing the Old-Celtic anlaut, which agrees with that of Skr. *dvāra, dvārakāṇi*.

No. 320. Root θυ. To this belongs Ir. *duine* 'homo,' W. *dyn*, as the 'thinker' (cf. Lith. *dù-ma-s* 'gedanke'): the diphthongal plural of *duine* (*dóini*) either shows an abnormal enhancement of the root-vowel or belongs to No. 308.

No. 324. Root VADII, ὁθ, ὠθέω. Add Ir. *fod-b* in *ra*[*t*]*-tregdastar mar thregdas fodb omnaid*, LL. cited in O'Curry's Manners and Customs, iii. 448, where it is rendered 'he pierces [leg. pierced] thee as the felling axe would pierce the oak.' O'Clery has *fodhbh* .i. *gearradh no teascadh*.

No. 326. Root πενϑ. For the words which Windisch here erroneously refers to the root BHADH, we may substitute the following:—

From the unnasalised form, we have Ir. *buiden*, O.W. *bodin* pl. *bodiniou* (gl. phalanges), *byddin* 'a band,' 'a troop,' O.Ir. *basc* 'monile' (= **bad-co*), Corm. 7, with which W. *baich* 'a burden,' 'bundle,' Br. *bech* = Lat. *fascis* (ex **bhadei-s*) may, I think, be connected.

From the nasalised form we have Ir. *band* .i. *dliged* 'lex,' in the Vocabulary in the Lebar Lecain (= O'Clery's *bann* .i. *dligheadh*),[a] *for-bann* 'bad or false law,' O'Don. Supp., pl. *forbanna*, Z. 874, *co-forbannach* ' κακονομιστί ' (if one may coin a Greek word), LB. 60b, and the adjective *bind* 'melodious,' *bindiu* (gl. sonorius), Z. 275, which is to be compared with Lat. *fides* 'the string of a musical instrument,' and the nasalised forms *of-fend-ix, of-fend-imentum*.

No. 338. ἕρπω. The W. *sarff* is identified by Ebel (Beitr. ii. 158) with Skr. *sarpa*: but it is probably a loan from *serp(ens)*, just as *prudd* is from *pru(dens)* and *ysplan* from *splend(ens)*.

No. 341. Root λυπ. Cormac's *rop* 'animal *rumpens*' (gen. sg. *ruip*, LL. *robb*, LL. 78 b 2, acc. pl. *rupu*) may belong to this Number[b]: his *rap* 'animal rapiens' to λαμβάνω, root RABH, (see infra, at No. 536b). From *rop* we have the abstract *roptene* .i. *gairge* in H. 3, 18, p. 73, col. 3.

---

[a] So Corssen refers Lat. *lex* (Osc. abl. sg. *ligud*) to the root LIG 'im sinne der bindenden satzung.'
[b] Another instance of *pp* from *mp* is *popp* LU. 97a = *pampinus* (*popp do birur for each cúach* 'a sprig of watercress on every cup'). This is probably a loanword.

No. 343. παγ, πήγνυμι, Skr. pac. The Ir. aicc 'bond,' O'Don. Supp., aigter (leg. aicther) 'is tied,' 'is fastened,' ib., aice .i. trebhaire 'a surety' (vas, vadis) ib., aicde .i. cumtach 'a structure,' Corm., aicde airgit .i. dealg no fail 'a pin' (cf. πάσσαλος, palus) or 'ring,' O'Don. Supp., aicce ab accula (leg. acula 'a little needle') H. 2, 16, col. 88, all appear to have lost initial p and to come from the root PAK.

No. 345. παλάμη and palma are represented not only by the Irish lám (= *plāma), but by the adjective dīlmain 'liber' (= *di-plāmani, lit. 'e-man-cipatus'), compar. dīlmainiu (gl. liberius), Ml. The noun palf, which occurs in Welsh, Cornish and Breton, is no doubt a loan from palma. Hence too the Ir. palmaire 'helm,' 'tiller' (ansa gubernaculi) O'Cl. = M. Br. palvesenn an reuf.

No. 350. The p of πατέομαι, pasco, etc., is preserved in the Old-Irish compound ír-phaisiu (gl. cancer, morbus), Z. 268, where paisiu is identical with (perhaps borrowed from) pastio, and ír (.i. olc, Cormac) is cognate with πύθω, pūs, etc. No. 383. The Ir. caithim 'consumo' here cited I would now connect with Goth. skathjan, A.S. sceadhan, NHG. schaden.

No. 351. Stem παυ. Add W. poues (gl. quies), Z. 1053, and the Cornish s-pauen mor (gl. equor), where the s is prosthetic, as in Corn. s-quenip (Fr. 'guenipe'), Bret. s-clacc (Fr. 'glace'), s-claer (Fr. 'clair'), Irish s-túag, τόξον, s-cipar from Lat. piper, and s-préidh 'cattle' from Lat. præda.

No. 352. πελός. The Ir. alad 'speckled' (gen. sg. m. alaid, LH. 34a. 2) = Skr. palita, πελιτνός, may have lost initial p.

The Ir. lí 'color,' (gl. gloriam), Z. 623, W. lliw m., Br. liu, belong to livor, cited under this Number.

No. 353. πέλλα (ex *πελνα). Cf. Ir. lenn (gl. sagana vel saga), Z. 1063, O.W. lenn, ib., ex *plenja, Lith. plëne 'haut,' Fick, Spracheinheit 338.

No. 355. In O.Ir. ál 'proles,' gen. áil, = OHG. fasal, A.S. fäsl 'fœtus' we have the Celtic cognate of πέ(σ)ος, pasas, pe(s)nis. From ál comes ultimately alachta 'prægnans,' LH. 9b, Goid. 100, the passive participle of a verb *alaigimm, or *alaigiur 'prægnantem facio,' which I have not met.

No. 356. περάω, περήσω, πορθμός. The Gaulish rito-n, O.W. rit, now rhyd, 'a ford,' may belong to this Number, if we assume the loss of p.

No. 357. The W. pell 'far' (pellach 'ulterior'), Br. pell 'procul' certainly belong to this Number. As to the liquids, O.Ir. ire, Z. 277, is = περαῖος = pell, just as O.Ir. ferr 'better' is = Skr. varíyas = W. guell.

No. 359b. Ir. earc .i. breac 'speckled,' O'Cl., is identical with πέρκος.

No. 360. πέρυσι. The form in-uraid (with one n), here cited from the Táin bó Fráich, is incorrect. It is an accusative of time, and should be inn-uraid or better (as in O'Mulconry's Glossary, No. 748, H. 2. 16, col. 117), inn-uraith.

The Celtic representative of the Gothic fairni-s, 'old' here cited seems the Old-Ir. iarn in Cormac's iarn-bélre or iarm-bélre 'an obsolete word' (see s. vv. cloch, fern). Here, as in the next words, we have loss of initial p.

No. 363. Root πι, πίων. Add O.Ir. *ith* 'fat,' O'Don. Supp. and Cormac s.v. *itharnae* 'a rush-light' (*filum scirpeum*): Corn. *itheu* (leg. *iteu*), gl. ticio, Br. *eteô* 'brandon.'

No. 366. Root πλα. Add Irish *com-all* 'pregnant,' acc. sg. f. *comaill*, Brocc. h. 39 (Franciscan copy): *comhaille* .i. *at bronn* 'pregnancy,' lit. 'tumor ventris,' O'Cl. The form *rochomall* here cited by Windisch means *implevit*, not *implevi*.

Ir. *lúa* 'fulness' (?), Goid[2]. 104, *lour* 'sufficiens,' *loure* 'sufficientia,' *loon* (gl. adeps) Z. 33 are cognate with πλοῦτος and come from a root PLU, PUL.

The original *p* seems retained in Corn. *pals* (*goleow pals leas myll*, P. 165, 3) and Br. *paot*[a] 'beaucoup,' 'plusieurs,' which point to a primeval British *palti*, whence probably the Gaelic *pailt* is borrowed.

No. 367. With πέλας, πελάζω here cited Windisch (Beitr. viii. 7) connects several Irish verbs from a stem (*p*)*alā*, to which add *r-alastar* LU. 11a, *ar-id-r-alastar* 'ei occurrit' .i. *ar-r-āle* Fiacc's h. 45, *intan conhualai* (*con-n-do-fo-alai*, *nh* = *nn*) ib. 65, *ad-ella*, ib., *con-id-ru-alaid*, Brocc. h. 49.

No. 371. Root πο, πι, πω. W. *yfed*, Br. *evaff* 'boire' should be put with Ir. (*p*)*ibimm* = 'bibo,' and W. *di-od*, Br. *di-et* 'boyre,' Mid.-Corn. *de-w-es* = O.-Corn. *diot*, with Lat. *potare*.

The Ir. *at* .i. *laith* 'milk,' O'Cl., *án* 'a drinking-cup,' Corm., and *ól* (*an ól meda* 'the drink of mead,' Brocc. h. 85), whence *rô-ôlach* (gl. crapulatus vino) Goidel[2]. 59, have all probably lost initial *p* and are connected with this root.

No. 378. Root πρα. Add Ir. *láth* 'heat of animals in the season of copulation,' O'Don. Supp., W. *llawd* 'subatio,' *llodig* 'sus subans.'

The Ir. *luaith* 'ashes,' W. *lludw* come from a root (cf. Skr. *pru-sh*, *plu-sh* 'to burn') whose vowel is *u*.

No. 381. πρoτί, Skr. *prati*. This, I think, is the Ir. *la*, Z. 643. The *t* is kept in *leth-u* 'apud eos,' 'secum,' Tir. 10, Fiacc's h. 17.

No. 383. Root πυ, πύθω. Ir. *úr* .i. *olc*, Corm. = Goth. *fûl-s*.

No. 385. πῦρ. Add Ir. *úr* .i. *teine* 'ignis,' O'Clery, unless, indeed, we assume here a vocalization of *v*, and connect this word with O.Slav. *varŭ* 'warmth,' Fick 607, Eng. *war-m*, Goth. *varm-jan*, strangely placed by Curtius (at No. 651) with θέρος, *gharma*, and *formus*.

No. 386. Fick's suggestion (Spracheinheit 341) that πυρός may be 'das 'reine' Getreide'—cf. Lat. *purus*—derives support from the Irish *cruithnecht*, Corm. Tr. 33, which seems cognate with Lat. *scrutinium*.

No. 387. πῶ-λος. The O.Ir. dissyllable *haue* 'nepos,' Z. 229 seems to belong to this. The Irish form is deducible either from *(*p*)*ausio-s* (cf. Lat. *pūsion-*, *pusiola*) or *(*p*)*avio-s*, *(*p*)*aveo-s*. In favour of the latter speak the

---

[a] For the vocalization of *l* before *t* in Breton cf. *aut* 'ripa' = W. *allt* 'cliff,' Corn. *als* (gl. littus), Ir. *alt* (*alt in maro* 'the shore of the sea,' LU. 23b): *auten* 'rasorium' = Ir. *altain* (W. *ellyn*): *auter* 'altare' (W. *allor*): *faut* 'fissura' (W. *hollt*, spult): *sauter* = psalterium (W. *sallwyr*, *llaswyr*), *stautet* 'mingere,' O.Fr. *estaler* etc. The modern *paotr* 'garçon,' which Bopp, *Gloss. Sanskr.* and Diefenbach, *Origg. Eur.*, compare with Skr. *putra*, is really for *paltr*, and connected with Eng. *paltry*, Low-Germ. *palt* 'lappen.' This vocalization is perhaps due to French influences: cf. *haut*, *autant* (aliud tantum), *autel*, *autre*, *loyauté*, *psautier*, *saut*, etc.

Ogham on the Killeen Cormac stone (Beitr. v.), which Rhys reads *Duvtanos avei Sahattos*, and another, newly-found, which he reads *Maqi Decceddas avi Toranias*.

No. 389. Root σπαρ. To this Number belong Ir. *spréd* 'a spark,' Cormac, s.v. tenlam, and LU. 85b: *spreite arfed senlebor* 'scattered throughout old books,' Rawl. 514, etc. Here too I would put both πτάρ-νυ-μαι and πτύρω, in which (notwithstanding Curtius, 696) I venture to think that the πτ is not = the *st* of Lat. *sternuo, -sternare*, but comes regularly from πτ̂, πj (Kuhn, Zeitschrift xi. 310), σπj, ΣΠ (Curtius, p. 683). The root SPAR-G (whence Lat. *spargo*) also seems to belong to this Number. From SPARG come W. *ffreuo* (ex SPREGAM) 'to gush,' 'to spout,' and *ffroen*, Br. *froan* 'naris,' Ir. *srón* 'nasus' (ex SPROGNA).

No. 390. σπλήν. Br. *felch* 'rate,' 'splen,' Cath., is identical with Ir. *selg* ex *spelgâ, the *g* becoming provected and then aspirated after the liquid,[a] and the combination SP regularly producing *f* in the British languages, and losing *p* in Irish. See No. 156.

No. 391. Root *svap*. Here the initial *sv* has, as usual, given rise both to *s* and to *f* in Irish. The verbal forms *fiu* (= *fefup) 'sopivit,' pl. *feótar* (= *fefup-antar), *foaid* (= *fupata-i) 'sopiebat,' Goidel². 87n., deserve to be quoted: also *socht* (= *sop-to) 'silentium,' *sochtid* 'silet,' Corm. prull, and *sochtais* 'siluit,' LU. 22b, to be compared with σιωπή (σι-σϝωπή), and the MHG. *swift* 'schweigend,' Fick 418. For the change of Indo-European *pt* to *ct* cf. *secht(n)* 'septem,' *necht* 'neptis.' The British forms W. *hun* 'sleep,' Corn. *fun* in *dy-fun* 'sleepless,' D. 2204, agree with the double form in Irish.

No. 393. The reflex of ὑπαί, as well as that of ὑπό, is found in Irish, namely *faoi-sin* .i. *fo no samhail sin* 'under or like that,' O'Cl. This form (spelt *foisin*) is found more than once in LU., e.g., *tanic in bliadain ass foisin*, 41a. So in LH. 16b (Goid². 135) *foe-sein*. So in a copiously glossed copy of *Beati immaculati*, formerly in St. Isidore's, Rome, now in the Franciscan monastery, Dublin, fo. 4 a, 'agulum *binntén*. Coagulum compositum a con et agulum vel agelo cogilatum *foe-side*.'

No. 395c. βομβυλίς. Add O.Ir. *bólcha* (gl. papulas), Parker 134.

No. 400. W. *am*, Z. 674, keeps the original vowel of ἀμφί, etc.

No. 404. ὀρφ-ανό-ς. Add O.Ir. *ad-r-arbbai* 'he abolished, expunged or left out,' O'Don. Supp. (*arbai* = 'orbavit'?).

No. 405. ὀ-φρύ-ς. The Irish gen. dual *brúad* occurs in the following passage from Lebar na huidre 113b, describing the hero Cúchulainn: *Atá limsa bá frass donemannaib roláid inachend. Dubithir leth dubfolach cechtarde adá brúad deirgithir partaing a beoil*, thus rendered by Mr. Crowe: 'I should think it was a shower of pearls that was flung into his head. Blacker than the side of a cooking-spit [?] was each of his two brows: redder than ruby his lips.' The form *bra* or *brai* (cf. OHG. *bráwa*) .i. *mala* is given by O'Clery. This is spelt *bráe*, LH. 2a. Is it the nom. sg.?

---

[a] cf. *calch* 'reretrum,' = W. *caly* = Ir. *calg* 'sword' (cf. ON. *hlauna-sverdh*): *dalchet, derchell* 'tenere,' W. *daly*, Ir. *delg* 'brooch,' Skr. r. *darh*: *erch* 'nix' = W. *eira*; and the following loanwords: *guerch* 'virgo,' *herberch*, O.Fr. *herberge*, *marcharit* 'margerita,' *pirchirin* 'peregrinus.'

No. 406. ῥοφέω. The O.Ir. *srub* in the expression *srub muicci* 'a swine's snout,' Corm. Tr. p. 154, is surely cognate with *sorbeo*, etc. In *ro-leltar im srub* 'they stuck in my snout,' LU. 114b, Cúchulainn applies it to his own nose.

No. 407. Root φα, φημί. O.Ir. *ad-bo* .i. *urfocraim* ' I proclaim ' .i. *obaim* 'prohibeo,' O'Dav. 50. To the secondary root *bhan* belong Ir. *at-boind* 'he proclaims,' 'inhibits,' O'Don. Supp., (cf. O.N. *banna*, OHG. *bannan*, Fick² 809), 3d sg. pres. pass. *ad-bonnar urfogarthar*, O'Don. Supp.

No. 410. Root φεν. Add O.W. *et-binam* (gl. lanio), Z. 1052, *du-ben-eticion* (gl. exsectis), Mart. Cap. 42 a.a., Br. *benaff* ' couper,' Cath.

No. 412. Root φλα, *flare, flos*. Ir. *blor* (leg. *blór*) .i. *glor* ' noise,' O'Dav. 57, *blór* .i. *guth no glor*, O'Cl. belongs to the root φλυ. So the W *blew* ' crines,' Z. 109, Corn. *bleu*, Br. *bleau, bleuenn*.

No. 413. Root φρακ. The Ir. *bárc* .i. *iomad* ' a multitude,' O'Cl., is cognate with Lat. *farcio, frequens* here cited.

No. 414. φράτηρ. Add O.W. *braut*, Corn. *braud* vel *broder*.

No. 415. φρέαρ. As the Ir. *tipra* is an ant-stem, the ground-form cannot be *do-ad-bravat*, as Windisch conjectures. I know not whether the verbs *do-e-prannat* (gl. afluant), Ml. 39d, *toi-prinnit* (gl. influunt), Goidel². 70, *do-r-e-prend-set* ' emicuerunt,' ib., *do-n-e-prenn-et* (gl. quo... liquefiunt), Sg. 209b, are connected with Goth. *brunna*, but phonetically the connection is possible, for the Irish *p* is here a *b* provected by the lost *th* of the preposition *aith*, Z. 880.

No. 417. Root φυ. Ir. *both*, Corn. *bos* = Lith. *búta-s* ' house.' Ir. *bot* ' penis,' O'Don. Sup., = *but-va* (cf. *fu-tu-o*). The Ir. *bithe* (.i. *bannda* ' femininus,' O'Cl.) suggests that the Lat. *femina* should be transferred to this Number from No. 307. Ir. *budh* .i. *bioth no sáoghal*, O'Cl., may also come from the root BHU.

No. 419. Root ἀν, ἀνεμός. Add Ir. *anim* ' anima,' Z. 264, Br. *eneff*, Ir. *anam* in *anam-chara* ' doctor,' lit. ' soul friend,' and the Welsh *anaw*, which Davies explains by *cerddor* ' musicus,' ' poeta' : but which other lexicographers say means ' poetic genius.' Compare Horace : ' Totum muneris hoc tui est.... quod *spiro* et placeo,' i. e., quod movet me poeticus spiritus.

No. 421. ἀνά. Cf. the intensive prefix *an-, en-* in Corn. *an-auhel* (gl. procella) = W. *en-awel*, Br. *am-pref-an* ' rubeta,' Ir. *an-fad* ' storm.'

No. 422. ἀ-νήρ. Add W. *nerth*, O.W. *nerthheint* (gl. armant), Juv. 89.

No. 423. γίνυς. Add W. *gên* ' gena,' ' mentum,' Corn. *gen*, O. 2712, Br. *guen* ' g.ioue l. gena ' Cath.

No. 424. ἔνεκ. The root NANK is in O.Ir. *coim-nac-mar* ' potuimus,' and other forms, Z. 451. The root ANK is in Ir. *t-ic, tair-ic* ' vĕnit,' *r-ecam*, *t-ecam* ' eamus,' ' veniamus,' *t-anac, r-anac* ' vēni,' W. *di-ange*, M.Br. *di-anc* ' deviare,' Cath., Ir. *tecm-ang* (gl. fors), *agad* (gl. fors), *tocad* (gl. fors), *do-thoicdib* (gl. fatis).

No. 425. ἐνί, *antar*. Add O.W. *permed-interedou* (gl. ilia), Juv. 35 : Corn. *enederen* (gl. exstum), O.W. *ithr*, Beitr. vii. 398 = *inter*.

No. 428. ἔνος. Add Ir. *sinit* ' senectus,' Ult. 11, O.W. *hen-c-assou* (gl. monimenta), Juv. 49.

No. 429. Add to the derivatives from the root MAN the O.Ir. *ro-ménair* 'putavit,' Fiacc's h. 67, *do-ru-meoin,* Amra Chol. 108, *cui-mne* 'memoria,' *in-main* 'carus' (cf. OHG. *minna* 'amor'), *múnud* 'instructio' (gen. *múnta*, LU. 46b, dat. *munud,* Z. 229), *muntith* (gl. eruditor) Z. 25. In Ir. *taith-met* 'commemoratio,' Fél. Ep. 131,235, *foi-mtiu, toi-mtiu* 'opinio,' Z. 42, and perhaps *miad* 'honor' the *n* is lost before a dental.

With the roots $\mu\alpha\theta$, *madh,* the Ir. *modh* .i. *fear* 'vir' and *modh* .i. *obair* 'opera,' O'Cl., seem connected.

No. 430. ναῦς. Add *noere* 'nautas,' O'Cl.

No. 431. Root νεμ. Add Ir. *nemed* (gl. sacellum), Z. 10, Gaulish *Vernemetis* 'fanum ingens,' and *nanto* (gl. valle), Beitr. vi. 229.

No. 432. Ir. *nett,* gen. *nit,* Goidel[2]. 84, W. *nyth* 'nest,' ex **netto-s* **nes-to-s, *nes-do-s,* may, like Lat. *nidus* ex **nis-dus,* be cognate with ναο(σ)ίω. Other Irish examples of *tt* from *st* are apparently—

áit 'place,' F.A. 312,= A.S. *ord,* NHG. *ort,* O.N. *odd-r,* from **usda,* Fick,[2] 704, who compares Skr. *astá* 'geschoss:'

aittenn 'furze,' Corm., gen. *atinn,* 1 SM. 66 = W. *eithin,* cognate with Lat. *pastinum,* whence another plant-name (*pastinaca*) is derived:

att 'tumor,' Fél. Prol. 18, Z. 949, (gl. tuber) Sg. 61b: cf. ὄζος (ex ὀσδος, Goth. *ast-s*), properly the *nodus* from which a branch springs:

bét 'culpa,' Corm. Tr. 20, LU. 49a, ex **besdo-* [βδέσ-μα, βδό(σ)λος], as *úr* .i. *olc,* 'malus,' Corm., from root *pū* No. 383, as *púdar* 'harm,' 'error' from Lat. *putor:*

brot 'stimulus,' LU. 64b, n. pl. *bruit* LU. 93, Br. *brout* = urdeutsch **brosda,* Fick[2] 822:

dretall .i. *trén* (I have not the reference to this gloss), W. *drythyll,* cognate with Skr. *dṛshta* θρασύς, No. 315:

etiuth (leg. *étiuth*) = *vestitus,* Z. 802, *étach* 'vestis,' Z. 810:

fut, fot 'length,' *fota* 'long': Lat. *vastus:*

gataim 'rapio'[a]: cf. Skr. *hasta* 'hand'; (so Lat. *manuor* from *manus*):

itu 'thirst' ex **istat,* root IS, No. 617:

lott 'meretrix,' Corm. Tr. 101 = λάστη· πόρνη, Hesych.

lott 'ver-*lust*,' No. 546: *loitim* 'lædo,' 'noceo':

maide 'baculum,' Corm. Tr. 118, O.Ir. **maitte,* OHG. *mast,* O.N. *mastr:*

rét 'res,' Z. 18, ex **ré-s-tu* (as *áis* ex **aiv-as-tu*):

rot, Corm., W. *rhwd* = *rust:*

sotal 'proud,' 'puffed-up'[b] ex **spustala,* as W. *ffothell* = (s)*pustula.*

The Corn. *banathel* 'genista,' W. *banadl* = **gvanastla,* Ital. *ginestra,* Lat. *genista,* and the loanwords Mod. Ir. *madadh* 'dog' (Eng. *mast-iff,* Ital. *mastino*) and Manx *paitt* 'plague' from *pestis,* may also be examples of this change, which we find in the Bœotian ἴττω, ἔττασαν, ἔττια for ἴστω, ἔστασαν, ἰστία (Grundz. 656).

---

[a] *ro-gat side dimsa,* Ml. 132a, *gutaid Cúchulainn inn-gai ass* 'C. snatches the spear out of him,' LL. 78a 1.

[b] i. *uallach no dimeach,* O'Dav. Cf. μέγα φυσᾷν magnum spirare. From *sotal* comes the abstract noun *sotlae* acc. *sotlai,* Fél. Ap. 28, Sep. 15, Ep. 135, n. pl. *sotli,* Z. 767.

No. 435. νεφρός. If we may assume that O.Ir. *áru* (gl. rien), Z. 264, a fem. *n*-stem, = W. *aren*, has lost initial *n* like—
Ir. *eas, easóg* = *ness* 'weasel,' Corm. Tr. 126 :
Ir. *eascu, easgann* 'eel,' = *naisciu*, Corm. Tr. 126 :
Ir. *Ua-chongbhail*, the name of a town (Navan), for *Nua-chongbail*:
Br. *effou* 'heavens' = W. *nefoedd*, Ir. *nime*:
Br. *azr, aer* = W. *neidr*, Ir. *nathair*:
Br. *Ormant, Ormandi* = Fr. *Normand, Normandie*:
we might equate it with the Old-Latin **nefro*, pl. *nefrones* 'testiculi,' Festus, s. v. *nefrendes*, and thus connect it with OHG. *niero*, Gr. νεφρός.[2] For the loss of *b* before the liquid cf. *nêl* 'cloud' ex **neblo* and *grén* 'falcon' (?) ex **grebno*.

No. 443. Root *νυ, συν*. To this Number belong Ir. *snuadh* .i. *sruth* 'flumen,' O'Cl., *snuad* 'cæsaries,' Corm., W. *di-nëu* 'effundere,' Br. *di-nou* 'fondre.' From root SNA, come Lat. *nare, natrix* 'water-snake' = Ir. *nathir* (gen. *nathrach*, a fem. *c*-stem), W. *neidr*. In the Ir. *snob* (gl. suber) Sg. 64, *snamach* (gl. suber), Ir. Gl. 391, *ro-sná* .i. *dorinne snámh* (= W. *nawf*) 'a swim,' O'Cl. the *s* is preserved.

No. 448. ὦνος. The O.Ir. *uain (oc-uain* 'in commodando,' Z. 634) is = ὠνή, *vasna-m*. The Irish *oin* .i. *iasacht* 'loan,' O'Cl., O'Dav. 109, is certainly cognate with ὀνίνημι here cited.

No. 449. Ir. *sét* 'instar' (ex *sam-ta*), Fel. June 16, and O.W. *amal* 'ut,' Juv. 32, are all cognate with ἅμα. Ir. *samud* 'congregation,' Brocc. h. 13, is perhaps the Celtic reflex of Skr. *sabhā*, Goth. *sibja*.

No. 449b. ἀμάω, *meto*. Add O.W. *et-met* 'retonde,' Juv. 77.

No. 453. ἡμι-. Add the W. *hanter, hanner* 'half' ex SAM-ter, and the Ir. privative particle *am-*, Z. 860.

No. 459. Root μαχ. Ir. *mactadh* .i. *marbhadh* 'a killing,' O'Cl., seems to belong to this Number.

No. 461. Root με. Add O.Ir. *med* (gl. lanx) Sg. 20a, dat. sg. *meid* 'balance,' Brocc. h. 79, *methos* .i. *crich* 'a boundary,' Corm., dat. sg. *methus*, Corm. Tr. p. 109. From the extended root ME-N, we have O.W. *menntaul* (gl. bilance), M. Cap. 12b, and *montol* 'trutina,' Z. 1054. From the further extended root *MEN-S* we have Ir. *tomus* 'mensura' (= *do-fo-MENS-u*), O.W. *do-guo-misur*[*am*] (gl. geo), Z. 1052: Ir. *mesurda* (gl. modicum), Ir. Gl. No. 807, *mesraigthe* (gl. modestus), Z. 780.

With the Old-Lat. *mānus* here cited compare the Ir. *muin* 'good' (*adfenar olcc anmuinib, adfenar maith munib* 'which renders evil to the ungood, which renders good to the good,' SM. i. 256).

No. 462. The Ir. *magh* in *magh-lorg* .i. *mór-lorg*, O'Cl., is identical with μέγας. The Ir. *maighne* .i. *mór* 'magnus,' O'Cl., points to an Old-Celtic **magnio*.

---

[a] Manx, like all languages that possess an article ending in *n*, affords many instances of loss of initial *n* : thus *edd* (O.Ir. *nett* 'nest'), *iu* (=O.Ir. *neim* 'poison'), *aslan* (=O.Ir. *nescu*, gen. *nescoon*, 'eel'), *ullick* (= O.Ir. *notlaic* 'Christmas'). So in loanwords from English : *aptin* =: *napkin, ashoon* = *nation* and *uddan* 'a lump on the toe-joints,' from *knot*.

No. 466. Root SMAR, μερ, μαρ. From the sm (afterwards zm ? zv ? zb ?) with which this root begins, may come the b of many Celtic words in which the meaning 'think' is implied. I refer to Ir. *bara* 'affliction,' *brón* 'moeror' (μέρ-ιμνα), W. *brwyn* 'tristitia,' *bryd* 'animus,' *bwriad* 'intentio.' Some of the following may possibly be instances of the same phonetic change—

Ir. *balc* 'potens,' W. *balch* 'superbus' = Lith. *smarkùs* 'gewaltig':
Ir. *baire, barad* 'mors,' Lith. *smér-tis* (Curtius No. 468):
Ir. *becc*, W. *bach* 'parvus' ex *smi-n-co, *sma-n-co, σμικ-ρός (Rhys, Rev. Celt. ii. 189, Fick², 415):
Ir. *bolad* 'odor,' *boltigetar* 'odorem faciunt,' *bolordae, bolamair* 'odoratus': cf. Eng. *smell*, Ndd. *smelen* = 'smoul-der':
W. *baeddu* 'tundere' = A.S. *smîtan* 'percutere':
W. *ber-th* 'nitidus,' Eng. *smar-t, σμαρ-κόν* 'δριμύ, Grundz.⁴ 681, note:
W. *buan* 'velox,' O.N. *smugall* 'penetralis,' 'volatilis':
Corn. *bor* 'pinguis,' *berri* 'pinguedo,' A.S. *smĕru* 'adeps.'

No. 469. μέσσος for μεθjος. The prefix *mid-* occurs in at least four Old-Irish words: *mid-chuairt* 'mid-court,' Fél. Ep. 94, *mid-lái* 'of mid-day,' LU. 78a, *mid-nocht* 'mid-night,' Reeves' Culdees, 86, *im-mid-ais* 'in middle age,' LB. 71, lower margin. In H. 2. 16, col. 119 *leth* 'half' glosses *mid*.

The *ia*-stem *mide* occurs in LL. 58, a. b: *á dorblas na maitne muche go midi medoin lai.... a mide medoin lai go tráth funid nóna* 'from the twilight of the early morning till the middle of mid-day.... from the middle of midday till the hour of evenfall.'

No. 472. μήτηρ. The Gaulish dat. pl. *matrebo* of the inscription of Nîmes might have been quoted here.

No. 473. μῆχος. Add Ir. *mám* .i. *cumas* 'potestas,' O'Cl. Whether Ir. *mám* 'jugum,' Z. 17, Brocc. h. 56, *com-mám* .i. *bean* 'uxor,' O'Cl., *commamsa* 'matrimonii,' O'Dav. 70, belong to this Number, I do not venture to say. They are apparently cognate with OHG. *gi-mahhâ* 'uxor,' 'conjux,' O.N. *mâg-r*, Goth. *mēg-s*, which Fick². 828 brings from the European root *MAG* = Indo-Germ. *MAGH*.

No. 476. O.Ir. *moth* 'nomen virili membro,' Corm., belongs to the root MAT, whence μόθος, *mathāmi, möndull*, etc.

No. 478. With *mu-tire*, μῦ-θος here cited the Ir. *mo-th* .i. *guth*, H. 3, 18, p. 636, col. 4, is cognate.

No. 482. μύρμος. Add Ir. *moirb* .i. *seangán*, O'Cl. pl. *morbi* .i. *seghaind*, H. 3, 18, p. 636, col. 4.

No. 485. ὄμβρος, *imber, abhra*. Add O.Ir. *imrim* 'storm' (*sína sceo imrima raith*, Amra Chol. 58), *amor* 'a trough,' Corm. Trans. 15. The Gaulish river-name *Ambris* and W. *Ambir* are put by Glück (Neue Jahrbücher, 1864, p. 601) with ὄμβρος, etc. Add also Gaulish *ambe* (gl. rivo), *inter-ambes* (gl. inter rivos), Beitr. vi. 229. Perhaps also *Ambrones* 'gens quædam Gallica, qui subitâ inundatione maris' (Festus, cited by Diefenbach, Origg. Eur. 229) sedes suas amiserunt, though the Skr. *ambhṛna* 'gewaltig' 'schrecklich' (connected by BR with *abhram*) suggests that the name is due to the character and not the misfortune of this nation.

No. 491. O.Ir. *eirr* (gl. curruum princeps) Goidel². 57. gen. *erred* 'champion' is cognate with ἄρσην, the *rs* becoming *rr* as in *err = ars* (No. 505), *tarrach* ex *tarsáco*, root TARS (No. 244), *dorr* .i. *fearg*, O'Cl., root DHARSH No. 315, etc.

No. 492. Root ἐρ, ἀμφ-ήρης. The Ir. *imrad* (better *imrát*) here cited by Windisch is a 3d pers. plur. *present*, and not, as he renders it, a preterite. The 3d sg. *imm-a-rá* occurs in LU. 40a with an infixed pronoun. Add O.Ir. *rám*, Br. *reuff* 'remus' = W. *rhaw* 'shovel.'[a] Add also the Old-Irish verbal forms *fu-r-ráith* 'quod adjūvit,' Tir. 11, *fo-ro-raid* .i. *fortachtaiged*, Brocc. h. 75, *fu-m-ré-se* 'me adjuvabit,' Tir. 11, which in form and meaning remind one of ὑπηρετεῖν (*fu, fo* = ὑπό).

With the Skr. *ratha*, Lat. *rota* here cited, the O.Ir. *rath*, Brocc. h. 84, should be placed.

No. 493. Ir. *briathar*, a fem. *ā*-stem, is = Ϝρήτρα, *vr* becoming *br* as often. So in *brián* .i. *briathar*, H. 3, 18, p. 51b. The Skr. *brū* 'to speak' = Zend *mrū* here cited seems to occur in the Ir. *fris-brudi* 'renuit,' Ml. 44b, Goidel². 40, and O'Clery's *frioth-bruth* .i. *diultadh* 'negatio,' and in the British *co-brouol* (gl. verbialia), Z. 1065.

No. 494. With ἄρακος here cited cf. *ar-inca* 'frumenti genus gallicum,' Plin. Another Gaulish name for grain seems *sasia* (= W. *haidd*, Br. *heiz* 'orge,' Skr. *sasya*, Zend *hahya*), which I find in Pliny's corrupt *asiam*: 'secale Taurini sub Alpibus (s)asiam vocant,' Hist. Nat. xviii. c. 40.

No. 496. εἶρος, *vellus*. Ir. *folt*, W. *gwallt* 'hair' may also come from the root VAR 'decken.' Hence too Ir. *fearn* .i. *sgiath* 'shield,' O'Cl.; and, with the usual change of *vr* to *br*, *brat* 'pallium.' In Ir. *ulaidh* .i. *srathar* 'packsaddle,' O'Cl., the *v* seems vocalised.

No. 499. εὐρύς. The Ir. *ferr* = W. *guell* 'better' = *variyas*. The positive may be in the Old-Celtic names *Veru-cloetius* (Εὐρυκλῆς, *cloetius*, like κλειτός from root CLU?) and *Veru-lamium*.

No. 500. Root ὀρ, *orior*. The O.Ir. *aur-ur-as* 'cursura,' Goidel². 32, *com-thur-ur-as* 'incursus' (*com-du-air-UR-asta*), Z. 887, belong to this. Hence too the common word *turas* (= *do-ur-asta*) 'iter,' 'peregrinatio.'

No. 501. Root Ϝορ, ὁράω. The Ir. *aire* 'vigilance,' Fel. Prol. 15 (now *faire* with prosthetic *f*, O'Don. Gr. 327), whence *airigur-sa* 'animadverto,' Z. 438, has lost initial *v* (*f*), vide infra No. 589.

Ir. *fili* 'poet' seems cognate with W. *gwelwr* 'seer,' as Ir. *filis* (.i. *seallais* 'vidit,' O'Cl.) is = W. *gwelas*.

The Ir. nominal preposition *hi-fail* 'near,' LU. 9a, *in-a-fhail-sium* 'near him,' LB. 61a, may also be added. If *fail* here means (as I conjecture) 'oculo,' cf. the W. phrase *ar-lygad hanner dydd* 'very near noon.'

---

[a] So W. *llaw* = Ir. *lám*, W. *mawaid* 'handful' = Ir. *mám*, W. *ffaw* borrowed from Lat. *fāma*.

No. 502. ὀρ-μή. Add the O.Ir. noun *sel* in the phrase *cach-'la-sel . . . in sel aile* 'modo . . . modo,' Z. 560, and the verb *con-selai* .i. *ro-elai*, Brocc. h. 62, *co-selastar*, LU. 9a (where it is wrongly explained by *dorat* 'dedit').

No. 503. ὄρνις, Lith. *erēlis*. Add W. *eryr* 'eagle,' also *erydd*.

No. 505. Ir. *err* 'tail' (from **erso*) LL. cited in Rev. Celt. i. 258, is certainly = ὄρρος, OHG. *ars* 'anus.' See at No. 491.

No. 507. From the root VART here mentioned comes the O.Ir. verb *ad-bart-aigiur* (for *ad-vart-aigiur*) 'adversor,' of which many forms are given by M. Nigra, Rev. Celt. i. 152.

No. 510. οὖρον, *vâri*. The O.W. *di-di-oul-am*, gl. micturio (not 'glisoυ'), Z. 136, 1052, like O.Ir. *fual*, is cognate with οὖρον, and this Welsh form supports Windisch's theory that the *f* in *f-ual* is prosthetic. The original *r* seems kept in the Old British river name *Varar* (*Vārar ?*), Οὐάραρ Ptol. 11, 2, in the Ir. *ferath* 'humor' (*ocuturgabail fri fual ocus ferath* 'raising thee up from water and wet,' O'Curry's Manners and Customs iii. 375) = W. *guyraut* 'liquor' (now *gwirod*), Corn. *gwyras*, Z. 842, 843, W. *gweren* 'liquamen.' So in the O.Ir. *-fera* 'pluit' (*ni fera cid oen banne*, Z. 952, *tech hina fera flechod* 'a house wherein wet showers not,' St. Paul, Goid². 177), *ferais* 'pluvit,' (*ferais anmich* 'it poured with rain ª,' Brocc. h. 30, *ferais snechta mór forru* 'a great snow showered upon them,' Táin LU. 58a), *ferthain* 'shower,' and *diorain* (**di-for-ani*) .i. *snigheadh no siledh feartluana no fleachaidh* 'the pouring or dropping of a shower or of moisture,' O'Cl. So perhaps in *foirthiu* (gl. marmora), Tur. 65, and *breisiu* 'flowing' (*br ex vr*), Corm. Tr. 26.

With this Number I would also put Ir. *fliuch* 'liquidus' = W. *gulip*, *gwlyb*, Ir. *flesc* = W. *gwlŷch* 'madidatio': W. *gwlaw*, Corn. *glau* (gl. pluvia), and Lat. *(v)liquere, (v)liquor*, etc., which Curtius places with λείπω, No. 625.

No. 523b. Root ἀλ, *alo*. Add O.Ir. *ail* 'esca,' Z. 527.

No. 524. ἄλλος. Add W. *all* 'alius,' *eil, ail* and *eilydd* 'secundus' = Ir. *aile, ala*, Z. 309.

No. 527. Root Fελ, *volvo*. Add W. *olwyn* 'rota,' (Rhys) and perhaps W. *bl-wydd* (ex **blêdâ, *vlêda*), Ir. *bliad-an* 'annus,' W. *bl-yn-edd*: the *bl* coming from *vl* as in *ro-leblaing*: cf. 'volventibus annis.' Aen. i. 234.

No. 529. ἔλαφος. O.Ir. *elit* 'doe,' Corm. Tr. 68, and W. *elain* 'hind' belong to this Number. So also, perhaps, the Macedonian ἀλίη · κάπρος. Pictet's *arr* 'hirsch' belongs either to No. 491, or to OHG. *far* 'taurus' ex *fars*, No. 376.

No. 536b. W. *lleibio, llepio* 'to lick' and Br. *lipat* point to nasalised forms like **limbiăm, *limbata*, where **limb-* is ex *lingv-*, Lat. *linguo*, Prisc. x. 11. So W. *lleipr* 'flaccidus' is = Eng. *limber*. See Rhys, Rev. Celt. ii. 191, 192, where the last syllables of W. *cyffelyb* 'such' (*com-he-lip*), Br.

ª Cf. the Latin *lacte pluisse*. Here *ánmich* is the dat. sg. of *ánmech* (O'Clery's *ainbheach* .i. *deura iomdha no fearthain* 'plenteous tears or a shower') gen. *ánbige*, Brocc h. 33, a fem. ā-stem ; cf. the use of the datives *ceill* and *biuth*, Z. 917, 918.

hevelep (**sama-lip*) are explained as ex **limb*, **lingv*, Skr. *liṅga*. Irish examples of *bb* (*p*) from *mb* are apparently—
babb, an interjection of intension, Corm. Tr. 19, *babl-óir* 'garrulus,' O.Ir.
**babblóir*, a nickname for S. Patrick : cf. βόμβος, βαμβαλίζω : *cepóc*, some kind of song or music, σκομβ-ρίσαι γογγύσαι, Lith. *skambù*: *gob*, O.Ir. *gop*, ' mouth,' Skr. *jambha*, Gr. γαμφή, No. 125 : *rap* 'every animal that drags to it,' Corm. Tr. 144 : λαμβάνω, root *rabh*.

No. 540. *Losc* .i. *bacach* 'claudus,' Corm. Tr. 104, acc. pl. *luscu*, Fiacc's h. 34, is identical with λοξός, Lat. *luxus*. So *lesc = laxus*.

No. 541. With λι-μός 'hunger' here cited the O.Ir. *lia*, Fiacc's h. 29, may be cognate.

No. 544. With Latin *glis* (stem *glit*) I would connect the Irish *lestar* 'vas,' Z. 166, W. *llestr*, from **lit-tro*. Here, as in *lomm* No. 135, initial *g* seems lost.

With ὁ(σ)λιβ-ρός and OHG. *släffar* (lubricus) the Irish *slemon*, Z. 776, (ex **slib-no*), W. *llyfn* 'smooth,' 'sleek' are probably cognate. So too the Lat. *lu-m-bricus* and the W. *llymriaid* 'sand-eels.'

No. 545. *Líbhearn* .i. *clann no crodh* 'children or goods,' O'Cl., is cognate with the Lat. *libet, liber* here cited. The nom. pl. occurs in a note to the *Amra Choluimbchille* (LU. 13b):—

Nech frisbert athigerna	"Whoso hath betrayed his lord,
nirba(t) ile a-liberna	His children will not be many,
corrucait namait achend	So that foes carry off his head,
agabair is adubcend ª.	His steed and his sword."

No. 546. λύω. The Old-Welsh *lou* 'louse' in *leu-esicc* (gl. cariantem), lit. 'louse-eaten,' Beitr. vii. 388, now *lleu-en*, pl. *llau*, Br. *louenn* 'pediculus,' like the German *laus*, belongs to the extended root LU-S, whence Goth. *fra-liusan* 'ver-lieren.' Hence, also, the Ir. *lott* 'damage,' 'hurt,' Corm., (ex **lus-ta*, No. 432), and the verb *loitim*, whence *ro-loiti, ro-loitestar, loitithe*, SM. i. 304, 160, 174, *loitfes*, Reeves' *Columba*, 67.

No. 547. λῦμα, λούω. The Gaulish *lautro* (gl. balneo), Beitr. vi. 229, should be connected with λούω. So M.Br. *louazr* 'alveus,' *loet* 'mucidus,' *loedaff* 'mucidare,' Cath. The Ir. *lunae* ' to wash,' O'Don. Supp., and *con-luan* .i. *cac na con* 'dogs' dung,' ib., are also connected with the words here cited.

No. 548. λύγξ. Ir. *loisi* .i. *sionnaigh* 'foxes,' O'Cl., seems cognate with the OHG. *luhs* 'luchs' here cited.

No. 551. μέλας. Add O.Ir. *for-molad* 'obscuring or darkening a word by adding a syllable thereto,' LU. 7a, where it is exemplified by *tereda*, *gandón* ('ón hic exemitur') and *annón*, fabricated, respectively, from *terc*,

---

ª AMRA, ed. Crowe, p. 56, where this easy quatrain is ludicrously misrendered thus :
One who betrayed his lord,
His offspring were not numerous,
Until (*sic*) enemies carried off his head,
His 'grey' and his 'black-head.'
It is cited by O'Clery s.v. *frismbeart*, where O'Clery (thinking of the Latin *liburna*) renders *libhearna* by *longa* 'galleys.' O'Clery also explains *ni-r-bat* by *narab* 'ne sit' : but it is a future (= *ní* + *ropat, rubat* 'erunt,' Z. 498), not an imperative.

gand and *ann*. So in a poem contained in a note to the Félire Jan. 15, we find *dothisatán* fabricated from *dothisat* 'adierint.' Many examples of a similar artifice are given by Nigra in his essay on the jargon of Val-Soana (in Piedmont) printed in the third volume of Ascoli's *Archivio glottologico italiano*, 1874.

No. 555. With οὐλή, *vol-nus*, Skr. *vraṇa* 'wound' here cited I would put W. *gweli* 'vulnus,' 'plaga.'

No. 558. Root σφαλ. W. *pall* 'failure,' *pallu* 'to fail' is, like Ir. *all* in *di-all* 'casus,' cognate with OHG. *fallan* here cited.

No. 569. ἴσος, *vishu*. Cf. Ir. *fiu* (ex *visu) .i. *cosmail* 'similis,' O'Cl.

No. 571. Root σα. The Ir. *síl*, W. *hil* 'suboles,' 'proles': W. *had* 'semen,' Br. *hadaff* 'serĕre' may be added to *sēmen, saian* and the other derivatives here mentioned.

No. 574. σόβη. The Ir. *fobhaidh* .i. *luath no ésgaidh* 'swift or nimble,' O'Cl., and perhaps the W. *chwyf* 'motus,' *chwyfio* 'movere' seem connected with the words here cited.

No. 577. Root *strang, strag*. The Ir. *sreang, sreangaim* here cited are genuine words, though Pictet probably took them from O'Reilly : *srengais* 'traxit,' LU. 26a, *sreangadh* .i. *tarraing (do-air-sraing)* 'tractio,' O'Cl., *dosreggat*, LH. 21b (*gg = ng*). The root *strag* has in Irish lost the *s* : *tracht* (ex *trag-ta, *stragta) .i. *neart* 'strength,' O'Cl., *rith tar tracht* 'running beyond strength,' O'Don. Supp., *di-thraicht* .i. *aimhneartmhar* 'strengthless,' O'Cl., *truag in maten ... rosbí mac damain dithraicht*, LL. 60, b. a.

With Lat. *tergo* we may put W. *teru* 'tergere,' *têr* 'tersus,' *mêl têr = 'mel tersum*,' i. e. purgatum.

No. 578. Root συ. The O.Ir. *úaim* 'seam' (*cen-úaim*, LH. 6a, Goid. 65) may have lost initial *s*. See No. 280.

No. 579. σῦς. With this the Ir. *socc* (in *socc-sáil*, gl. loligo, Z. 30) = W. *hwch*, Corn. *hoch*, Br. *houch*, an Old-Celtic *succo-s*, seems cognate. Grimm's theory of a borrowing here by Celts from Germans (Eng. *hog*, NHG. *haksch*, Beitr. ii. 175) is overturned by the Irish form with *s*.

One of S. Patrick's four names, *Succet-us*, Lib. Arm.9a. 2,[a] later *Succat*, LH. 15b, is explained in the latter MS. as meaning 'god of war' ('deus belli a-laten'). But it must be the name of some Old-Celtic war-god. Have we here a derivative from *succo-s ?* The Romans sacrificed pigs to Mars (Preller, Röm. Myth. 2te aufl. 299), and that the Gauls did so too may be

---

[a] The context is: 'Inveni .iiii. nomina in libro scripta Patricio apud Ultanum episcopum Conchuburnensium—sanctus Magonus qui est clarus : Succetus qui est [ ]: Patricius: Cothirthiacus quia servivit .iiii. domibus magorum.' In the Tripartite Life, Rawl. B. 512, fo. 6 b. 2, we find : Cethrar linmurro rocendaigseom. óin dibside Miliuc. is dó sciu arróctsom iuninm is Cotraigi iarsindí foruigenai do cet[h]artreb. rotecht dana ceithir anmand fair .i. Sucait aninm otustidib. Cothraigi diambaí icfognam docethrur. Magonius a Germano. Patricius, id est primus civium, a papā Celestino. 'Now four persons bought him: one of them was Miliuc. From him Patrick received the name Cothraige, because he served four houses. So he had four names, to wit, Sucait, his name from his parents : Cothraige while he was serving four persons : Magonius [cf. Skr. *maghavan*] from [his teacher] Germanus; and Patricius from Pope Celestine.' Windisch (Beitr. viii. 218) ingeniously tries to explain the late form *Succat* as εὔμαχος ; but he had not then before him the above quotations from the Book of Armagh and the Tripartite Life.

conjectured from the inscription MAR. ET SVI (de Betouw, *De aris et lapidibus ad Neomagum et Santenum effossis*, etc.).

No. 582. *áξων*. Add W. *echel* 'axle,' Br. *ahel*.

No. 583. *αὔξω*. O.Ir. *ásaim*, Mid.-Ir. *f-ásaim* 'cresco' = *vakshāmi, for-as* .i. *biseach* 'incrementum,' O'Cl., *for-ásaim* 'proficio,' *for-ásat* (gl. proficiunt) Ml. 40b, 46d, *for-r-assais-siu* (gl. profecisti) Ml. 43d. The same root appears as *fosc* for *focs* = Skr. *vaksh* in *do-n-foscai* .i. *ro-tho-di-usca* 'nos resuscitet,' Sanct. 5.

No. 584. *ἕξ*. The O.Ir. *fes* in *mórfeser* 'a heptad of persons,' Z. 313, lit. 'a great hexad,' *mor-fesser*; LU. 21a, dat. sg. *morfessiur*, Fél. July 18, should have been cited, as well as the forms beginning with *s*. See Windisch, Kuhn's Zeitschrift xxi. 428.

No. 585. *αἰές*. In the Ir. *étte* .i. *aois* 'ætatis,' *aos éta* .i. *daoine aosda* 'aged persons,' O'Cl., we probably have another instance of the assimilation of *s* to a following *t* noticed above at No. 432.

No. 586. The Irish reflex of the Zend *av* 'to protect' *au-dio* and other words here cited is in the third sg. pres. *-ó,-ói,-óei* or *-ai*, all meaning 'servat.' Examples are numerous: *ni-m-ó do-legend-so* 7 *ní-m-chobrathar.side* 'non me servat lectio tua (sacrarum literarum) neque me hæc adiutat,' Goidel². 180, (where it is wrongly rendered), *dobeir dig con-ói ríg dogní echt* 'dat potionem quæ servat regem facinus committentem,' LU. 98a, *con-n-oi* 'qui servat,' Z. 431, *co-ta-ói* 'servat id,' ib., *for-ta-com-ai-som* 'servat id ille,' ib. So O'Clery: *connáoi* .i. *coimhédaidh no cumdaighidh*: 3rd sg. pret. *con-r-óeth biu bath* 'is qui servavit vitam mortuus est,' Amra Chol. LU. 8b. : 3rd pl. pret. *con-r-oitatar*, Rev. Celt. i. 74. Passive: *for-dom-chom-aither* 'servor,' Z. 482, *co-tam-r-oither* (*cotamroether*, B.) 'sine ut server,' Fél. Ep. 69.

The Welsh reflex of *au-di-o* is *ewi* 'to listen.' We can hardly separate the W. *ewyllys*, Bret. *eouel* (ex *avelo) 'voluntas,' Cath., from the Lat. *av-i-dus* here noticed.

Ir. *sáith*, LH. 13b, Goid. 104, *sathech* 'satiatus,' Brocc. h. 28, should be put with *ἄω, ἄμεναι*, Lat. *satur, satis*, which Curtius notices under this Number.

No. 587. Root VĀ, *aF*, *ἄω*. Add Ir. *athach gaoithe* 'a blast of wind' (.i. *sidhean*, O'Cl.), Corn. *an-auhel* (gl. procella), W. *en-awel* (as to the prefix see No. 421), and O.W. *aguen*, now *awen*, in *tat aguen*.

No. 589. *ἔαρ*. Add O.W. *guiannuin* (gl. vere) ex **visantêna-*. See Beitr. vii. 235. In the Irish *errach* for **(v)esráca*, initial *v* has been lost, as in the following :—

ail = *vara*, *vol-un-tas*, No. 659.
aire 'heed,' OHG. *wara* 'consideratio,' 'cura' :
ásaim 'I wax,' Skr. *vakshāmi* : *for-an-asa athirni* 'whereon a calf grows,' LU. 8a., *asait clanda* 'crescunt plantæ,' H. 2. 16, col. 90 :
ascid 'request,' *toisc* (*do-osci*) 'desire,' Skr. *vañcha*, OHG. *wunsc* :
athach 'a blast,' Skr. *vāta*, Lat. *ve-n-tus*, No. 587 :
égem, iachtad, root VIC, infra No. 620 :

— 38 —

ess 'ox,' W. *ych*,[a] pl. *ychen* = Goth. *auhsa* from *vexan* :
ess, 'cataract,' gen. *essa*, ex *ved-tu*, root VAD, No. 300 :
espartain 'eventide,' O'Don. Gr. 268, from *vesper* and Ir. *tan* :
ĕt-ach ' ves-ti-s,' *étiud* = *vestitus* :
iath .i. *mind* 'diadem,' root VI, No. 593 :
Icht = *Vectis*, in *Muir n-Icht*, 'quod dividit Galliam et Britanniam,' Z 68 :
olann (W. *gulan*) 'wool,' *vellus* :
on 'defect,' Tir. 11, *on-mit* 'oaf,' Corm. Tr. 132, W. *yn-fyd*, O.N. *van* in *fjör-van*, *vanar-volr* [b] :
root *org*, *orc*, 'cædere' (*orcun* 'occisio,' Z. 738), Fρήγ-νν-μι :
ordu, gen. *ordan*, 'thumb,' 'great-toe,' *orddu lámae* gl. pollex, Z. 765, root VARDH [c] :
oss 'cervus' = Skr. *vasta* 'goat' :
remmad 'distortio,' ῥέμβω, ῥόμβος, *(v)rengvātu*, A.S. *vringan*.

Both *guiannuin* and *errach*, like the Latin substantive *vernum*, may have been originally adjectives used with some word equivalent to 'tempus': cf. Lucr. v. 802 'ova relinquebant, exclusæ tempore verno.'

No. 591. With ἰάομαι here cited Diefenbach, *Origg. Eur.* 339, connects W. *iach*, Ir. *ícc*.

No. 593. With ἰτέα, *vi-men*, *vitex*, etc., the following Celtic words are cognate : Ir. *fiamh* .i. *slabhradh* 'chain,' O'Cl., *iath* .i. *mind* 'diadema,' Goid. 159, W. *gwden*, Corn. *guiden* (gl. cutulus, i. e., catulus 'a kind of fetter').

No. 595. ὄις, *ovis*. Another form of O.Ir. *ói* is in the masc. *ia*-stem *ae-gaire* 'shepherd,' where *-gaire* (also in *in-gaire*), like the 3rd sg. pret. *ar-gair-t*, Brocc. h. 33, is to be compared with ἀ-γείρω from *σα-γερ-ίω*, NHG. *kehren*, A.S. *cordhor* 'heerde,' 'schaar.'

Curtius and Benfey connect ἀμνός with ὄις, which, no doubt, is phonetically possible (cf. σεμνός). But where then would be the Greek reflex of *agnus* ? Fick, *Spracheinheit* 53, brings ἀμνός from *ἄβνος, *ἄγνος ; and, if he is right, ἀμνός, *agnus*, Slav. *agnĭcĭ*, and the Irish diminutival ending in *-án* [d] all go together.

No. 602. Root *i*, *si*. Add Ir. *sín* .i. *muince* 'monile,' H. 3, 18, p. 73, col. 3, *sion* (= *sinu*) .i. *idh no slabhradh* 'collar or chain,' O'Cl., *sinann* .i. *slabradh*, H. 3, 18, p. 17 : *sên* = W. *hwyn* 'a springe.'

No. 603. The locative of the pronominal stem *sa* occurs with the suffixed demonstrative *na* (cf. Lat. *si-c*) in the O.Ir. adverb *sin* .i. *as amhlaidh*, O'Cl., who cites *IS sin téid an mal in a theach righ* 'thus the king went into

---

[a] A second instance of loss of initial *v* in Welsh is *llysg* 'virgula,' Ir. *flesc*; and if W. *llewa* (= Ir. *longud* ' edere ') be connected with Lith. *valgyti*, we have a third.
[b] So *ut-* in *ut-mall* seems = O.N. *vanta*, Eng. *want*.
[c] So Eng. *thu-mb*, OHG. *dû-mo* from the root TU 'to swell.'
[d] This seems the Old-Celtic *agnos*, of which the gen. sg. *-agni* frequently occurs on the Irish Ogham inscriptions, e. g. *Mailagni*, *Talagni*, *Ulccagni*. The last word is = *Olcáin*, cf. the Gaulish name VLKOS, Rev. Num. 1861, p. 341. and perhaps Skr. *ulkâ* 'meteor,' 'firebrand.' VLCAGNVS, the nom. sg. of Ir. *Ulccagni*, occurs (according to Rhys) on the Welsh stone at Llanfihangel-ar-arth. *Maglagni* (= the Ir. *Mailagni* ? a Gaulish *Magilagni*?) occurs on the Llanfechan stone.

his palace.' So in the Amra Chol. 124: *sin* (leg. *siu*) *incdim* .i. *is amlaidsin dogniim a aisneis* 'thus do I announce him.'

No. 604. Root *ú*, ὔει, ὑετός. O.Ir. *suth* .i. *lacht* 'milk,' *ont-suth* .i. *on loimm*, Corm. s. v. *uth*, *toth* (= *do-su-ta*) .i. *sugh*, H. 3.18, p. 638: *suba* .i. *fuil* 'blood,' LU. 50a: *Sabrann* (the name of the river Lee near Cork) = W. *Hafren*, *Sabrina* (*br* ex *vr*), Gaulish *Savara*, *la Sèvre* (Pictet) are all from the root *su* here noticed.

No. 605. υἱός. Root *su*. Add the O.Ir. *too*, *toud* 'gignere,' O'Cl., (= *do-soo, *do-soud) : *fuil nuitlige*[a] *iar too* 'the blood of a cow after calving,' ib., 3d sg. pret. *gur-thoi* .i. *go rug* 'genuit,' O'Cl.

No. 608. ὑσμῖν-. The O.Ir. *idnae* Corm. s. v. nith, (acc. pl. *idnu*: *bruid idnu buden mbáeth* 'he crushes the weapons of vain hosts,' LU. 47b: dat. *taithniomh oir aran-iodhnoibh* 'the sheen of gold on their weapons,' Petrie's *Tara* 166), the adj. *iodhnach* .i. *armach no cathach*, O'Cl., and the O.W., Corn. and Br. *iud*, the first element of many proper names of men, are cognate with Skr. *yudh-ma*. In Ir. *idnu* the semivowel has become *i*. But it is preserved in three instances, viz., *iúg* in *iúg-suide* (gl. tribunal), Z. 183, *iunad* gen. *iunta* 'coitus (avium),' O'Don. Supp. (root *yu* 'jungere'), and *iúr* .i. *orgain* ' occisio,' O'Cl., (cf. Skr. root *YU-SH* ' verletzen,' BR.).

No. 617. Root ἴς, Skr. *ish*. Add the Gaulish god-name *Ésu-s*, Rev. Celt. i. 259, ii. 203, the O.Ir. noun *ítu*, gen. *ítad*, ' sitis ' (= Slav. *choti* ' verlangen ' ' begehr ' Fick[2] 401) and the woman's name *I'te*, Skr. ishṭâ.

No. 620. Root Ϝεπ, VAK. Add the following Irish words from O'Clery: *foch-t* .i. *iarfaighi(dh)* 'quæstio'; *fuigheall* .i. *briathar* ' verbum '; *fachain* .i. *foeighemh no glaodh* ' monitio vel clamor '; *fa-n-g* .i. *fiach* ' corvus.' The verbs *du(fh)acthar* (gl. loquitur) Ml. 51c., and *ateoch* (= *ate-vacu) ' precor,' Br. 95, also belong to this root.

The form *fiach* 'corvus' is from *vēco*, root VEC (VIC ?), to which Curtius refers Lat. *convīcium, in-vi(c)-tare*.

No. 621. Root SAK, ἑπ. Add O.Ir. *soich fír* .i. *rosheichestar in fír* 'he followed the truth,' Amra Chol. 110, Goid. 169, and the verb *siachtaim*, whence *o-ro-siacht tra brenainn co-brigit* ' when Br. drew nigh to Brigit,' LH. 16b. *siachts-um* (= *siachtais -um*) *donend 7 úacht* ' storm and cold drew near me,' LU. 40a.

With the Ir. *saigim* 'adeo,' Goth. *sokja*, here mentioned we may perhaps put O.Ir. *sog* ' greyhound,' the acc. pl. of which occurs in the Amra Chonroi, H. 3. 18, p. 50: *x. soga soleicdi* (.i. *milchoin soleicthi*) *asa-slabraduib findruine no airgit hi segraide oss neng* ' ten greyhounds easily slipt from their leashes of white-bronze or silver after deer.'

No. 627. Root AK. ὐπ. Add O.W. *ein-epp*, O.Ir. *ag-ed, ag-id* ' facies,' and *ugail* ' oculi,' LU. 50a, unless this be a loan.

No. 628. ὀπός, *sucus*. In O.W. *dis-suncnetic* (gl. exanclata ' pumped out, sucked out'), Mart. Cap. 3, a. a., the *s* of the root SVAK is preserved. In other Welsh words (*chwaeth* ' savour,' ' taste,' ex *svakta, chweg* ' sweet ' ex *sveka) the combination *sv* has regularly become *hv, chw*.

---

* Is this cognate with O.N. *naut* ' bos ' ?

No. 630. Root KVAKV, πεπ. Other British words from this root are W. poeth, Br. poaz = πεπτός, Br. poazat 'coquere.' Add also Ir. coicc 'coquus' and cucenn 'coquina.'

No. 631. Ir. can .i. tan no úair, O'Cl. = Goth. hvan, Eng. when, should be added.

With ἐκεῖ, ci-s, ci-tra mentioned in the Note to this Number I would connect the Ir. cé (used in the phrase for bith ché 'on this world,' cen- in cen-alpande 'cisalpinus,' Z. 870, cen-tar 'pars citerior' and cen-tarach (gl. citimus, gl. citra), Z. 72, 781.

No. 632. Root σεπ. The Old-Welsh hep, hepp 'inquit' occurs often in the Capella Glosses, and should be cited in preference to the Mediæval Welsh heb. The Ir. cosc (= *con-seca), co-tob-sechfider 'instituemini,' Z. 483, aithescc, Z. 67, 'answer' (*ati-s-co) = W. atteb (ex at-hep) and Ir. tairmescc, Z. 67, 'prohibitio,' not 'perturbatio,' *tarmi-s-co, should be added.

No. 633. Root TARK, τρεπ, torqueo. Add W. treigl 'revolutio,' treig-lo 'volvere.'

With the Skr. ap, Lat. aqua, Goth. ahva, which Curtius cites after this Number, we may place the Ir. ia-stem oiche .i. uisge 'water,' O'Cl.

No. 634. Root βα. Add Ir. béim .i. céim 'step,' O'Cl. The Lat. vādere here cited may come from *va-n-dere = Ir. fonnadh .i. foghluasacht no siubhal 'moving or travelling,' O'Cl., just as vācillare from vancillare, Schmidt, Vocalismus 104. Anyhow vādo cannot be separated from vadan, the Celtic reflexes of which are Ir. do-faid 'ivit,' Fiacc's h. 9, in-baid (b for v) Ult. 8, W. ad-wedd 'reversio,' 'reditus,' Davies.

No. 640. W. bwyd, Br. boet 'cibus' = βίοτος. The W. buch in buchedd 'life' is, according to Rhys, ex *gvivanca : cf. Skr. jivaka, Lat. (g)vivax.

No. 642. βοή, βοάω. The O.Ir. bóu in the phrase ni torbe do bóu (gl. ad nihil utile, verbis contendere), Z. 23, may perhaps be cognate.

No. 643. Root βορ. Ir. broth 7 bruith .i. feoil 'caro,' O'Cl., gen. bruithe, also belong to this Number, the br coming from vr as often. And the old g appears in for-diu-guilsiter (gl. vorabuntur), Ml. 84, fordiucailsi 'absorpti,' Ml. 59, and other such forms, Goidel[2]. 25, fordiuglaim 'devorare,' LU. 111a, fordiuglantaid 'devorator,' O'Mulc. Gl. No. 780, and in gleith .i. caitheamh 'consumptio,' O'Cl.

No. 651. Root θερ. With ghransa-s (ghrāsa-s?) 'sonnengluth' here cited, and perhaps χρυσός, I would connect a number of Irish words with s ex ns:—gris 'fire,' O'Don. Supp., grísach 'burning ember,' etc. Words like *gris 'fire' (gristaitnem na gréne, O'Don. Gr. 286), with short i, for *grid-ti, seem connected with χλιδή, χλίω, A.S. glítan, etc. Hence gresaim 'incito,' 'excito.' The O.Ir. gronn and gorn 'firebrand,' Corm., are also from the root ghar.

No. 652. The Welsh ffwn 'breath' (Gen. vii. 22, Dan. x. 17), ffwn 'a puff,' 'sigh,' (ex SPUNA), ffothyll = Lat. (s)pustula (see No. 432, supra), Ir. sotal (= *spustala) 'proud,' whence sotlae 'pride,' support Curtius' theory that φῦσα and the other words here cited come from a root SPU.

No. 654. Here Curtius (I venture to think) confounds two roots: VAG, whence Fάγ-νυ-μι and Ir. fann, W. gwann (ex *vag-no) 'weak,' 'zerbrechlich,' and BHAG, whence Skr. *bhanajmi*, Ir. *comlaig*, to which add from O'Clery *bugh* .i. *briseadh* 'fractio,' *buich* .i. *briseadh*, *com-bocht* .i. *dobris* 'fregit.'

No. 655. Here also two different roots are dealt with as one: VRAG, whence *Ρήγνυμι* 'I *wreck*' and the Ir. root *ORG*,[a] whence *orcun*, and BHRAG, whence Lat. *frango*, Goth. *brikan*. The W. *brau* 'fragile,' and perhaps Ir. *braigim* 'pedo,' if *br* is from *vr*, are cognate with *Ρήγνυμι*; if *br* represents an Indo-European BHR, they are cognate with *fra-n-go*, *brikan*. The Ir. *brissim* and *brossnae*, which Windisch doubtfully quotes here, belong (with Ir. *brosc* .i. *torann* 'thunder,' O'Don. Supp., *im-bresan* 'conflict,' Corn. *bresel*) to the OHG. *brestan*, and (if Fick be right) to the Gr. $\phi\lambda\acute{a}(\sigma)\omega$.

No. 656. Root ἀλ. The Ir. *salt* .i. *léim* 'a leap,' Corm., is possibly not a loan. It occurs in Irish topography. *So-alt* (i. e. *so-salt*) .i. *soiléim* .i. *léim maith* 'a good leap,' O'Clery, who also has *alt* .i. *léim*.

No. 657. ἅλς. Ir. *sál* 'sea' should be added. It occurs in the Book of Leinster, fo. 19. a. 2:—

In-tocéb mo-curchan ciar	'Shall I launch my black skiff
for-inn-ocian n-uchtlethan n-áin	On the ocean broad-breasted, splendid?
in-rag a-rí richid réil	Shall I go, O King of bright heaven,
as-mo-thoil fein ar-in-sál [b].	According to my own desire, on the sea?'

The gen. sg. *sáil* seems to occur in the objective compound *socc-sáil* (gl. foligo), Z. 30, where the *ái* (an infected *á*) is, wrongly, I think, treated as a diphthong, the acc. sg. in the Félire, at Mar. 5, Aug. 25, Sep. 10. The cognate *ia*-stem *sáile* occurs with the same meaning at July 9.

No. 658. Root VARDH, βλάστη. From the root VARDH comes, with loss of initial *v*, Ir. *ordu* 'thumb,' with metathesis and change of *vr* to *br*, Ir. *brú* gen. *bronn* 'venter,' Z. 264, (W. *bru*): *bruinne* 'mamma,' 'pectus,' (W. *bronn*) acc. pl. *bruinniu*, Z. 653; and *bruinnech* 'mater,' Corm.

No. 660. Root Fελ, Skr. *var*. The following Irish words belong to this Number: *félmae* (gl. sæpes), Z. 770, *fál* 'hedge,' Z. 953, SM. i. 236.

No. 665. Root SVAR. The O.Ir. *selam* .i. *neam* 'heaven,' (Lebar Lecain Glossary, No. 301) is cognate with σέλας, *ser-enus*, etc.; so also *sellad*, Goid. 159, or *silled*, 'to see,' *sellach* 'eyewitness,' SM. i. 240, *sella* 'eyes,' T. B. Fr., where *ll* = *ly*, *ry* as in "Ελλη = *svaryā* (Kuhn). So perhaps in *aislinge* 'a vision,' *ad-sell-ang-ia*, Corm. Tr. 13.

---

[a] *orgait in dun fochetóir* 'they wreck the fortress forthwith,' Táin bó Fráich, LL. 189. b. 1.

[b] This is misquoted and the verbs are mistranslated in O'Curry's Manners and Customs of the Ancient Irish iii. 388. But this is nothing to a passage in the preceding page, where a prose proverb (*maraith seroc céin mardda aithne a máellecán* 'manet amor quamdiu manent opes, O M.' Nigra. Rel. Celt. 22) is printed as verse and translated thus: '"Twas my much-loved long-coveted treasure, to understand their warbling.' Take another specimen from the same book: King Conchobar, in the Táin bó Cualnge, after seeing the feats of the boy Cúchulainn, says regretfully, 'If (only) he had (i. e. could perform) the deeds of championship, even as he hath the boy-deeds!' *Nicumdas arád, ur Fergus, feib atré in mac bec atresat a gnima óclachais leis*, LL. 47 a. 2. 'It is not meet to say that;' says Fergus; 'as the little boy will grow (literally 'rise') up, his deeds of championship will grow up with him.' O'Curry (ii. 362) renders this easy passage thus: 'It is not proper to speak so,' said Fergus, ' for, according to the manner in which the little boy has performed his actions, (it is clear) he must (already) know the feats of championhood.' A few more of the many mistakes in this book are noticed infra, Appendix H.

No. 664. Root σκαλ. Ir. *scailt* 'a cleft,' *ro-ccachladar* (leg. *ro-che-chlatar*) .i. *do-tho-chladar* 'fodierunt,' O'Cl., *forroichlaid* (*fo-ro-ce-chlaid*) gl. effodit, Ml. 24c, *focechlaitis* .i. *rotochlaidis* 'fodiebant,' Transcript of Laws by O'Curry 2044, *ro-cloth a both* 'fossa, fundata est ejus casa,' Br. 70, and the noun *cail* in the following passage from Lib. Arm. 11, a. 2: 'et sepultus ibi in quo dicitur *Cail Boid-mail* usque in hunc diem.'

Having thus suggested addenda to most of Curtius' Numbers, I will now mention some of the phonetic changes in which the Neo-Celtic languages resemble Greek. Windisch, Grundzüge, pp. 894, 415, notices the regular Welsh, Cornish and Breton change of initial *s* before a vowel to *h*. But there are many more.

1°. The weakening of a vowel-flanked tenuis to a media, which we find in ἀρήγω, κραυγή, Ἀρτέμιδος (= Doric Ἀρτάμιτος), καλύβη, and other words cited by Curtius, pp. 522—530. This is the rule in the British languages.

2°. The loss of *s* in the combinations σρ, σν, σμ, Curtius, p. 681. This is common in Welsh: cf. *rhes* with Ir. *sreth* 'series'; *nedd* 'nit,' *nawdd* 'protection,' *nawf* 'a swim,' *noden* 'thread,' (Br. *neut*) *notuid* 'needle,' with Ir. *sned, snádud, snám, snáthe, snáthat*; cf. too W. *nyddu*, Br. *nezaff* 'filer' with (σ)νήθω and ἔννη (nebat) ex ἔ-σνη; W. *mug* = Ir. *múch* (*ainm dileas do dheataigh* 'a name proper to smoke,' O'Cl.), Br. *moguet*, with σμύχω for *σμύκω, Fick 416; Ir. *much* .i. *toirse* 'tristitia,' O'Cl., with ἐπι-σμυγ-ερός; W. *mynawyd* 'awl' with σμινύη.

3°. The change of ν to μ before the labial nasal (ΤΕΜ ΜΥΣΙΑΝ, ΤΩΜ ΜΙΣΘΩΣΕΩΝ, Curtius, p. 532): cf. O.Ir. *am-mag*, Z. 214, *innam-miled*, *innam-moge*, Z. 216, *diam-mennut*, Tir. 8, 9.

4°. The hardening of a medial by a following spiritus asper (Curtius, p. 425), as in ἄνθος *ant-h-os* = Skr. *and-h-as*. So the Old-Irish article (*s*)*ind* becomes (*s*)*int* wherever infected *s* (= *h*) follows[a], Beitr. i., Z. 44. So the preposition *ind* (Gaulish *ande*) becomes *int* before infected *s*, Z. 878. So in the preposition *imb* = ἀμφί the *b* changes into *p* before infected *s*: *impu* = *imb-su*, *impod* = *sód*, etc.

5°. The change of ρj, λj to ρρ, λλ, Curtius, p. 652, is paralleled by the Ir *ferr* 'better,' = W. *gwell* = Skr. *varîyas*, and by the W. *peil* 'far' ex *peljo-s* = περαῖος, and *oll, arall* = Ir. *uile, araile* (Rhys).

6°. As regards the generation of parasitic sounds, the British languages afford four interesting parallels to Greek: first, in the change to *p*, through the intermediate stage *kv*, of the *K* corresponding with Skr. and Zend *k, ch*, Greek (κF) κ, κκ, π, ππ, Lat. *qv*,[b] (see Fick, *Spracheinheit* 6, 7, 62);

---

[a] In the nom. sg. masc. *int-ech* (e. g.) comes from *(*s*)*ind-h-eco*, *sinda-s-ecvo-s*.

[b] And compare Windisch, Beitr. viii. 35—48. To the instances there given of W. *p* = Ir. *c* add—

W. *pás* 'tussis,' Ir. *cas-achtach*, A.S. *hvósta*, OHG. *huosto*;
W. *ar-pet, arbed* 'parcere,' *arpeteticion* 'parcis,' Z. 1055, Ir. *air-chissi* (gl. parcit) Z. 183, (*are-cet-tit*).

secondly, in the growth of v to gv [a] (Curtius, pp. 584, 586) both in anlaut and inlaut (*neguid* 'novus,' Ir. *og* ('ovum'); thirdly, in the growth of g to gv, which combination has then become b: this is found both in Irish and the British languages; fourthly, in the change of j into dj and then into d. This fourth change (the brilliant discovery of Mr. Rhys [b]) is, so far as I know, confined to Welsh, Cornish and Breton.

III.—NOTANDA.

I shall now mention some 40 Greek words which have apparently their cognates in the Celtic languages, but which, with three exceptions, are either not noticed in Curtius' book, or only referred to for non-comparative purposes:—

ἄρδις, Ir. *aird* 'point,' 'place,' Tur. 138, *in cech 6en aird in hére ambia asil* 'in every single place in Ireland wherein his seed shall be,' LU. 115a. *cipe aird do airdib in domain* 'whatever be the point of the points of the world,' LU. 111a;

βρόγχος, O.Ir. *bráge* (gl. cervix), Z. 255, (an ant-stem), W. *breuant* 'windpipe';

γοργών, γοργός, Ir. *garg* 'fierce,' Corm. Tr. 88, also *gearg* .i. *garg*, O'Cl.;

γῦρος, Ir. *giugrann* (ex *gi-gur-ann*) 'anser bernicula,' Z. 21, Corm. Tr. 88, W. *gwyrain*;

ἐρείκη, (ἐFρείκη), Ir. *froech*, gen. *froich*, Z. 918, W. *grug* 'heath'; ἐρείκω, *rec* (gl. sulco), Z. 1063, (Mod. W. *rhyg* 'notch,' 'groove'): cf. ἤρεικον χθόνα;

εὗρον = O.Ir. *fuar*, Brocc. h. 98, LU. 40 a, εὗρε = *fuair*, O'Don. Gr. 242, ζειά, Skr. *yava-*, Lith. *javaí*, Ir. *eo-rna*;

ἠΐθεος, root VADH 'heimführen,' 'heirathen,' Fick 179. O.Ir. root VOD in *in-bod-ugud* 'nubere,' *in-both-igetar* 'nubent,' Z. 1034, *in-botha* 'nuptias' (*th* for *dh*), Tur. 48, Corn. *d-om-eth-y*, BM. 327 = Br. *d-im-iz-iff* 'soy marier,' 'nubere'; cf. the Skr. *vadhū* 'sponsa,' *vadhitra* 'qui facit sponsalia' (Kern, Rev. Celt. ii. 158: more in Joh. Schmidt's Verwantschaftsverhältnisse der indogerm. Sprachen, 49);

ἤν, Lat. *en*, O.Ir. *énde*, Corm. Tr. 69, = O'Clery's *énne* .i. *féch no fionn* 'see or know!';

---

[a] In O.Ir. *derbb* 'certus,' Z. 60, = Goth. *triggv-s* the *gv* has become *b*, the root is DRU, whence Goth. *trauan*. To the same root belong O.Ir. *derb* 'certus,' 'verus,' Fél. Jan. 3, Mar. 25, etc., *der(b)-bráthir*, Z. 263, now *dearbh*, where the *b* (*bh*) is = *v*, and the O.Ir. *drui*, pl. *druid*, W. *derwydd*, Gaul. *druis*, pl. *druides*, which simply means ' *soothsayer*,' ' *wahrsager*,' and has nothing to do with δρῦς or any other kind of tree.

[b] See Revue Celtique ii. 115, where Rhys equates *haidd* 'barley' ex *hakja* with Skr. *sasya*; *ardd-u* 'to plough' with Goth. *arj-an*; *Iwerddon* with *Iverjon(em)*; *trydydd* for *tritija*; Skr. *trtíya* and *llonedd*, *caredd*, *chwerwedd*, *gwyledd*, *llyfredd*, *moeledd*, *truedd*, *trugaredd* with the Irish fem. *yā*-stems *láine*, *caire*, *serbe*, *féle*, *lobre*, *máile*, *tróige*, *trócaire*. To these may be added *leguenid*, *llawenydd* 'laetitia' = Ir. *láine* .i. *medhair*, O'Cl.: *an-hawdd* 'difficilis' = Ir. *anse*: *emid*, *efydd* 'aes' = Ir. *umae*; and *eilydd* = Ir. *ala*. So W. *-ebedd* in *wyn-ebedd* 'superficies' is = ωπια in ἐν-ώπια.

The Welsh plurals in *edd* (Corn. *-eth*, Br. *-ez*) appear to have been originally collectives identical in formation with Greek δωρ-ιά, ἀνθρακ-ιά, μυρμηκ-ιά, νεοττ-ιά and Skr. *gav-yā* 'a number of cows,' Grundzüge 595.

θολός, θολερός, Goth. *dval-s*, Eng. *dull*, = Ir. and W. *dall* 'blind,' Ir. *cluas-dall* 'deaf,' lit. 'ear-dull,' O'Cl., s.v. *athaile* ;

ἰσχ-νό-s, ex *σισκ-νοs, W. *hysp*, f. *hêsp* 'dry,' 'barren,' Ir. *sesc*, W. *hespin* 'a yearling ewe' = *seisc*, Corm., s.v. Oi. pl. *sesci* 'dry cows, SM. ii. 120 ;

κέντρον, (ex *κεντ-τρον) W. *cethr* 'clavus,' Br. *quentr*, Ir. *cinteir* (gl. calcar), Z. 67, ex *cens-tri, *cent-tri, as— *cainte* 'satirist,' ex *cans-tia, root CANS in Lat. *censeo, cens-or*, *daintech* 'dentatus,' Z. 811, from *dans-tica, *dant-tica, *mant* 'gingiva,' Corm. Tr. 115, from *mans-ta, *mand-ta (Lat. *mandere*), *sant*, Z. 42, W. *chwant* 'desiderium,' from *sva-n-stā (root SVAS,[a] Skr. çvas, Gründz.[4] 560) :

The O.Ir. *cét* 'a blow' (*col-dam aidid crist na cét* 'I know the death of Christ of the blows,'[b] Harl. 1802, fo. 9b) = O'Clery's *céad* .i. *béim*, is cognate with κεντέω, O.N. *hnjódha*, 'obtundere malleo,' NHG. *nieten*, Fick 31, 730 ;

κέρκος 'cock,' Hesych., Fick 35, Ir. *cerc* 'hen' ;

κλᾶϊος, = A.S. *holt*, NHG. *holz* (Fick, Spracheinheit, 310), Ir. *caill* 'sylva,' Z. 183, 815, gen. *calle*, Fiacc's h. 16, but dat. *caillid*, LL. 10. b. 2, a *t*-stem (*caldit-), W. *celli* ;

κνήμη, Ir. *cnam* 'os,' nom. pl. *cnamai*, Z. 1003 ;

κρόμνον, Ir. *crem*, W. *craf* 'garlic' ;

λαχαίνω, Lat. *ligo*, Ir. *laighe* 'spade,' O.W. *liou* (gl. ligones) Juv. 25 ;

λό-γ-χη, *la-n-cea*, O.Ir. *laigen*, W. *llain* 'gladius,' 'lamina' ;

μαστός, 'a swelling breast,' Ir. *máss* 'buttock,' 'the bottom of a vessel' (*cen mas isin dabaig*, note to Fél. Nov. 24), also used in topography, for a long low hill (Joyce 508), as μαστός is used for a round hill or knoll ;

μάταιος = Ir. *madae*, Fél. Ep. 227, *in-madae* (gl. sine causa), Z. 609, *ho ru-maith* 'eum fregit,' Ml. 51c., *asa-to-roi-med a-sruáim* 'e quo erupit τὸ flumen,' Z. 24. *Co-róe-mid ceo mór dia chind* 'so that a great mist burst forth from his head,' LU. 58 ;

μέ-μ-φ-ομαι (= *μεμέφομαι according to Pott), O.Ir. *mebul* 'shame,' Z. 711, ' pudendum muliebre,' O'Dav. 107, W. *meflu* ' to disgrace ' ;

μόρον, Lat. *mōrum*, Ir. *merenn*, W. *mer -wydden* ;

ὀθόνη, root VADH ' binden,' ' winden,' ' kleiden ' Fick 179. To this root, and not to BHADH, Windisch should have referred O.Ir. *co-beden* 'conjugatio,' *co-bod-las* 'conjunctio,' *coi-bd-elach* 'necessarius, amicus.'

---

[a] This root is also unasalised in the Latin *vensica* from *sve-n-s-tca. Other Celtic derivatives from it are :—
  Ir. *fet* ' fistula ' W. *chwyth* ' halitus,' ' flatus,' *chwythell* ' whistle ' :
  Ir. *sétim* ' flo.' ' spiro,' *siataire* ' vesica.'
See for other examples of hard *t* from *s-t*, supra p. 30.

[b] See Matth. xxvii, 67 : Mark xv. 9 : Luke xxiii, 63, 64 : John xix. 3. In Dr. Reeves' edition of the Codex Maelbrigte, O'Curry renders *aidid crist nacét* by ' the fate of all ruling Christ ' ! *Aidid* means ' death by violence.'

Other derivatives from this VADH are: Ir. *fedan* 'jugum,' Corm.' Tr. 79, W. *gwedd*, Ir. *feidm* 'jugum,' gen. *fedma*, Ir. *fascud* (ex *vadcatu), Corm. Tr. 79, Br. *goascaff* 'stringere'; Ir. *fadb* LU. 7a, or *fodb* .i. *édach inmairb* 'the dead man's dress,' O'Dav. 55, s.v. resclad: *teora camsi hi foditib* (.i. *hi cenglaib*) *impu* 'three bedgowns (*camisiæ*) in belts about them,' LU. 94;

ὄρχις, Ir. *uirge* 'testicle';

οὐτάω, ὠτειλή, Ir. *futhu* 'stigmata,' *fothib* 'facibus,' *co-fothea-sa* (gl. ut mordeam), Z. 1005, *foccul gonas nech fothuind*, Amra Chol. ed. Crowe p. 70, *diothach*, Amra 86, and *diuthach, diuthainn*, Corm., Lith. *voti-s* 'wound';

πέτ-ρα, πέτ-ρος, Ir. *áith* 'fornax,' W. *od-yn*. So κάμινος and Skr. *açmanta* 'oven' are cognate with *açman* 'stone.' " Die ältesten öfen sind jedenfals steinerne herde oder in stein gehauene löcher gewesen, wie sie es zum teil bis auf den heutigen tag gebliben sind. Daher nante man sie auch 'steine'." Schmidt *Die Wurzel AK*, 66;

-πλοος, -πλους in ἀ-πλόος, διπλοῦς, Ir. *dia-bul, tri-pulta*, Ir.Gl. Nos. 930, 931;
πολλός, (Lat. *pollere, poll-ex*), Ir. *oll* .i. *mor*, O'Dav. 109: compar. *huilliu*, Z.² 275;

ῥῦμα, O.W. *ruimmein* [a] (gl. vincula), Juv. 55: cf. NHG. *riemen*, Fick, *Spracheinheit* 359;

σκαμβός, Old-Celtic *cambo-*, Ir. *camm*, Z. 857, W. *camm* 'curvus,' Br. *cam* 'boiteux';

σπαργή, σπαργάω, (Skr. *sphurj*), W. *ffrau* 'torrent,' 'gushing.' That σπαργάω is connected with Lat. *turgeo* (Curtius 619) seems very doubtful;

τηράω, O.Ir. *táid*, 'thief,' *táin* 'cattle-spoil';
τῖλος 'stercus liquidum,' W. *tail* (Davies);
Τριτο(γένεια), etc., Ir. *triath* 'sea,' Corm. Tr. 156, *trethan* (gl. gurges), Z. 264, gen. *trethain* .i. *mara*, Fél. Nov. 23;

φαλλός = Ir. *ball* 'membrum,' Z. 222, (Siegfried):

χάλιξ ex σκαλ-ιξ, O.Slav. *skala* 'stone,' Fick 408, Ir. *calad* 'hard,' O.W. *calat*, Ir. *cailte* .i. *cruas* 'hardness,' O'Cl.

χρέμπτομαι, χρέμψις ex *σκρε-μ-π-τις (Lith. *skreplei*, Lat. *scrapta*, Fick 409), Ir. *crontaighim* 'I loathe, abhor, detest,' Lhuyd and O'R., *crontaile* or *crointile* [b] 'pituita,' ex *scro-m-p-tal-ia*, as Br. *prount* ex *promptus*.

One might easily lengthen this list of wild Celtic words; but *boni venatoris est plures feras capere, non omnes*. I now present this paper to Windisch in hopes that he will criticise my work as freely as I have criticised

---

[a] The MS. has '*cuinhaunt irruimmein* quæ det pœna eterna super illos.' Other such plurals are *cemmein* (gl. gradus), *enuein* = nomina, Mart. Cap. 11 a. a, 11 b. b, Rhys, Rev. Celt. ii. 119, and *drummein* = Ir. *drommann : ar drumain mor* ' on the sea's ridges,' Cynddelw cited by Pughe under the forged word *truman*.

[b] The spellings *crontshuile, crointsheile* rest on one of Cormac's absurd etymologies, Corm. Tr. 36.

his, that he will choose from my citations what seems to him worthy of Curtius' admirable book, and that he will pardon my presumption because of my strong desire that nothing unsound should be added to that book, and that no unsteady superstructure should be raised on the foundation so well and truly laid by Zeuss and Ebel. It is, unfortunately, hard to criticise without seeming to assume a certain superiority. But this, as regards Windisch (who has already taught me much and who, I trust, will teach me more), I assuredly cannot claim. On the contrary, I am convinced that if I had made the Celtic additions to the *Grundzüge*, he would have been able to point out many more faults than I have indicated in the present paper.

SIMLA, *Nov. 1st*, 1874. W. S.

ADDENDUM TO No. 64, *supra p.* 9.

dinn 'hill,' ex **dig-ni*, Skr. *dehî*, τεῖχος, No. 145:
fann, W. *gwann* 'weak,' 'zerbrechlich,' ex **vag-no*, cf. Fάγνυμι, No. 560:
lainn 'desire,' Crowe's *Amra*, p. 18, ex **lag-ni*: cf. λάγ-νος 'lustful,' No. 146:
linn 'pool,' '*liegendes* wasser' ex **ligno*, No. 173:
mann 'great,' O'Dav. 105, 107, ex *mag-no*, Lat. *magnus*, No. 462.

II.

ON THE CELTIC COMPARISONS IN BOPP'S *COMPARATIVE GRAMMAR*.[a]

THE Celtic words—genuine or fabricated—noticed in Bopp's *Comparative Grammar* are seventy-five in number. Of these twelve are cited either for the ending or for the treatment of the terminal letter of consonantal stems. These are :—

Ir. *athair* 'father,' Z. 262 : retains the *r* of the stem : *brathair* (leg. *bráthair*) 'brother,' Z. 262. Same remark : *comharsa* 'neighbour,' gen. *comharsan*, the modern form of *comarse* : *is dia mo-chomarse* 'God is my neighbour,' LU. 16b : *geallamhuin*, gen. *geallamhna* 'promising' : a stem in *-mani*, Z. 277 : *geanmhuin, ginmhuin* 'engendering' : ditto : *geineamhuin* 'birth' (*geinemhain*, gl. generacio) H. 2. 13 : *guala* 'shoulder,' gen. *gualann*, Z. 264 : *leanamhain, leanmhuin* 'following' : a stem in *mani* : *mathair* (leg. *máthair*), 'mother,' Z. 262 : retains the *r* of the stem : *naoidhe* 'child,' 'gen. *naoidhin*,' O.Ir. *nóidiu*, gen. *nóiden*, Z. 264, 265 : *ollamh* 'princeps poetarum,' gen. *ollamhan* : a stem in *n*, Z. 264 : *scaramhain* 'separation,' a stem in *-mani*.

Ten seem fabrications or blunders of O'Reilly, Shaw or other Gaelic lexicographers, namely :—

Ir. *aisk*, i. 89, 'request.' This is Shaw's *aisg* 'petitio.' But there is no such word. The word meant is *ascid* or *aiscidh* s. f., which has probably lost initial *v*.[b] It occurs in O'Don. Gr. 106 : *ni h-aiscidh carad ar charaid*, and in LU. 41a, (Rev. Celt. ii. 88) : *tucad disi ind ascidsin* ('that request was granted to her'). Cognate with this is *toisc* 'voluntas' [=*do-(v)ansci*] and both belong to the Skr. *vañchá*, OHG. *wunsc*, Eng. *wish* :

beasach 'l'adjectif *beasach* signifie éclat,' i. 267,[c] where it is connected with Skr. *bhâs* 'briller.' There is no such word. *Bésach* (now written *béasach* or *beusach*) is a derivative from *bés* 'mos,' and means 'moral,' 'modest,' 'well-behaved.' It can have nothing to do with *bhâs*. The Ir. *bótt* 'fire,' Corm. Tr. 52, may come from this root, see supra p. 30 : *gailleamhain* 'offence.' I know of no such word except in O'Reilly :

---
[a] Vergleichende Grammatik ...... von Franz Bopp, zweite Ausgabe, Berlin, 1857—1861. Grammaire comparée des langues indo-européennes ... par M. François Bopp traduite sur la deuxième édition ... par M. Michel Bréal. Paris, 1866—1872.
Francis Meunier. Registre détaillé, Paris, 1874.
[b] The initial vowel forbids us to connect *ascid* with Skr. *ichâ* ex *iskâ*, the European form of which is *aiská*, Fick², 511.
[c] Here, as elsewhere, I cite from M. Bréal's translation.

gnia, gnic 'connaissance,' *gno* 'ingénieux,' i. 259. I doubt if there is any such word as *gnia* 'connaissance.' O'Reilly doubtless cites it from O'Clery, who has *gnia aithne. cia dognia .i. cia doaithéonta,* whence it would seem to be a verbal form. As to *gnic* I know it only from O'Reilly and Lhuyd. As to *gno* (leg. *gnó*) it means 'remarquable,' not 'ingénieux':

logha 'brillant,' i. 58. This is from O'Reilly, but I know of no such word. Perhaps *lóche* 'lightning' (gen. *lochet*) gave rise to this forgery:

ollamhain 'instruction.' This is from O'Reilly. I have never met it, except as the dat. or acc. sg. or nom. pl. of the *n*-stem *ollamh* 'chief-poet':

ruadh 'force,' 'vailleur,' et comme adjectif 'fort,' 'vaillant,' iv. 291n., where it is connected with Skr. *ruh* 'grandir' for *rudh*. This may be right as to the adjective *ruadh*, which O'Clery explains by *trén no láidir*. But (though it occurs in O'Reilly) I know of no such substantive as *ruadh* 'force,' 'vailleur':

rud 'wood.' From O'Reilly, who gives a gloss, '.i. *coill no fidh*,' found nowhere else, so far as I know:

ruigheanas 'éclat,' connected by Bopp with Skr. *ráj*. This also is *unbelegt*, and is almost certainly a forgery or a blunder. (Can it be = *ro-genas* 'great chastity'?):

There remain fifty-three, of which the following twenty-four are (I venture to think) wrongly compared:—

Ir. *am* 'time,' W. *amser*, Br. *amzer*, Vergl. Gr. i. 492: I cannot find it in the French version, ii. 77, 80, to which the index refers one. Bopp compares the Skr. *amasa* 'tempus': but the hardness of the *m* in the Celtic words (which are genuine) points either to the root AMB *ambati* 'gehen,' which however is not *belegt*, or to the root AG, through the form *a-n-g-va*, (see p. 20—21 supra) cognate with the Oscan *angetuzet, angit*:

anal 'breath,' iv. 269n, is compared with the Skr. *anila* 'wind.' The Irish word meant is *anál* = W. *anadl*, an O.Celt. *anatlo*, which is only radically connected with *anila*:

anochd 'noctu,' 'hâc nocte,' ii., 333. 'Here,' says Bopp, '*a* est employé comme thème démonstratif.' But *a-nochd* is a mere modern corruption of the O.Ir. *in-nocht*, Z. 609, where *in* for *inn* is the acc. sg. masc. or fem. of the article, of which the stem is *sinda*:

arasaim 'j' habite,' i. 59. Bopp compares the Skr. *â-vasâmi*, assuming a change of *v* to *r*. But this is impossible in Irish. I have never met with *arasaim* except in O'Reilly's Dictionary. If it be a genuine word, it is a denominative from *aros* 'a dwelling' (= W. *araws* 'a staying') which seems compounded of the preposition *ar* and *foss* = *vastu*, Curtius No. 206:

as 'hors de,' iv. 394n, is compared with the Skr. adverb *âvis* 'offenbar,' 'vor augen.' But terminal *s* is never preserved in Irish. *As-* (which is only found combined with the article and pronouns or in composition) is = Lat. *ex*, Gr. *ἐξ*: and (like ὀμφαλός, *umbilicus*, *imbliu*: ὄνυξ, *unguis*, *inge*) may be quoted as a relic of the Græco-italo-celtic unity:

beosaighim 'j'orne,' 'j'embellis,' i. 266, where it is compared with Skr. *bhûshayâmi*. As *s* between vowels disappears in Irish, this comparison must be wrong. I have not met with *beosaighim* except in O'Reilly's Dictionary:

bhus 'il sera,' iii. 301, when it is compared with the Lith. *bus*, Skr. *bhavishyati*. But Ir. *bhus* means 'qui sera,' and is the modern 3d. sg. *relative* future, the Old-Irish *bes*, Z^2. 498. Compare Keating cited in O'Don. Gr. 161, *oir as tu bhus aoin-bhean damhsa óso amach* 'car c'est toi qui sera ma seule femme dorénavant,' in Old-Irish *air istú bes-óenben damsa óso immach*. Whatever may be the *s* in *bhus*, it can have nothing to do with the *s* in *bus* or the *sh* in *bhavishyati*:

bleachd 'lait' is explained as from *bo-leachd*, *bo* (leg. *bó* 'vache'). But here, as in *blith* and other Irish words, *bl* is from *ml*, and *bleachd* is from *mlecht* (cf. *bo-mlacht*, Corm. Tr.) and cognate with ἀ-μέλγω, &c.:

bri 'parole,' iv. 276, note 4. This should be *brí*. Bopp connects it with the Skr. root *BRÛ* 'parler'; but the vowels do not agree; and *bri* like *briathar*, is cognate with Γρῆ-μα, Γρῆ-σις, Γρή-τρα:

cac, cacach, cachaim, scachraith, i. 351, are compared with Lat. *caco*, etc. The first three words would be better spelt *cacc, caccach, caccaim* : cf. W. *cach, cachu*, where *ch* = *cc*. As to *seachraith* or *sechraid* (.i. *salchar* 'filth,' O'Cl., O'Dav. 116) it has obviously nothing to do with the other words, and seems a derivative from the preposition *sech* :

dasachd 'ferocité,' 'courage,' i. 150, iv. 269, (O.Ir. *dásacht*) is connected with θρασύς, Skr. root *DHARSH* 'audere.' But this is impossible. *R* never is lost in Celtic. *Dásacht* properly means 'insania,' Z^2. 805. Its etymology is quite obscure:

déagh, deich 'dix' are equated with *daçam, decem,* i. 52. Here *déagh* is a mistake for *déag* = O.Ir. *déac* 'ten,' a dissyllable, the etymology of which has not been explained. It is used as the absolute form of the numeral, while *deich* is used with substantives:

deanaim (leg. *déanaim*), vide infra p. 52, s. v. *dan*:

dear 'fille,' i. 333, is quoted as an example of the preservation of the final *r* of the theme. This is very unlikely. The Old-Irish form *der* occurs in Cormac's Glossary, s. vv. *ainder*, and in the Lebar Brecc 85: *petronilla der petair* 'S. Petri filia.' So in numerous women's names ; *Der-inill*, LB. 17a, 22a, *Der-mor* 17d, *Der-chartaind* 19c, *Der-lir* 22a. *Der* may perhaps be the Neo-Celtic reflex of the Gr. θάλος, which in Homer always means 'stripling.' It cannot possibly be = θυγατήρ, *duhitā*, &c. :

fiafruighim 'je demande' is connected with Skr. *pṛchasi* 'tu demandes,' and Bopp says it appears to contain a reduplicative syllable. Here, as often in modern Irish (and modern Ireland), appearances are deceptive, for the Old-Irish form is *iar-faigim*. Hence we see that the first *f* in *f-iafraighim* is only prosthetic, that the *r* has undergone metathesis, and that the root, instead of being (as Bopp supposes) *PARSK*, is *VAK*: *grith* 'cri,' i. 264, is connected by Bopp with Goth. *grêta*. He is possibly right if we assume that in Old-Celtic there was a nasalised root GRA-N-D = Skr. *hrâd* ' tönen ' (see infra s. v. *nadu*). It seems more likely that *grith* (= W. *gryd*) descends from **gariti*, a derivative from the root *GAR*, whence γῆρυς, OHG. *kirru*, etc., Curtius No. 133 :

mile (leg. *mîle*), W. *mil*, 'a thousand,' ii. 243, is treated as a loanword from Lat. *mille*. But, first, the quantities of the penults differ; secondly, in Latin loanwords *ll* is represented by *ll* (cf. *cella* 'cell '), and, lastly, the genders differ, for *mîle* is a feminine *iâ*-stem :

piuthair 'sœur,' i. 333, is stated to be for *spiuthair* (*piusthar*, ii. 323) ' avec endurcissement du *v* en *p*, comme dans *speur* 'ciel' qui répond au Sanscrit *svar*.' So far as concerns *piuthair* this is right ; but *speur* or *spéir* (gen. *spére*, O'Don. 11) is a loan from *sphaera* (cœlestis). *Piuthair* is still living in Scotland, but in Ireland I have only met with it in the gen. sg. in the following extract from LU. 59b : *Cia th-ainm-seo ol-conchobar. Setanta mac sualtaim atomchomnaicse 7 mac dechtere do-phethar-su* ' What is thy name ? ' says Conchobar. ' Setanta, son of Sualtam, am I, and son of Dechter, thy sister' :

raidim 'je dis,' i. 59n, is put with OHG. *far-wâzu* 'maledico' and Skr. *vad*. This is obviously wrong : *v* never becomes *r* in Irish. *Raidim* (recte *ráidhim*) is the O.Ir. *-ráidiu* or *-ráidiu*, Fél. Ep. 358, and is = the Goth. *rodja* (*rodjan* λαλεῖν, λέγειν, etc.) :

roid 'race' (recte 'cours') is connected with Skr. *ruh* 'venant de *rudh* grandir.' As this connection is obviously due to Bopp's having taken O'Reilly's 'race' to mean ' genus,' ' progenies,' whereas it means 'cursus,' nothing more need be said on the subject save that *rôid* and O'Davoren's *ruitech* .i. *rith* may come from a root *RAS*, Fick.² 842. See supra, p. 30 :

seasamh 'se tenir debout.' Bopp separates *seasamh* thus : ' *seas-a-mh*, l'a est la voyelle charactéristique, le *mh* est probablement un reste de *-mhuin*.' This is all wrong. *Seasamh* (= O.Ir. *sessam*) is a reduplicated form, and stands for **se-stam-a*, a derivative from the extended root *STAM* (*STA*, Skr. *sthâ*), whence Ir. *samaigim* 'pono,' W. *sefyll*, *safiad*, Br. *seuell* :

smigeadh 'le sourire,' i. 261. Bopp compares this with Skr. *smayati* ' il rit' and says 'le *j* est endurci en *g*.' This can hardly be, as *smigeadh* (with its hard *g*) points to an O.Ir. *smiced* :

speur, vide supra s.v. *piuthair* :

staighre 'pas,' 'degré,' is connected with the root *STIGH* 'monter,' Greek στιχ. But *staighre* is a loanword from the Eng. *stair*, A.S. *stäger*, *stegher*. The *st* in anlaut in Irish either loses *s* or assimilates *t*. The root STIGH appears as *tiagu*, στείχω, Curtius No. 177 :

Bopp also notices the following British words :—
cais 'contentio,' 'labor,' i. 34, he connects with Lat. *quæro*, for *quæso* and Skr. *cheshṭ*. But *cais* means 'conamen,' 'tentative' (*rhoi cais ar beth* 'to make an attempt on a thing') Davies :
danhezu 'mordre' (recte *dannheddu*) is connected by Bopp with δάκνω, *lacero*, Goth. *tahja*. But it comes from *dantedu, and is cognate with ὀδούς, *dens* and *tunth-u-s*, Curtius No. 289 :
nadu 'crier,' iii. 538, when it is connected with Skr. *nad*, *nânadati*, 'ils résonnent.' The Ir. *nath* (*taithmet fiadat ferr cech nath* 'commemoration of God is better than any *nath*,' some kind of poem, Br. 94), seems cognate with W. *nadu*, *nâd* 'sonus,' 'strepitus,' 'clamor.' As *nadu* ('sonare,' 'strepere,' 'clamare,' Davies) points to an Old-Welsh *natu, it cannot be right to refer these Celtic words directly to the unnasalised *nad*, Curtius No. 287b. But possibly Bopp meant to deduce them from an Old-Celtic root *nand* = the Skr. frequentative *nânad* 'to roar.' Compare O.W. *i-strat*, Ir. *srath* with Eng. *strand* (Rhys, Rev. Celt. ii. 190). So perhaps

Ir. *maith* 'good' ex *mandi, root MAND, Fick[2] 145 :

Ir. *lith* 'stone'? ('jewel' O'R.) Corm. s.v. adba othnoe = *plinda, Fick[2] 377, whence πλίνθος and *flint*, and

Ir. *grith* 'cry,' W. *gryd* ex *grandi : cf. Lat. *grando*, Goth. *grêta*, Skr. *hrâd*, Curtius No. 181.

The etymology of all these Celtic words is still highly uncertain :
tyvu 'croître,' ii. 9n. (leg. *tyfu*) is compared with Vedic *tavisha* 'fort, *tavishî* 'force.' But this is impossible, as the *v* would have been vocalised. *Tyfu*, like *twf*, *tyfiad* and *tyfiant* 'incrementum,' seems cognate with Lat. *tumeo*, root TU, Curtius No. 247.

The rest of the words are rightly compared :—
a 'ejus,' *a-n* 'eorum,' ii. 334. Of these pronouns Bopp equates *a* 'his' with Skr. *asya*, and *a* 'her' with Skr. *asyâs*, 'dont le *s* final est joint en Irlandais, sous la forme d'un *h*, au mot suivant, si celui-ci commence par une voyelle : e. g., *a hathair* 'ejus (au féminin) pater,' pour *ah athair*.' But this *h* appears only in Middle-Irish MSS. In the Old-Irish *a-altram-si* 'nutritionem ejus, mulieris,' Z[2]. 337, it does not appear at all, and in *tria h-esséirge-som* 'per resurrectionem ejus, Christi,' it occurs after the masculine form. It is however worth noticing that in Welsh (not in Cornish nor in Breton) 'si secuntur vocales, *h* præmittitur post pronomen [possessivum] femininum, abest post masculinum,' Z[2]. 386. Thus, in Old-Welsh *hi h-ataned* 'her wings' gl. Ox., Ovid's Ars Amatoria, but *i anu* 'his name,' MC. 11, a. b :
cluas 'ear,' i. 261. is rightly connected with ϙru, κλυ, *clu* :
con, *cona*, i. 333. The former word is the gen. of *cú* (not *cu*) 'hound' ; the latter, the acc. pl. of the same noun :

creanaim 'j'achète,' W. *pyrnu*, iv. 237 note, is rightly compared with Skr. *krīṇāmi*. See further comparisons by Windisch, Beitr. viii. 38, where, however, *perchenokyon* 'possessores,' Corn. *perhenek* 'possessor,' should be connected rather with Lith. *perkù* 'kaufe':

cru. The index to the French translation refers to i. 167. The word, however, is not to be found there. In the German edition, i. 92,d, Bopp rightly connects *cru* (leg. *crú*) 'blood,' W. *crau* with O.Slav. *kruvi*, Skr. *kravya-m*. See Curtius No. 74:

daghaim 'je brûle' is, (at i. 38 and iii. 418,) rightly equated with Skr. *dahâmi*. But at iii. 134, where Bopp equates *daghamaid* or *daghamaoid* 'nous brûlons' with *dahâmahe*, he falls into serious error from not knowing the Old-Irish form of the modern suffix *-maoid*. This is *mi-t*, which cannot possibly be the same as *-mahe* from *-madhe*, Gr. -μεθα:

dan 'œuvre,' i. 259 (*dan* .i. *obair*, Leb. Lecain Vocab. No. 446), and *deanaim*, leg. *déanaim* (O.Ir. *dénim*) 'facio,' are rightly connected with Skr. *dhâ*, θε, &c. See Curtius No. 309:

dearbh 'certain,' iv. 47, (*bh* for *v*) is equated with OHG. *triu*, now *treu*. This seems perfectly right. (The O.Ir. *derbb*, with hard *b*, is the Goth. *triggvs*.) I would add O.Ir. *drui* (a *d*-stem), W. *derwydd*, and the Old-Celtic *druis*, gen. *druidos, which means merely soothsayer, *wahr*-sager, and has nothing to do with δρῦς. The Ir. adj. *dron* (= *dru-na) .i. *direach*, O'Cl., belongs to the same root:

eile, i. 58, is rightly equated with 'alius,' ἄλλος. The older form is *aile*:

fasaim 'je crois,' i. 236, iv. 49, is put with the Skr. *vakshâmi*. The Irish word meant is *fásaim*, where the *f* is prosthetic, as we see from the O.Ir. *ásaimm*, which has lost initial *v* (see above pp. 37, 38):

fasamhuil (leg. *fásamhuil*) 'crescens,' is rightly explained as *fás-amhuil*, the latter part of the word signifying 'semblable' (*fás* 'growth,' O'D. Gr. 98):

feadhaim 'je rapporte,' iii. 76, (where it is misprinted *feadheim*) is connected with Skr. *vad* 'parler.' I do not know the Irish word given by Bopp. O'Reilly has *feadaim*, Lhuyd *feadam*:

fearamhuil 'semblable à un homme,' iv. 49, is rightly explained as a compound of *fear* = vir and *amhuil* = similis:

garaim 'j'échauffe,' i. 47. This verb (in O.Irish *goraim*, *guirim*) is here rightly connected with Skr. *ghar-ma*, Russian *gorju* 'je brûle':

genteoir (leg. *geinteóir*) = Lat. *genitor*, i. 334. This word, if it really exist (I know it only in O'Reilly and Lhuyd), must be a masc. *i*-stem, and is therefore wrongly quoted by Bopp as preserving the final *r* of the base:

gradh 'amour,' 'charité,' i. 150n. is connected with the Skr. root *GARDH*, the Goth. *gairnja*, the Eng. *greedy*. This may be so:

graidheag (leg. *gràidheag* = Ir. *gráidheóg*) 'femme aimée,' i. 156. This is a Highland derivative from *grádh*, vide supra:

— 53 —

gus 'désir,' i. 265 is rightly connected with Goth. *kus* 'choisir.' It stands for **gus-tu* :

macamh 'garçon,' and *mag* (leg. *mac*) 'fils' are connected by Bopp ii. 250, with the Skr. root *MAGH* 'croitre,' Goth. *magus* 'garçon,' *mavei* 'fille,' *magath* 'virgo.' These comparisons seem quite right. The Indo-European speech had apparently a root meaning 'to increase' in two forms,—the primary one *MAGH* whence Skr. *mah*, and the nasalised *MANGH*, Skr. *manh*, W. *magu*. From the former come Ir. *mug*, Corn. *maw* = Goth. *magus*, and Goth. *ma(g)vei* and *magath* : from the latter, Ir. *macc*, W. *map*. The oghamic **maqo-* = *mac-va*, *mang-va* :

min, mion 'petit,' ii. 212, is rightly connected with Lat. *minor*, etc. The Irish word is *mín* (Corn. *muin*, Br. *moan*, Z². 99). It occurs often in composition, e. g. *min-chasc* 'Low-Sunday,' 'Pascha minor,' *min-cethra* 'menu bétail,' S.M. i. 190 :

ruaidhneach 'cheveu,' i. 266, where it is connected with the Skr. root *RUH* from *RUDH* 'grandir.' The word intended is *ruainne* (*ruainne im a fiacail*, S.M. i. 174, *ruaindi* gl. pilus, Ir. Gl. No. 463). The etymology is obscure :

samhuil 'semblable,' iv. 49, is rightly put with Skr. *sama*, Gr. ὁμός, Lat. *similis* :

siol 'sémence,' *siolaim* 'je sème,' iii. 257, are connected with the Goth. *seths* 'seed' and the Skr. *sáti* 'don.' This is right enough as to *seth-s* :

suidiughaim 'je place,' 'je plante,' *suidhim* 'je suis assis,' iii. 414, are connected with *sádayámi* and *saditi*. This is right, but when Bopp goes on to say that in *suidiughaim* (O Ir. *suidigim*) 'le *gh* . . . comme en général dans les causatifs Irlandais, représente le *y* Sanscrit,' he errs, for this *gh* is for *ch* ; compare—

cuiligim (gl. prosto) with *cuilech* (gl. prostibulum) :
intonnaigim (gl. inundo) with *tonnach* 'undosus' :
ru-s-madaigset 'se frustrârunt,' with *madach* gl. cassa :
cumachtaigim (gl. potior) with *cumachtach* 'potens' :
dephthigim 'dissideo' with *debthach* 'dissidens.'

ver / *tar, tair* 'au delà, à trans, pardessus,' ii. 175, *tri* 'trans, par,' iv. 415. Bopp compares these prepositions (of which the Old-Irish forms are *tar* and *tri*) with Lat. *trans* and Goth. *thair-h*.

MR. CROWE'S PUBLICATIONS.
(*Vide supra* p. 2.)

SIX of this gentleman's works are before me,—all, save the first and the last, published by learned Societies in Ireland. This circumstance gives them an importance which (he will excuse me for saying) they would not otherwise possess. I shall notice only such mistakes as will be obvious to any one having (like myself) merely a slight knowledge of the Old or Early-Middle Irish vocabulary and grammar:—

I.—SCÉLA NA ESÉRGE.
Dublin, 1861.

TEXT	MR. CROWE	READ
p. 8, *trachtaid*	'interprets,'	'handles,' (*tractat*)
folaid	'notion.'	'substance.'
p. 10, l. 13, *comthóither*	'shall return.'	'shall be converted.'
p. 12, *is[s]ochma*	'it is easy.'	'it is possible,' *or* 'there is power.'
„ *todochaide*	'expectation.'	'future.'
p. 20, *lucht ind remeca*	'the previsionists.'	'the prematurely dead.'
p. 22, *triasinderna*	'through which were made.'	'through which he made.'
„ *diafil in forbairt ocus in beógud*	'which goes to decay and revives.'	'which has the increase and the quickening.'
p. 24, *atchichestár*	'shall be worshipped (?)'	'shall be seen.'

The printed Irish text of this publication, which the Editor (p. 26), asserts to be 'an exact reproduction of the original' (LU. 34a—37b), is very inaccurate. Omissions of marks of length, bisections of words, wrong insertions or omissions of marks of aspiration, occur in almost every line; and I have noticed the following graver errors:—

p. 4, l. 4 from bottom, for *cinudu doenda* read *ciniud ndóenda*:

p. 6, l. 23, for *roeirete* read *roerrete* (recté *roesrete*):

p. 8, l. 23, for *feisin sin iarndligud* read *féisin iarndligud*; l. 3 from bottom for *ni* read *in*:

p. 12, l. 4, for *háisi* read *báis* ('mortis'):

p. 14, l. 8, for *thechtfat* read *thechtfat*; l. 24, for *aniail* read *amail*; l. 25, for *innosa* read *innossa*; ll. 30, 32 for *uair, uair* read *úar*:

p. 16, l. 18, for *fdchraic* read *focraic*; last line, for *Elsi* read *Elesi*:

p. 18, l. 6, for *for[sh]airind* read *fkairind*; l. 12, for *dcus* read *ocus*; l. 14 for *tortromad* read *tórtrommad*; l. 25, for *sorordai* read *forordai*:

p. 22, l. 5, for *ség* read *fég*; l. 15, for *ocur* read *ocus*; l. 17, for *beógad* read *beógud*; l. 20, for *sairend* read *fairend*; l. 23, for *sum* read *som*; l. 28, for *sirenaib* read *fírenaib*; l. 30, for *innosa* read *innossa*:

p. 24, l. 5, for *araltib* read *ariltib*; l. 14, for *ra sualchi* read *na súalchi*; l. 17, for *emiltiuf* read *emiltius*

II.—Aided Echach maic Máireda.

(Journal of the Royal Historical and Archæological Association of Ireland, January, 1870, pp. 94—112.)

Text	Mr. Crowe	Read
p. 104, *siachtsum*	'we reached.'	'there came to me' (*siachtais-um*).[a]
„ *baithium anfud*	'I plunge into my storm.'	'a storm overwhelmed me' (*baithi-um*).[a]
„ *múr*	'sea.'	'wall' (*murus*).
p. 106, *bes*	'perhaps.'	'certainly.'
p. 108, *robaisted*	'he baptized.'	'(she) was baptized.'
p. 110, *angaisced fair* [MS. *for*] *an otraigib*	'their heroism on their filths.'	'their weapons on their ordures.'
p. 112, *da dam allaid*	'Two wild oxen.'	'Two stags.'

The text of this piece (LU. 39a—416) is also inaccurately printed. Thus—

    p. 96, for *Echac* read *Echach*; for *maithi* read *mathi*; for *ailges* read *algis*; for *Dobert* read *Doberat*:

    p. 98, for *mairfed-sa* read *mairfetsa*; for *fácthai* read *fágthai*; for *Ddber* read *Dober*; for *haithigid* read *hathigid*:

    p. 100, for *snaidfed* read *snaifid*; for *ar din sceng* read *ard in sceng*; for *mho* read *mo*:

    p. 102, for *bhadna* read *bliadan* or *bliadua*:

    p. 104, for *Siacht-sum* read *siachtsum*; for *baithiu'm* read *baithium*:

    p. 106, for *fri etal* read *frim etal*; for *adbu* read *adba*, for *Muir-gen* read *murgen*:

    p. 108, for *ben-se cech* read *ben secech* (i. e. *sech-cech*); for *line* read *lín*:

    p. 110, for *fodera* read *fotera*.

III.—Siaburcharpat Con-Culaind.

(Journal, &c., January, 1871, pp. 374—399.)

Text	Mr. Crowe	Read
p. 376, l. 4, *solam*	'easy.'	'swift.'
p. 378, l. 1, *bruitne*	'Goadlets.'	'A goadlet.'
„ l. 26, *latrechtmecho*	'with speed.'	'with thy faithful ones.'[b]
„ l. 28, *ná túadaig tond talman torut* (= *na tudaich tond talman torut*, p. 398)	'that a wave of earth may not dash ['come,' p. 399] over thee.'	'that earth's surface (or 'skin,'—*tonn* = W. *tonn* 'crusta,' 'cutis') may not come over thee.'

---

[a] Cf. *berthium, ainsium, snaidsium, tathum*, Beitr. vii. 41.
[b] *rechtmecho* is by metathesis for *chretmecho* the acc. pl. m. of *cretmech* 'fidelis,' Z. 811.

Text	Mr. Crowe	Read
p. 380, *Ba mesi a laucúrad cartais* [a]	'I was their little hound whom they used to love.'	'I was their little champion, *cúrad*, (whom) they used to love.'
p. 382, *adfét*	'he shall tell.'	'let him tell.'
p. 384, *diálád hi tír scaith*	'for plunder to the Land of Scath.'	'when I went into the land of Scath.'
p. 386, *sonnach*	'rampart.'	'palisade.'
p. 388, *rósnaidet*	'they strong-swim.'	'they swam.'
„ *for a muin*	'upon his shoulder.'	'on her back (or neck).'
p. 390, *gai bolgae*	'the bellows-dart.'	'the belly-spear.'
p. 392, *formna na lath ngaile*	'the most of the heats of steam [champions].'	'the choice of the champions of valour.'
p. 394, *rochluinethar*	'be it heard.'	'who has heard.'
„ *creitted*	'who would believe.'	'let him believe.'
„ *bad mór a déne*	'great would be his strength.'	'let his speed be great.'
p. 396, *band*	'bound.'	'deed,' (*bann* .i. *gniomh*, O'Cl.).
p. 398, *latrechtmecho*	'with speed.'	'with thy faithful ones.'

The text of this piece, too, (LU. 113a—115a) is printed with great carelessness: for example—

p. 374, for *Torchomraic* read *terchomraic*:

p. 376, for *bámár* .... *fúathu* ... *demhis* ... *dergithir* read *bámmár* .... *fúatha* ... *demis* ... *deirgithir*:

p. 378, for *cles Daire* .... read *cless Daire*:

p. 380, for *norúmed* read *norúined* (i. e. *noshrúined*, *no-shróined*):

p. 384, for *rofherussu-sa* read *rofherussa*:

p. 392, for *consmat* read *consniat*:

p. 394, for *scar-su* read *scarsu* (the 1st sg. of the absolute form of the s-preterite of *scaraim*, Beitr. vii. 37):

p. 396, for *dodrathbeoagastar* read *dodrathbeogastar*:

p. 398, for *la trechtmecho* read *lat-rechtmecho*; for *blidain hi talain* read *bliadan* (or *bliadna*) *hi talam*:

p. 400, col. 2, for *Dub-thaige, Maie Lir, Midgnai,* .i. *Midgin, Erimóin* read *Dubthaigi, Maic Lir, Midgni, Erimoin*.

"In conclusion" (says Mr. Crowe, p. 373) "I beg to tell the Irish student and the antiquary, that I guarantee the perfect accuracy both of text and citations."

---

[a] Mr. Crowe prints *a lau-cú radcartais!*

I have already noticed his text. Here are some specimens of his citations:—

p. 423, l. 7, for *lúamaipecht* read *lúamairecht*; l. 30, for *issn* read *issin*:

p. 424, l. 3 from bottom, for *trig* read *tiug*. [The context is *o thana a tháib co tiug a ochsaille*, literally 'from the thin of his side to the thick of his armpit.' Mr. Crowe renders this (p. 426): 'from the waist of his side to the pit of his arm']; l. 2 from bottom, for *foierditchs* read *focherditis*:

p. 425, l. 1, for *rogabastára[fh] úathroic sreb-naide* read *rogabastár a-úathroic srebnaide*; l. 10, after *cóicrind* insert 7 *a-saigetbolg*; l. 12, for *dub-depg* read *dubderg*; l. 14, for *imge-ir* read *imgéir*; l. 22, for *geiniti* read *geniti*; l. 4 from bottom, for *muueóil* read *muineóil*:

p. 430, l. 29, for *bruinui* read *bruinni*; l. 33, for *Dond-fciath* read *Dond-sciath*; l. 4 from bottom, for *is in* read *issin*:

p. 432, l. 13, for *Ite* read *Int*:

p. 433, l. 1, for *sian chupad* read *sian churad*:

p. 436, for *fcraithmenadar* read *foraithmenadar*:

p. 438, last line, for *tiagat* read *tiagait*:

p. 439, l. 2, for *poth* read *roth*; l. 7, for *ochtaig* read *hochtaig*:

p. 444, l. 11, for *conid atá* read *conid de atá*.[a]

So much for the 'perfect accuracy' of the citations. The renderings of those citations are equally erroneous. Thus, p. 419, *tria drochu na carpat* 'through the wheels of the chariots' is rendered 'through the wheels of the chariot,' as if *carpat* were the gen. sg. *Feotár* 'they slept' or 'they rested' is rendered by 'They sat down'; p. 423, *oss-lethar* 'leather made of deer-skin,' is rendered by 'ox-leather'; p. 424, *cethr-ochair* 'four-pointed,' (*ochair* = ἄκρος, in form ἄκρις) an epithet for Cúchulainn's helmet, is rendered by 'four-adjustment' (*sic*), and (*f*)*úathroic* 'girdle' by 'kilt'; p. 427, *formna secht ndamseched* 'the choice of seven ox-hides' is made 'the shoulder of seven ox-hides,' and *cathbarr* 'helmet' is rendered by 'battle-head'; p. 431, *siricda* 'silken' (Lat. *sericus, sericeus*) is rendered by 'Syriac.'

The worst of all, however, is in p. 426. The Irish romancer is describing Cúchulainn's girdle with its golden fringe '*fria-frimóeth-ichtur a-medóin*.' Here the second *fri* is obviously an instance of 'dittography,' (like the second *ib* in *saib-ib-em*, Z. 278), and the Irish words should be rendered thus: 'against the soft (*móeth* = Lat. *mītis*) lower part of his middle,' *i. e.*, some part of his belly. Mr. Crowe actually renders the Irish words just quoted by 'to his chief-liver at the bottom of his middle.' Cúchulainn was, no doubt, a remarkable personage, but I believe that there is no evidence (except Mr. Crowe's) that he possessed more than one liver.

---

[a] The facsimile here has *itá*.

IV.—Echtra Condla Cain.

(Journal, April, 1874, pp. 128—133.)

This, the shortest of Mr. Crowe's works, has naturally the fewest mistakes. But at p. 133 *taidbred* ('would give back') is rendered 'would deign,' *aithesc* 'answer' is rendered by 'song,' and *ni fes* 'it is not known' by 'the gods only know.' *Fadib* is rendered in the text by 'prophets,' in the footnote by the 'Lat. *vadum*, the pl. used poetically for *sea*.' In p. 132, l. 6, the words *Asbert Condla* have been omitted. In the prefatory remarks, p. 119, note 1, the following passage about Leviathan (LU. 85b): *adchomaic a erball do thóchur in betha tar-a-chend* is wonderfully rendered thus :—'that strikes his tail *against the embankment of the world before him.*' But *tóchur tar cenn* (which occurs also in the *Crith Gablach*, O'Curry's Manners and Customs iii. 489) is only a variant of the common phrase *cor dar-cenn* 'to overturn' (literally 'ponere trans caput,' i. e. 'quod deorsum est sursum facere'). Thus, in the homily on St. Martin, LB. 60b, Rop áil do martan *cor dar-cend* araile tempail moir amboi fdaladrad 'Martin desired to overturn a certain great temple wherein was idol-worship.' Mr. Crowe should therefore have rendered the last seven words thus : '. . . . his tail to overturn the world.' I am not sure of the meaning of *adchomaic*.

V.—Táin Bó Fráich.

(Proceedings of the R. I. Academy, Irish MSS. series, Vol. I, pp. 136—157.)

Text	Translation	Read
p. 136, *finda ói-derga*	'white-eared.'	'white, red-eared.'
p. 138, *bes sáiniu* (MS. *bess áiniu*)	'which is more distinguished.'	'which is more splendid.'
„ *dobor-chona*	'water-dogs.'	'otters.'
p. 140, *dobor-chon*	'of water-dogs.'	'of otters.'
p. 142, *for a dernaind*	'On his haunches.'	'On his palm.'
„ *is maith rongabus*	'It is well we have been entertained.'	'It is well I am.' (See Z. 922.)
p. 144, *ni fhil dot-daidbrisiu nach-imm éta-sa om-muntir*	'There is nothing of thy display that I have not learned from my family.'	'It is not for thy poverty (*daidbre*) that thou dost not win me from my family.'
P. 146, *linn*	'flood.'	'pool.'
„ *brissis*	'breaks.'	'broke.'
p. 148, *dóitib*	'wrists.'	'hands.'
p. 150, *condessar chuca* [Mr. Crowe prints con dessar chucann]	'it will be set to us.'	'it will be asked of her' (*condessar* is the 3d sg. s-fut. passive of *cuindigim*).
„ *fóidis*	'sends.'	'sent.'

Text	Translation	Read
p. 152, *ni béoda do ḟhectas dochoas*	'Not active of journey hast thou gone.'	'Not lively (has been) thy journey which has been performed [lit. has been gone.']
p. 154, *conaccatar fraccnatain* [Mr. Crowe prints *fracc na tain*]	'they saw the woman of the herd.'	'they saw a girl.' (*Fraccnatan* is a double diminutive of *fracc* 'woman.')
„ *bés*	'perchance.'	'certainly' (*bes* .i. *derb*, H. 3. 18, p. 51b).
„ *toisc*	'errand.'	'desire,' 'wish.'
p. 156, *reiss*	'has come.'	'will come.'
„ *tistai-si*	'come thou.'	'ye shall come.'

Some of the mistakes in the printed text have been already mentioned. Here are some more :—

p. 136, for *rígh* ... *comcutrumma* .. *cho* ... *ermitiuda* .. *gabar* the MS. has *ríg* ... *comchutrumma* .. *co* ... *eirmitiuda* .. *gabor*:

p. 140, *forri* 'on it': the MS. has *óir* 'of gold':

p. 142, *deibthir*: the MS. has *deithber*:

p. 144, *chucut-sa*, MS. *chucutsu*: *asbeir is corrodalláus*, MS. *asbér is cor rodalláus*: *cummblegitar*, MS. *cummel[ge]tar*:

p. 148, *a béoil*, MS. *abbéoil*:

p. 150, *arfiti* ... *cdnfiu* .. *uaidi* ... *decmaig*, MS. *airfiti* .. *confiu* ... *uadi* ... *decmaing*:

p. 152, *oc a* ... *immim* ... *catnocaib* ... *diaid-siu*, MS. *oco* ... *immum* ... *cotnócaib* ... *itiadsiu*:

p. 156, *lein* 'ours': MS. *lem* 'mine' (lit. 'apud me').

The notes to this edition (pp. 158—170) are equally inaccurate :—

p. 158, for *taidbi* read *taidbsi*:

p. 160, for *tuigi* (l. 5), *con-chobuir* (l. 18), *archapúr* (l. 21), *carrmocuil* (l. 23), *dec* (l. 26), *immacuaird* (l. 27); read *tugi*, *chonchobuir*, *archapur*, *carrmocail*, *deac*, *immacúairt*. The verb *contóitis* is rendered 'used to turn'; it means 'they used to be silent':

p. 163, for *nonburn aile friu*, the MS. has *nónbur naile friu anair*, for *Find-adair* (l. 22) read *Findabair*: l. 7 from bottom, for *Rogellsom* 7 *in fili* read *Rogellsom ol Mongán* 7 *in fili*:

p. 164, for *nónbos cacha urchara* (l. 18) read *nónbor cacha urchair;* fo *ha* (l. 4 from bottom) read *ba*:

p. 168, for *teglath* (l. 10) read *teglach*:

p. 170, for *Ba* read *Buí*, for *indrong* read *androng*; for *gulbencha* read *gulbnecha*.

VI.—AMRA CHOLUIMBCHILLE.

(Dublin 1871.)

Text	Translation	Read
p. 10, *resinn-ibar aniar-thúaid*	'By the yew in the north-west.'	'To the north-west of the yew.'
p. 12, *roth craed*	'wheel-poetry.'	'the circle of science.'
„ *fo érind*	'over Erin.'	'throughout Erin.'
„ *a chubus con a anim glan*	'O tree of hounds, O pure soul, ('O conscience with its soul pure,' p. 76).	'O clear conscience, O pure soul.'
p. 14, *dochendnaib*	'of headlets.'	'extempore.'
„ *abela*	'rapidity.'	'adulation.'
p. 16, *agur águr*	'I ask, I ask.'	'I fear, I fear.'
„ *formolad*	'superabundance.'	'darkening' (a word by adding a syllable thereto).
p. 18, *ten-d*	'stroke.'	'fire.'
„ *gand-ón*	'narrow this.'	'scanty.'
„ *imbite ann-ón*	'in which there is plentiness.'	'in which they are there.'
p. 20, *múr*	'rampart.'	'abundance.'
„ *immed*	'fence.'	'abundance.'
p. 26, *arcraib cernine*	'on branch of *cernine*.'	'quickly on a dish.'
p. 28, *in ía[th]*	'to Hí.'	'into the land (of heaven).'
p. 30, *nolaiged*	'He used to be.'	'he used to lie.'
„ *slicht*	'form.'	'trace.'
p. 32, p. 52, } *dubrécles*	'black church.'	'dark cell.'
p. 32, *i[n]ré assidrócaib* [a]	'on high he departed.'	'when he upraised himself.'
p. 34, *nad accestar*	'he saw not.'	'is not seen.'
„ *écnach*	'oppression.'	'carping.'
p. 42, *ralastar*	'he poured.'	'he came.'
p. 44, *dordaid dam*	'ox murmurs.'	'stag belleth.'
„ *gair arrith*	'cry is attacking.'	'short is her (the sun's) course.'
„ *rath*	'raying.'	'fern.'
„ *moscle* (leg. *moscél*)	'very wretched.'	'my tale.'
p. 46, *frim anthuaith*	'facing me on the north.'	'to the north of me.'
„ *atber cet*	'prophecy says.'	'who says *cet* 'permission.'
p. 52, *nodgeilsigfe*	'has associated him.'	'will take him into (his) family.'

[a] The MS. (LU.) has *ire assidrochaib.*

Text	Translation	Read
p. 54, *la docetul*	'with music.'	'with a double music.'
„ *it i[i.]chlais*	'in the chief choir.'	'there are two choirs.'
p. 62, *ic Tói toil-rig*	'at Toy with king's will.'	'with Tay's high king.'
p. 66, *cerd Cuind*	'the profession of Cond.'	'Conn's part'[a] (*i. e.*, the northern half of Ireland).

The oddest mistake is in pp. 42, 43. The Gaelic notes on the *Amra* are obviously a compilation from several, and sometimes discordant, commentaries. Here the annotator is dealing with two consecutive passages of the poem:—

glinsius salmu (he, Columba, 'illustrated' or 'learned' the psalms).
sluin[n]stus léig libru libuir ut car Caseon.

On the latter passage, he first gives the following note:—

.i. *rosluinnestar na salmu ic a tichtain iarna foglaim* 'he, Columba, explained the psalms, understanding them after having learned them.'

The annotator then adds: *isúas in sluinnsius foisin* 'and according to that, the *sluinnsius* is above,' *i. e.*, belongs to the preceding paragraph. Mr. Crowe, not seeing this, prints the last five words thus: '7 *is úas in sluinn, sius fo isin*,' and translates thus (without revealing his bisections of *sluinnsius* and *foisin*): 'and above the explanation: poetry under that.'

Absurd as this mistake is, it is surpassed by the following which, unfortunately, I am too ignorant to be able to correct:—

p. 17, 'May thy monument at dawnbreeze be after thy deathwound a sail ever to be driven':

p. 19, 'Advance from lakes for a net of twists':

p. 67, 'The conweb he figulated from deed he followed':

„ 'The profession of Cond broke grief through his going for a stay of greatness of good':

p. 69, 'He cried a melodious lion in a snow's new meeting':

p. 75, 'Great circles of great turnings, great poems of heaven to me sunless is not a suitableness':

I suppose it is because I live so many thousand miles from Ireland; but I cannot, for the life of me, understand how publishing such nonsensical guesswork can either advance Mr. Crowe's reputation or promote the cause of Irish literature.

In the printed text I have noticed the following errors, some of which, e. g. *feig* p. 20, *fresthal* p. 30, *rochualamniar* p. 46, *nerbo* p. 48, *drumiu* p. 60 (leg. *féig, frestal, rochualammar, uerbo, druiniu*) are due to carelessness, others to ignorance of the proper way to resolve contractions. To the latter class belong the following:—

pp. 8, 12, 14, 18, 20, *imm.* leg. *immurro*. Mr. Crowe prints *immoro*. The word is written at length thus: *imuro*, in Laud 610, fo. 82b, col. 1, left margin; but the modern *iomorra* shows that this is a clear case of 'singling':

---

[a] *cerd* (= *cerdd*, Amra LII, 33b, 1) is for *cert* in *des-cert* (W. *deheu-barth*) and *tuais-cert*.

p. 22, *nufhiad.*, leg. *nufhiad*naise, the common word for 'New Testament.' Mr. Crowe prints *nufhinad*:

pp. 36, 40, 46, *o cholum c.*, *do cholum c.*, *o chollum c.* Here '*c.*' stands for the gen. sg. of the fem. *ā*-stem *cell* and should be resolved thus: *chille.* Mr. Crowe actually prints *chilliu*:

p. 52, *slicht na cetri suis.*, leg. *suis*célaigthe 'the track of the four evangelists.' Mr. Crowe prints *suiacht* (sic) and renders this false coin by 'wisdoms';

p. 68, *s.* (i. e. *acht*) *luch 7 sindach* 'except a mouse and a fox.' Mr. Crowe prints *sed luch 7 sindach* and translates 'a flock of rats and of foxes.' He must have known that there is no authority for this rendering of *sed*, and he ought to have known that *luch* 'mouse' (= W. *llygod-en*) which he treats as a gen. pl., is a *t*-stem (gen. sg. *la tabairt na lochad inna beólu*, LL. 207, a. 2, acc. pl. *mani estais na lochtha*, ib.), and that its gen. pl. would therefore be *lochath-n* or *lochad-n*.

APPENDIX B.

Facsimiles of Neo-Celtic Texts.

[*Vide supra*, p. 6, note c.]

I refer in particular to some of the facsimiles published in the supplement in Appendix A to Mr. C. P. Cooper's *Report on the Foedera* and to the facsimile of part of the Book of St. Chad given in the *Liber Landavensis* at p. 273. The latter has misled Ebel (G. C. 662—663). Here is the true reading according to Mr. Bradshaw, our greatest living palæographer:—

Ostendit ista cons[c]ripsio
nobilitatem mainaur med
diminih et mensuram *eius*
ap*er* huer
di c*um*guid maun
di toldar i*n* guodaut [a] clun
di rit cellfin
di libe [b] maur
di bir main i*n* cluenide
di pul ir deruen
di cimer di ap*er* ferrus

di pennant ir caru
di boit bahne
di guotin [c] hen lann
dir hitir melin
di margles
di rit braugui
di ap*er* istil [d]
di licat
di pul retinoc
di minid di ap*er* heru. [e]

(See *Archæologia Cambrensis*, July 1874.)

---

[a] guoilaut, Rhys. [b] libor, R. [c] guoun, R. [d] pistil, R. [e] huer? R.

The facsimiles recently published in Ireland are better, but far from what they might be. Thus, I noticed the following errata on cursorily collating with the original codex the lithographic copy of Lebor na huidre which the Royal Irish Academy has published as 'an exact lithograph of the original.' Many more mistakes would doubtless be discovered by any one with time and inclination to look for them :—

1	col. a	l. 44.	Facs.	ahaims*i*de	Ms.	ahainms*i*de
1	„ b	l. 37.	„	for*o*enici	„	f*h*oenici [a]
11	„ b	l. 22.	„	th*o*dgarach	„	to*n*dgarach
30	„ a	l. 15.	„	do	„	tic
37	„ b	l. 42.	„	nec*u*stos	„	necmui*s*
50	„ b	l. 1.	„	-bod	„	-bad
51	„ a	L. 33.	„	-fuitis	„	-faitis
	„ b	l. 17.	„	molbthuch	„	molbthach
52	„ b	l. 11.	„	brio	„	bric
53	„ b	l. 34.	„	ani	„	ani*m*
58	„ a	marg.	„	s. (i. e. *acht*)	„	for
67	„ a	l. 43.	„	ag*ai*d	„	lug*ai*d
72	„ b	l. 4.	„	tubrait*er*	„	tabrait*er*
		l. 33.	„	dobi*n*d	„	dob*er*id
91	„ b	l. 13.	„	becda	„	becdu
109	„ a	l. 11.	„	iarth*us*	„	arth*us*
113	„ b	l. 15.	„	for*s*erg	„	for*s*eng
114	„ a	l. 9.	„	norúnied	„	norúined
		l. 39.	„	úasa úibnanech	„	uasaúib nanech
121	„ a	l. 5.	„	lugha*n*d	„	beith a*n*d

Eight more I did not verify, but (if we bear in mind the similarity in Irish handwriting of *n*, *r* and *s*, of *m*, *in* and *ni*, of *ss*, *rs*, *sr* and *is*) the corrections are obvious enough :—

10	col. a	l. 32.	Facs.	edbar éil	*read*	ed ba réil
12	„ a	l. 5.	„	rogi*n*saig	„	rog*r*essaig
13	„ a	l. 26.	„	nidligtecha	„	indligt[h]echa
14	„ b	l. 16.	„	lalam	„	balam
		l. 30.	„	magne	„	magre
73	„ a		„	Dirim	„	Turim
127	„ a	l. 17.	„	comallastas	„	comallast*r*
130	„ a	l. 5.	„	ecít	„	eóit.

The fact is that, except when the process is purely mechanical (as in the case of photography or a thoroughly ignorant facsimilist) to copy an ancient Irish MS. correctly requires considerable knowledge of the language. How much of this accomplishment is possessed by the gentlemen connected with

---

[a] Here, as elsewhere, I have to represent the dotted *f* by *fh*.

this publication may easily be guessed from the prefixed 'Description,' in which we find—

TEXT	TRANSLATION	READ
p. xiii, *dorrogus*	'I beseech.'	'I shall have besought.'
,, *dian-da tairle mo-lorg-sa*	'should you follow my track.'	'if my club reaches them' (*mairfidus* 'it will kill them).'
p. xv, *sin*	'thy condition.'	'that.'
p. xxii, *adfet in scel so*	'are told in this story.'	'this story relates.'
p. xxiv, *amne*	'you are.'	'thus.'
p. xxv, *tucait baile Mongán*	'account of Baile Mongán or Mongan's residence.'	'the cause of Mongán's madness.'

They have obviously a smattering of the language, but only enough to lead them astray. In the 'Contents' prefixed to their facsimile of *Lebar Brecc*, Part I, (Dublin 1872), are equally remarkable errors:—

TEXT	TRANSLATION	READ
p. 1, *foitnech*	'wise.'	'patient.'
p. 3, *de die pentecosti*	... ...	... de die pentecos*tes*
,, *coem*	'faithful.'	'dear.'
,, *im-da-huli*	'through all the.'	'by all thy.'
,, *condagar da*	'are essential to.'	'are required by.'
p. 4, *fáth airic*	'cause.'	'cause of invention.'
,, *imrordus*	'I celebrate.'	'I have meditated.'
,, *re sil dálach*	'With the race of Dalach' (*sic*)	'before (men's) multitudinous seed.'
p. 6, *amne*	'alone.'	'thus.'
,, *don tarmchrutta*[a]	...	... [*liachtu in ta*]*rmchrutta* ('lectio τῆς transfigurationis').
,, *cacht* ('question')	... ...	... *cest*.
p. 7, *erim nglan*	'with pure wisdom.'	'a pure course.'
,, *mic n-Israel*	... ...	... 'mac n-Israel.'

APPENDIX C.

'*Ignorant and reckless Native Scholars.*'

[Vide supra, p. 6.]

These are hard words, but no one, I think, who reads the Appendices to this pamphlet respectively marked A, B, and H will say that they are undeserved. I do not of course refer to the dead O'Donovan or the living

---

[a] This gibberish is rendered 'Of the Transfiguration.' It is about as good Irish as τῷ μεταμορφώσεος would be good Greek.

Hennessy, O'Grady or O'Mahony. Of these I can truly say *Nolo esse laudator, ne videar adulator.*

To Mr. Hennessy in particular, every student of the early Irish literature, language and mythology is deeply indebted. He has so much of the spirit of a true scholar, that I am sure I cannot lighten my obligations more agreeably to himself than by correcting a few slips in his paper on the Ancient Irish Goddess of War, *Revue Celtique*, i. 32—57 :—

p. 35, 'Cormac states that *Fea* meant everything most hateful.' The word thus explained by Cormac is *fé:*

In p. 39, *amaite* is rendered by 'idiots,' and, lower down, *amati adgaill* is rendered by 'witches.' At p. 50, Mr. Hennessy, quoting LL. 77a. 1, and again thinking probably of *onmit* 'oaf,' says that Cúchulainn meets 'three *female idiots* blind of the left eye,' *teora ammiti tuathchaecha.* The nom. sg. is *ammait.* Surely we have here a cognate of the O.N. *amma* 'grandmother,' the OHG. *ammā*, NHG. *amme,* the Lat. *amita.* We should therefore probably render *amaite, amati* or *ammiti* by 'crones' :

p. 40, *frasa* 'masses,' *read* 'showers' :

p. 42, in the quotation from LU. p. 57a, for *samam, fathaigh, focedoir, slógh, Medbh* read *sámmam, athig, focétoir, slóg, Medb.* In the quotation from LL. 54b. 1 for *os, Do fainig, namad, ced* read *uas, dofainic, námat, cét* :

p. 43, *faindeal* 'panic,' *read* 'wandering about':

p. 45, in the quotation from LL. (50a. 1) for *sidaib, mani, rabuid* read *sídib, meni, robuid.* And in the quotation from LU. (74a.) for *oinmgorti, haurusa, comrac, firu, ath* read *ainmgorti, haurussa, comruc, firiu, áth* :

p. 46, l. 1, for *maile derce, eit* read *máile dérce, éit* [a] : l. 2, before *forsnai* insert *ort; nim-aircecha-sa* 'thou shalt not find me' *read* 'thou shall not see me' (*aircecha* is the 2d sg. reduplicated fut. act. of a verb from the root *CAS*) :

p. 47, in the quotation from LU. (76b) for *Dauautat* (.i. *buailis*) read *Danautat* (.i. *búalis*), for *slúaga* read *slúagu,* for *ind sod mactire* read *int-sod maic tíre,* for *muitte* read *muitti.* And surely *sod maic tíre* means 'she-wolf' and not (as Mr. Hennessy renders the expression) 'wolfhound'; *sod* 'bitch,' gen. *soide* LU. 74a, a fem. *ā*-stem, comes from the root *SU* (Curtius No. 605) :

p. 48, *ni airciu* is rendered 'I see not,' though it is glossed by *ni rochim* 'non adeo,' and may well be the 1st sg. pres. indic. act. of the verb whence *ercid* 'ite' LU. 32a, *arecar* 'invenitur' Z. 987 :

p. 49, in the quotation from LL. 54a, 2, for *sidaib, Choinchullaind* read *sídib, Choinchulaind :*

p. 50, lines 9, 10 for *Emain . . . afrithis* read *Emuin, afrithisi.* In l. 25 *uasa erra oen-charpait* is rendered by 'over the chief in his chariot.' But *erra*

---

[a] *éit* 'cattle' (*eit* .i. *nomen cethrae,* O'Mulc. 456) 'pecus,' n. pl. *éiti,* dat. pl. *éitib* or *étaib.* Is not this cognate with the Oscan *eituās* 'pecuniæ,' *eituam* or *eitiuvam* 'pecuniam' ?

is the acc. pl. of *err* 'a spike,'ᵃ and the passage means 'over the spikes of the one (or unique) chariot':

p. 51, line 2, for *conbad* read *combad*: l. 4, for *Cairpre* . . *m'atarsa* read *Carpri* . . *m'atharsa*; l. 7, for *imchoimét in céin* read *imchomét i céin*; l. 8, for *ruathar* read *ruathra*; l. 11, for *dolliud* read *dolluid*; l. 12, for *Carpre* read *Corpri*:

p. 52, in the quotation from LU. (p. 27a.) for *im, rodlebaing, escada,* read *imó, rodleblaing, escata.* And for *dober fir nolnecmacht in riastarthu do animm,* which is not Irish, read *doratsat fir nólnécmacht in riastartha do anmum* (LU. 72a) 'the men of Connaught gave him for name 'the Distorted:''

In p. 51 is what seems to me a mistranslation of the following passage from the Book of Leinster, 78, a2: (Cúchulainn, wounded unto death, is standing in Loch Lamraige.) *Dodechaid iarum crich mór ond loch síar. 7 rucad a rosc airi. 7 téit dochum coirthi cloiche file isin-maig co-tarat a-choimchriss immi na-ra-blad na shuidiu nach ina-ligu com-bad ina shessam atbalad.* Mr. Hennessy renders this passage thus:—'He (Cuchullainn) then went westwards, a good distance from the lake, and looked back at it. And he went to a pillar-stone which is in the plain, and placed his side against it, that he might not die sitting or lying, (but) that he might die standing.' But surely the true version is this:— 'Now there went westwards from the lake a great mearing, and his eye litᵇ upon it, and he fared to a pillar-stone which is in the plain, and put his waistbelt around it, that he might not die sitting nor lying down, (but) that he might perish standing.'

Why, too, does he write (pp. 35, 41) the nominative *plural* of the name of his nation 'Gaeidhel,' when it is 'Gaeidhíl' or (in Old-Irish spelling) 'Góidil,' and the name of his national hero 'Cuchullain' or 'Cuchullainn,' when the real name is Cúchulainn or Cú-chulaind, literally 'Culand's Hound'?

So much for corrigenda to this valuable and most interesting paper. As addenda I would mention the quatrain cited supra, p. 22ᶜ from LU. 50a, the statement made by O'Curry (Manners and Customs, ii. 50) that the Mór-Rígan was the wife of the Daghda, and the following passage from the *Bruden Da Derga*, LU. 94:—

Imdai nam-badb.

Atconnarc triar nocht hi-cléthi in-tigi a-tócsca fola trethu. 7 súa*nemuin* an airlig aram-braigti.

Rus-fetursa olse. tri ernbaid úagboid triar orgar la cach naim insin.

ᵃ The gen. pl. occurs in LU. 79a: *ic díchur gai 7 rend 7 err 7 sleg 7 saiget* 'casting off spears and spear-points and spikes, and javelins and arrows'; the dat. pl. in LU. 80a: *in-a-chathcharpat serda con*-erraib *iarnaidib* 'in his sithed battle-chariot with iron spikes.'
ᵇ Literally, 'was borne.'
ᶜ Should we render *mná tethrach* .i. *badb* by 'Tethra's wife i. e. Badb'? Tethra was king of the Fomoire. O'Clery and the *Forus Focal* cited by O'R. s. v. *Troghan* are in favour of the rendering at p. 22; but Irish glossographers are by no means infallible.

This seems to mean:

'*The room of the Badbs.*
'I saw a naked Three in the top of the house. Their streams of blood (ran) through them, and the ropes of their slaughter (were) on their necks.'
'I know them,' says he. 'Three awful slaughterers (?): three that (themselves) are slain at every time are those.'

What are the 'ropes' here mentioned? May we compare *Salomon and Saturn*, ed. Kemble, p. 164?—

hwæt beódh dha feowere	What be the four
fǽges rápas	ropes of the doomed man?
Salamon cwædh.	Solomon quoth:
Gewurdene	Accomplished
wyrda, dhá beódh	weirds, these be
dha feowere	the four
fǽges rápas.	ropes of the doomed man.

Or are they equivalent to the *wridhene wæl-hlencan*, 'twisted chains of slaughter,' of Elene 47?

Badb and Nemaind, who so often appear in Irish battle-stories, had been slain by a Fomorian (*Rev. Celt.* i. 35). Were these wargoddesses capable of coming to life again?

APPENDIX D.

GOIDELICA, SECOND EDITION.

CORRIGENDA.

[*Vide supra*, p. 6, note.]

Pref., line 3, *for* 'codex' *read* 'Berne, Leyden and Carinthian Codices':
p. 7, gl. 58, *for* 'pray' *read* 'utter thanks'; gl. 65, *for* 'seas' *read* 'waters':
p. 9, gl. 87, *for* 'decoration' *read* 'robe':
p. 12, gl. 118, *for* 'he offended it' *read* 'it denied him (*dodrolluind = do-dro-sluind*), Ebel, Z. 874'; gl. 127a, *read* 'taccmungad aadbrann(u)— 'which reached his ankles''; gl. 128, *for* '. . . .' *read* 'a kid (?)', and with *innaric* cf. O.W. *enderic* 'juvencus,' Beitr. vii. 411':
p. 13, gl. 141, *read* 'roglanad-e 'it, the East, was cleansed by this crown'' (of Christ's head); gl. 142, *for* 'he shone' *read* 'it, the North, was cleansed.' [So the South was cleansed by his left hand, the West by the soles of his feet, see *Anglo-Saxon Homilies*, ed. Thorpe, ii. 257]:
p. 14, note, *for* 'kindles' *read* 'warms':
p. 15, n. 87, *for* VI *read* VAS, *fethal* ex **vethra*, **vestra* = Skr. *vastra-*:
p. 16, *dele* the notes 103 and 111; l. 16, *for* 'goraim' *read* 'guirim':
p. 18, n. 22, *dele* 'O.Slav. *mladŭ*, βραδύς, Skr. root mṛd,' the Irish cognate of which is *mall* (Windisch). Also *dele* 'Lat. *mollis*,' the Ir. cognate of which seems *merb* = W. *merw* 'flaccid':

p. 19, n. 26, *for* 'apparent (*batoich* = *baddoich*)' *read* 'meet (*batoich conveniebat*, Z. 639)'; note 34, correct by reference to pp. 86, 91; note 41, *for* 'to be naked' *read* 'it be night.' (If we may read *cesu nocht is aldu de*, translate 'quamvis sit nox est pulchrior eo'); note 42, *for* 'he would not get' *read* 'there showers not even'; note 44, *for* 'dixit' *read* 'dixi':

p. 24, l. 18 from bottom, *for* 'road' *read* 'field':

p. 29, note 34r, *for* 'life' *read* 'soul':

p. 29, note 30r, *read* 'they deign not to inflict (?) upon them (any) other death but striking,' &c.:

p. 31, l. 16 from bottom, *for* 'the breast of a virgin' *read* 'a virgin's breasts'; last line, for *ro*[*fh*]*dsaiset* read *ro-dsaiset:*

p. 32, codex 18c, *read* '*conai*[r]*lemmarni*':

p. 33, codex 19d, *for* 'est' *read* 'erat'; 20a, *read* '*donai*[d]*bset*':

p. 34, l. 4, *for* 'debebant' *read* 'debuerunt'; l. 8, *read* '*bed*[d]*iachti*':

p. 37, codex 34d, *after* 'doircthi' *insert* '(leg. dóirthi?)':

p. 38, l. 11, *for* 'consumpsit' *read* 'consumptus est'; l. 5 from bottom, *for* 'forrarsissiu' *read* 'forrassissiu':

p. 39, l. 29, *for* '(leg. *artatar?*)' *read* 'i. e., coarctatus sum':

p. 41, l. 31, *for* 'condaérset' *read* 'condaér[soil]set'?

p. 45, l. 5 from bottom, *for* 'meritis' *read* 'id meruerunt':

p. 46, codex 63c, *omit* 'leg. dengatar?':

p. 48, l. 1, *dummaichisiu*, should this not be *dummaithisiu?*

p. 56, ll. 11 and 12, *cáith a uuair*. The translation and conjectural explanation are clearly wrong. Should we read *cáich a uuair* 'to (lit. of) every one in his turn'; and compare *nogonad-som cach fer díb a úair* LU. 73b, *is bith cáich arúair immaredisiu* LU. 114a, *bá cách arúair* LU. 43a:

p. 59, note on *lind*, omit '*teo*' (for *teo* is from *teu = *tepu, Skr. *tapu*):

p. 66, l. 28, *after* 'furnus' *insert* 'frenum':

p. 81, s.v. *fern*, *for* 'If this word,' etc., *read* 'The gen. pl. *fern* occurs in LL. 60b, a., and a derivative *fearnaidhe* .i. *feardha* 'manly' is given by O'Clery:

p. 82, last line but one, *for* 'If *ng*' etc., *read* 'It is borrowed from A.S. *sæcing*':

p. 85, note 6, *read* "*dir-ró-g-gel*, i.e. *dír-ró-n-chel, dír-ro-fo-n-chel* (cf. *doruaichill* .i. *dochennaigh* O'Cl., *dorúagell* Book of Kells, *doruaichli* .i. *derbchendaighes* O'Dav. 112), *dír* an adjective meaning 'due,' 'lawful,' in composition with the 3d sg. pret. act. from the root *OEL, CER*, (Beitr. viii. 38), *ro* the infixed particle, *n* an infixed pron. of 3d sg. infecting, Z. 330":

p. 87, line 15, *for* 'importsin' *read* 'inportsin':

„ note 17, line 9, *for* 'shame to the' *read* 'blemish to a':

p. 89, l. 4, *for* 'for' *read* 'far'; l. 5, *for* 'Conacolt to' *read* 'Conaclid with'; l. 21, *for* 'relationship' *read* 'family'; l. 31, *for* 'blackthorn' *read* 'bush':

p. 90, l. 2, and note 33, *for* 'given' *read* 'paid'; l. 14, *for* 'family' *read* 'province,' and correct Z^2. 639, l. 5, accordingly:

p. 91, line 8, *for* 'disgrace' *read* 'defect'; line 20, *for* 'reliquary' *read* 'credence-table (?)'; line 35, *for* 'marked out' *read* 'placed'; note 41, line 3, *for* 'on his forehead' *read* 'in front of him':

p. 96, l. 7, *for* 'leavest' *read* 'leftest.' Note 4, *for* 'this hymn was made' *read* 'he made this hymn':

p. 99, l. 8 from bottom, *for* 'came' *read* 'rose up':

p. 102, l. 12 from bottom, *for* 'there' *read* 'three':

p. 104, l. 27, *for* 'sooth,' *read* 'that'; l. 28, *for* 'It was not' *read* 'Nor was it':

p. 116, col. 2, s. v. comded, *for* 'with some,' etc., *read* 'of the preposition *con* and *midiu*, root MID, Curtius, No. 286':

p. 126, l. 15, *for* '15d' *read* '15b':

p. 128, l. 67 of the hymn, *for* 'nuabar' *read* 'núaba[i]r': in the Gloss, l. 6, *after* 'dogníth *insert* [leg. fognìth]':

p. 129, l. 1, *for* 'aracomthad' *read* 'aracomth[ó]ad': l. 8, *for* 'imlobor' *read* 'indlobor':

p. 129, l. 5 from bottom, *for* 'with his circuit' *read* 'to sojourn with him';

p. 130, l. 8, *for* 'at Sletty in the North-West' *read* 'to the North-West of Sletty':

p. 131, hymn, line 21, *for* 'druids' *read* 'soothsayers'; l. 29, *for* 'in (the) territory of Benn-Boirche' *read* 'north of Benna Boirche'; l. 31, *for* 'robe' *read* 'quilt'; l. 37, *for* 'to Hell' *read* 'with (the) Demon'; l. 48, *for* 'from' *read* 'out of'; l. 49, *for* 'at' *read* 'to'; note b, *for* 'tuaith' etc., *substitute* " Benna Boirche, 'Boirche's Peaks,' part of the Mourne Mountains, so called from Boirche, herdsman of Ross, King of Ulster, in the third century ;" note e, *for* 'jati' *read* 'gati':

p. 132, hymn, l. 67, *for* 'loftiness or arrogance' *read* 'a sign of vainglory':

p. 133, l. 12, *for* 'the great offspring of meadow-landed Erin' *read* 'Erin's meadow-lands, a mighty birth !'; l. 16 from bottom, *for* 'will ... shall' *read* 'would ... should'; l. 6 from bottom *for* 'inasoé' *read* "inanóe 'in his boat'?"

p. 137, l. 7, *for* 'through' *read* 'in spite of':

p. 138, hymn, l. 24, *for* 'niadorontai' *read* 'madoròntai' [I am indebted to Mr. Crowe for this valuable correction. *Non olet.*]:

p. 142, hymn, l. 3, *read* 'not much of carping was found (in her): with the noble faith of the Trinity (she lived)'; hymn, l. 10, *read* 'a town sheltered her: when she went (thence) it protected hosts'; l. 13, my translation of, and note on, *plea* are clearly wrong :

p. 143, hymn, l. 24, *read* 'If it hath been wrought for man, where hath ear of any one living heard [it]?' l. 25, *for* 'calling' *read* 'herd'; *for* 'in spring' *read* 'with first butter'; l. 26, *for* 'food' *read* 'stock'; *for* 'substance' *read* 'attachment'; l. 27, *for* 'marvel' *read* 'triumph'; l. 30, *read* 'there was dry weather till night[a] in her field, though

---

[a] *coidchi*, O'Clery's *chaidche .i. go hoidhche. amhail adeir an muimhneach* ('as saith the Munsterman') *cá rabhadhais la choidhche .i. ca hionadh ina rabadhais ar feidh an láoi gonuige an oidhche* ('in what place hast thou been throughout the day until the night ?').

throughout the world it poured with rain'; 1. 33, *for* 'storm' *read* 'rain'; 1. 40, *omit* '(for the poor)':

p. 144, hymn, l. 43, *for* 'to Brigit etc.' *read* 'it was one of her, Brigit's, miracles'; lines 51, 566 *for* 'sent' and 'helped' *read* 'directed':

p. 145, hymn, l. 64, *for* 'swift' *read* 'fluttering'; l. 73, *for* 'dwelt (?)' *read* 'refreshed her'; note *d*, *read* '*argenteum mare*':

p. 146, hymn, l. 84, *for* 'He' *read* 'There was'; l. 9, *for* 'come to' *read* 'help': l. 94, *for* 'knowledge' *read* 'poem'; l. 98, *for* 'She' *read* 'I':

p. 148, l. 2, *for* 'drochirnas' *read* 'drochinnas'; l. 13, *for* 'serca' *read* '*sancta*':

p. 149, l. 1, *for* 'me' *read* 'us'; l. 12, *for* 'love thou the sage,' *read* 'holy senior,' (*sruith*, like *flaith*, is feminine, though applied to a male):

p. 152, l. 32, *for* 'lusts (?)' *read* 'solicitations':

p. 156, l. 18, *for* '*seth' *read* 'sith':

p. 158, l. 6 from bottom, *after* 'demuir' *insert* '[leg. demuin]':

p. 159, the first quatrain should follow the second, and l. 4 should run on with the last line of p. 158:

p. 160, l. 10, *for* 'dedesion' *read* 'déde sion':

p. 171, l. 11 from bottom, *for* '143' *read* '141':

p. 175, l. 2, *for* '501' *read* '101':

p. 179, note 21, l. 4, *for* 'airshetal' *read* 'airchetal':

p. 181, last line, for 'a shrine which gold accompanies' *read* 'a holy shrine which gold bedecks'; and with *con-u-taing* cf. *co-ta-u-taing* 'eam protegit,' Ml. 36b:

p. 182, l. 2, *for* 'choruses' *read* 'melodies'; l. 10 *for* 'thou gettest' *read* 'pours'; l. 12, *for* 'an *udnacht*' *read* 'a palisade.'

See also M. Nigra's corrections of pp. 23—51, in the Revue Celtique i. 505, 506, and Prof. Windisch's in the Literarisches Centralblatt, 15 März, 1873.

The latter part of the story of the Devil and S. Molling, pp. 180, 181, is very badly rendered. It should run thus:—

'Wherefore hast thou come?' asked Molling.

'That thou mayst give me thy blessing,' says the Devil.

'I will not give it,' says Molling. 'Since thou deservest[a] it not, thou wouldst not be the better thereof. What good were it to thee moreover?'

'O Cleric,' says he, 'just as if thou shouldst go into a vat of honey and bathe therein with thy raiment, the odour thereof would be on thee unless thy raiment should be washen[b].'

'Wherefore is this thy desire?' asks Molling.

'Because, though thou givest nought of thy blessing to me, the benefit and goodness thereof will be on me externally.'

'Thou shalt not have it,' says Molling, 'for thou deservest[a] it not.'

'Well then,' says he, 'give me the full of a curse.'

'Wherefore wishest thou this?' says Molling.

---

[a] *·airle* for *airilli*: cf. *naichid airilset* (gl. non promerentibus), Ml. 54, *airilliud* 'meritum,' Z. 802.

[b] *nestá* 3d sg. secondary s-fut. passive of *nigim*, Curtius, No. 439.

'Not hard to say, O Cleric,' says he : 'on thy mouth will (then) be the venom and hurt of every mouth whereon gathers [a] the curse on me.'
'Go,' says Molling, 'to no blessing hast thou a right.'
'Better were it for me that I should have a right to it. How shall I earn [b] it?'
'By service unto God,' says Molling.
'Woe's me,' says he, 'I have not chosen [c] this.'
'A ... reading (of holy texts),' says Molling.
'Thy reading saves me not [d], and this does not help me.'
'Fasting then,' says Molling.
'I am fasting since the world's beginning. Not the better am I.'
'Making genuflexions,' says Molling.
'I cannot bend forward, for my knees are (turned) backward.'
'Go forth,' says Molling, 'I cannot save thee.'
Then said the Devil, '*He is pure gold*,' etc.

ADDENDA.

p. 20, line 14, *add:* "The idea of miraculous parturition by a male may have been suggested by S. Paul : 'Filioli mei, quos iterum parturio' (Galat. iv. 19) ; 'Etenim in Christo Jesu per evangelium ego vos genui' (1 Corinth. iv. 15). In the Lebar Brecc, p. 74, col. 4, Christ is thus addressed : *A mic roghenair fodíí* ('O Son, who wast born twice!') ; and in the same page, col. 2 : *A mic ind-athar aircisectaig cin máthair anim* ('O Son of the merciful Father, without a mother in heaven!') ; *A mic ina fire oigi muire ingine cin athair italam* ('O Son of the true Virgin Mary, the maiden, without a father on earth!')."

p. 71, note on *antach*, *add*: 'Cf. Philippe de Thaun, cited by Wright, *St. Brandan* 60 :

Cetus ceo est mult grant beste, tut tens en mer converse
le sablun de mer prent, sur son dos l'estent
sur mer s'esdrecerat, *en pais si esterat*.

p. 72, after line 35, *after* 'ingredient,' *insert—*
'And the following instances actually occur in extant Irish MSS.:—

(a) insertions of -*ua* :	*anuaim* for *anim*, Amra Chol. 99 : *coluain* } *conuail* } for *colinn*, ib. 110, 118 :
(b) insertion of .*uc* :	*uasucan* for *uasunn*, LB. 79 :
(c) addition of a letter :	*tend* for *ten* 'fire,' LU. 7a, line 9 :
(d) addition of a syllable { -*án* :	*cia dothísatán* 'though they should come,' LB. 79 :
-*ón* :	*gandón, annón*, LU. 7a, lines 20 [e], 21 :
-*da* :	*tereda*, LU. 7a, line 17.

---

[a] *targa* : cf. *tárgadh* .i. *tionol no cruinniughadh*, O'Cl.
[b] *do-sn-uilliub*, from *tuillim* 'I earn,' stem *do-pallia *do-palnia, Windisch, Beitr. viii. 5.
[c] This is a guess. I conjecture *rucaim* to be=*ro-ucaim* and connect it with *ucu* 'choice.'
[d] *ni-m-ó* for *ní-mm-ói*, vide supra, note on No. 586.
[e] Here the glossographer writes : '*ón* hic exemitur.'

p. 88, note 21, add "*Ata din neccodim isiu adnoculsa immo-chassaib stephanus martir* 'N. is in this grave at the feet of the martyr S.,' LB. 35a. Can *immo* = *ambi-ava* = Skr. *abhyava-* in *abhyavahāra, abhyavahārayāmi?* *Mo-an* 'around the,' 'around whom,' and *moalle* for *immó-alle* occur in Middle-Irish."

p. 96, line 22, to 'hifuterna' add a note 'in Whiterne (in Galloway).'

In p. 148, the following translation of the Irish part of the preface to Sanctáin's hymn was accidentally omitted :—

"'*I beseech the King.*'—Bishop Sanctáin made this hymn, and when he was going from Clonard westward to Matóc's Island [a] he made it. And he was a brother of Matóc's, and both of them were of Britain, and Matóc came into Ireland before Bishop Sanctáin. Now the *causa* is this : to save him(self) from enemies, and that his brother might be let come *in insulam* to him. *Scoticam*, etc.'

APPENDIX E.

[*Vide supra* p. 19.]

Additional Old-British Glosses.

(*a*) on Eutychius (Z. 1052—1053).

gruitiam (gl. grunnio), *preteram* (gl. perpendo), *crum* (gl. cerno, cernuus).

(*b*) on Ovid's *Ars amatoria* (Z. 1054—1059).

donec vel *cant* (gl. cum), *ir* (gl. quod), *penitra* (gl. tractat), *ircretuis* (gl. Cressa). These, like *hí hataned* supra p. 51, were discovered by Mr. Bradshaw.

APPENDIX F.

[*Vide supra*, p. 22.]

Corrigenda to the Old-British Glosses

as printed in Gr. Celt. 1052—1057.

p. 1052, *mergidhaham* (gl. euanesco), *read* (gl. besco [b]) :
  „   *didioulam* (gl. glisco), *read* (gl. micturio) :
  „   *lemhaam* (gl. arguo), *read* (gl. acuo) :
p. 1053, *gueig* (gl. testrix), read *gueg* :
p. 1054, *anguoconam* (gl. uigilo), *read* (gl. lacto [c]) :
  „   *orgarn* (gl. medio), read *orgarr* :

---

[a] An islet in the lake of Templeport, county Leitrim, (O'Curry's Lectures on the MS. Materials of Ancient Irish History, p. 27, and see Z. præf. xiii and Rel. Celt. 21).
[b] Connected, according to Mr. Bradshaw, with *rescus* 'poor,' 'shrivelled' (*vesca farra*).
[c] i. e. deficio in pondere.

p. 1055, *guorimhetic* read *guorunhetic* :
p. 1056, *trudou* (gl. ocellos) read *grudou* :
p. 1057, *ceinguodeimisauch* read *ceinguodemisauch* :
„ *cenitolaidou* (gl. natales) ; read *utolaidou* :
„ *cetlinau* read *cedlinau*.

The above corrigenda are also due to Mr. Bradshaw. The most important are *an-guoconam* (gl. lacto) and *utolaidou* (gl. natales). With the former Rhys connects *an-wogawn* 'invalidus,' *gwogawn*, *di-gawn* 'saturatio,' 'potens.' The latter is cognate with the Ir. *uaithne* 'puerperium,' SM. i. 194, 268, which O'Reilly erroneously explains as 'the monthly terms of a woman.'

APPENDIX G.

[*Vide supra*, p. 24.]

Parker Collection (Corpus Christi College, Cambridge), No. 279.

['This MS.', says Mr. Bradshaw, 'contains the 'Synodus Patricii, Auxilii et Issernini,' and a number of other Church canons of Irish origin. It is written in a continental, not in a Hiberno-Saxon, hand, and may be of the ninth century. Most of the other MSS. which contain these canons are now to be found in libraries in France. The glosses are in the handwriting of the original scribe.']

fo. 108, *tinolsiter* (gl. adplicabitur) :
fo. 109, *banessa* (gl. nuptias), *brotligi* (gl. uestimenta), *mariaranostar* (gl. si tria ista non fecerit) :
fo. 115, *indenim* (gl. debilitatum) : fo. 118, *indibbrit* (gl. in negotio) :
fo. 123, uassa uel *bŭnni* [gl. chitropedes (i. e. χυτρόποδες)] :
fo. 124, *ó cuidich* (gl. aucupio) : fo. 126, *iscuilech* (gl. incestus est) :
fo. 134, *bólcha* (gl. papulas), *trusci* (gl. scabiem), *reet* (gl. inpitiginem) :
fo. 156, *anre* (gl. colirio).

APPENDIX H.

On the Manners and Customs of the Ancient Irish.
London, Dublin and New York, 1873.
[*Vide supra*, p. 41.]

Vol. II	O'Curry	Read
p. 91n, ' cia tiassam cain temadar'(printed *Cia tiassa cain timadar*)	'wherever we go,—though great our numbers.'	'wherever we shall go, let him guard (us) well.'
p. 92, l. 6, 'fifth'	... ...	'eleventh.'
p. 192, *tir. . . hi fil rind*	'a land which is mine.'	'a land wherein is music ' (*rinn* .i. *ceol*, O'Cl.).

Vol. II	O'Curry	Read
p. 193, *amra tíre tír as-biur ní théit oac and re-siun*	'the only land to praise is the land of which I speak, where no one ever dies of decrepit age.'	'A marvel of a land is the land I mention. There the young goeth not before the old.'
p. 196, *ni bo sirsan intanad* (LU. 44b)	'Thy stay should not be long.'	'the delay was not good news.'
„ *domficfe uaimse*	'from me shall be sent.'	'will go from me.'
p. 253, n. *cairchiu 7 grindegar na saigidbolc*	'the music and harmony of the belly darts.'	'the din and ringing of the quivers' (lit. 'arrow-bags' or 'dart-bags').
p. 309, *fodb*	'lance.'	'hedgingbill'? (W.*gwddi*).
„ *conderna thuaig . . . de*	'so that he became a . . . rainbow (*sic*).'	'so that he made a giant of himself' (root TU).

Vol. III	O'Curry	Read
p. 18, *clethi*	'post.'	'rooftree.'
„ *la*	'way.'	'day.'
„ *dofeised for gúalaind conchobair*	'he sat at Conchobar's shoulder.'	'he rested on Conchobar's shoulder.'
p. 19, [a lady with her 50 women go out of the palace] *iar trummi óil*	'to take the cool air outside for a while.'	'after heaviness of drinking.'
p. 20, *tuargabsat a lénte co mellaib a lárac*	'they even took up their dresses to the calves of their legs.'	'they lifted their smocks to their buttocks' (lit. 'to the globes of their forks').
p. 21, *briatharchath*	'battle speeches.'	'wordfight' (λογομαχία).
p. 77, *combói forindotruch in-dorus ind-rígthige* (LU. 111a)	'so that he fell upon the bench [a] at the door of the royal house.'	'so that he was on the dunghill in the doorway of the palace.'
„ *do orgain inna cathrach* (LU. 111a)	'to come to the *cathair*.'	'to wreck the burgh.'
„ *má-s-tat carait co-ná-m-usn-ágat : ma-s-tat námait co-m-os-r-alat* [b] (LU. 111a)	'let them speak if friends; let them attack if foes.'	'if they are friends, let them not fight me; if they are foes, let them come to me.'

[a] This mistranslation is not due to ignorance, but (like those at pp. 19 and 20) to a desire to conceal a fact militating against theories of early Irish civilisation.
[b] This is the most wonderful example of polysynthesis that I have yet met in old Irish; *co-ná-m-usn-ágat* (literally 'that-not-me-they-fight') might almost be Basque or Accadian.

Vol. III	O'Curry	Read
p. 78, *adrolaic a-béolu con-dechsad óen na-rígthige in-na-croes* (LU. 111b)	'it so opened its jaws that the vat of a king's house might enter them.'	'It opened its jaws so that one of the palaces would go into its gullet.'
„ *foraithmenatar-som*	'He executed.'	'He calls to mind.'
p. 141, *húa smech có a imlind*	'from his chin to his waist.'	'from his chin to his navel.'
p. 143, *o adbrund co ur-glune*	'from his bosom to his noble knees.'	'from ankle to kneecaps.'
p. 145, *ríg-drúth*	'royal druid.'	'royal buffoon.'
p 146, *ix. mbuilc*	'nine shields.'	'nine bags.'
p. 147, *teora caimsi hi foditib impu*	'wearing shirts of full length.'	'three nightgowns girt (lit. 'in girdles') about them.'
p. 149, *folt derg forsind-laech 7 abrait deirg lais*	'the champion himself had red hair, and had a red cloak near him.'	'Red hair (was) on the hero and red eyelashes had he.'
„ *tri dorsaide ríg Temrach ... tri mic ersand 7 comlad* (LU. 96b)	'three door-keepers of the King of Teamair .... three sons renowned for valour and combat.'	'three door-keepers of the King of Tara .... three sons of Doorpost and of Valve.'
p. 152, *cumala bana .i. di argat*	'white *ancillæ* or anklets of silver.'	'white *cumals*, i. e. of silver' (see Tir. 6).
p. 185, *hi sedgregaib oss neng* (printed *hi sedghangaib oss nég !*)	'as fleet as roebucks.'	'in the tracks of deer.'

So far Professor O'Curry. For the following errors in the version of part of the *Táin Bó Cualngne*, vol. iii., p. 415, Mr. Sullivan has generously made himself responsible. ['With this object I (*sic*) made a literal translation from that romance of a complete episode recording the combats of Ferdiad and Cúchulaind, which, together with the original text, I have printed as one of the Appendices to vol. iii.']:—

Vol. III	Mr. Sullivan	Read
p. 414, *drúith*	'druids.'	'buffoons.'
„ *rat-fia*	} 'I will give.'	} 'thou shalt have' (lit. 'tibi erit').
p. 416, *rat-fiat*		
p. 418, *rodfia*		
p. 422, *dunaid*	'court.'	'leaguer.'
„ *dáil*	'challenge.'	'meeting.'
p. 426, *droich*	'roll.'	'wheels.'

Vol. III	Mr. Sullivan	Read
p. 426, *is demin donrua*	'he is [the presage of] bloody slaughter.'	'it is certain that he will come to us.'
pp. 426 & 428, *ó thánac ótig*	'since he came from his home.'	'since thou camest from thy house.'
p. 430, *is missi rat-gena*	''tis I that will do it.'	''tis I that will slay thee.'
p. 432, *robud*	'vauntings.'	'warning.'
„ *nít-fia luag na logud*	'nor pay nor reward hast thou received.'	'thou shalt not have pay nor reward.'
„ *gnathaig*	'respective.'	'usual.'
p. 434, *tiglecht*	'last end.'	'grave' (lit. 'final bed').
p. 436, *ropdar*	'we were.'	'they were.'
p. 438, *assa aithle*	'forthwith.'	'thereafter.'
„ *fri dé*	'at dusk.'	'daily' (cf. Fiacc. h. 28).
p. 440, *ele*	'incantation.'	'unguents.'
p. 450, *cach n-alt 7 cach n-áge*	'every crevice and every cavity.'	'every limb and every joint.'
p. 452, *leo ni bec bar mbith-scarad*	'to them seemeth not too small [the numbers] who have parted for ever.'	'not little to them (were) parting with you for ever.'
„ *mad iartais ind fhir sein*	'if thou hadst consulted these men.'	'if those men were asked.'
p. 454, *dar lind*	'we then resolved.'	'it seemed to us.'
p. 456, *is gat im ganem na im grian*	'it is putting a gad on the sand or sunbeam.'	''tis a withe round sand or gravel' (*grian* m. = W. *graian*).
p. 458, *beóil bána*	'angry words.'	'white lips.'
p. 462, *indar limsa fer dil dead is am diad rabiad go-brath*	'dear to me the beloved Ferdiad. It shall hang over me for ever.'	'meseemed that the dear Ferdiad would have been after me (i. e. survived me) for ever.'

More than fifty pages (549—604) of the third volume are occupied with a 'Glossarial Index of Irish Words.' 'In preparing it,' says Mr. Sullivan (Preface 15), 'I have taken advantage of the latest results of my inquiries and increased knowledge of the subject to improve the meaning (*sic*) and correct the spelling of several words.' The following are fair specimens of this glossary, which is worthy to rank with the most characteristic work of O'Reilly, Vallancey and Betham. I can give it no higher praise:—

1. '*Adid*, his two, iii. 497.' These two syllables commence the word *ad-idn-giallna* (iii. 497), where *idn* is an infixed personal pronoun of the 3rd sg. (Z. 330) and *ad-giallna* (ex *ati-giallnát) a verb meaning 'renders service.'
2. '*Airilliud*, good works, iii. 514.' This common word is singular, not plural, and always means 'meritum,' 'deservingness.' A similar

error is committed under *Aideadh ulad*, which is rendered 'the *deaths* of the Ultonians.'
3. '*Aitherach*, a gain, iii. 493.' Read *aitherrach* 'again.'
4. '*Alamu*, her hands.' The reference is to vol. i., p. ccciii, where we find a version of the following passage from LU., p. 42a : *Rochumtaiged dún ocan-druid andsin in-Almain 7 rocomled alamu dia-sund corbo aengel uli . . . . dond-alamain tuc dia-thig isde ata almu ar almain*. In the face of the dative singular *alamain*, this easy passage is thus rendered : 'The druid built a Dún then in Almhain and she rubbed her hands to its walls until it was all lime-white . . . . From the two hands which she rubbed on the house, it is from it *Almhain* was called *Almu*.' The true version is obviously : "Then a stronghold was built by the soothsayer in Almu, and *alamu* was rubbed on its house (lit. 'to its stake'), so that it was altogether white . . . . From the *alamu* which he gave to his house, hence ' Almu ' is so-called."ᵃ
5. '*Allaid*, a wild stag, iii. 428,' *allaid* is a common adjective meaning 'wild.' 'A stag' would be *ag allaid*.
6. '*Apdaines*, persons whose rank was proclaimed or legally admitted.' *Apdaine*, better *abbdaine*, is a common word meaning 'abbacy.'
7. '*Arfuin Arfoimsin*, accept thou (or I present to thee), iii. 221.' The words meant are *arfóim*, *arfóim-siu* 'accept thou.' Mr. Sullivan's correction in brackets reveals the intimate acquaintance with Irish conjugation which we shall find exemplified *infra* at Nos. 8, 9, 11, 14, 19, 20, 23, 26, 34, 37, 40, 41, 47, 48, 49, 52, 57, and 65.
8. '*Asatluí*, in revolt, aggressive, iii. 505.' And again '*Satluí*, revolt, aggression, iii. 505.' Here we have, not a preposition and a noun, but the common verb *aslui* 'effugit,' 'transfugit,' Z. 437, with the infixed pronoun *at*: cf. *ti-at* 'let him go,' *bath-at* .i. *ata aige*, O'Cl., where it is suffixed. The passage in which *asatluí* occurs (iii. 505), *slogud tar crich fri tuaith as-at-luí*, means 'a hosting over the border against a tribe that *deserts him*.'
9. '*Atchisiu*, I perceive, iii. 446.' It means 'thou perceivest,' *atchí-siu*.
10. '*Baar*, top or head.' The word meant is *barr*.
11. '*Barficfa*, will be fought, iii. 558.' This means 'he will fight (*ficfa*) you (*bar*).' Compare *no-bar-beraid*, LL. 46b, 2 : *ro-bar-tinoil* 'vos collegit,' LB. 8a : *do-bar-ruachtadar*, Leb. Buide Lecain, col. 647.
12. '*Bemmim*, a stroke, a blow.' This word (rectiùs *bémmimm*) is the dat. sg. of *béim*. It is here treated as a nominative: cf. *Duilemain* infra No. 27, *Ereman* No. 29, *Fidu* No. 36, *Gnimu* No. 42, *Ordain* No. 58, *Togarmand* No. 67, *Tomadmaimm* No. 68.
13. '*Berrach*, a junior barrister' (*sic*).

ᵃ Can *alamu* have lost initial *p* and be connected with *pal-ita*, πελ-ιτ-νός, Lit. *pal-va*, OHG. *falo*? It may possibly be not only cognate, but identical in meaning, with O.N. *fölski* (= **fal-viskan*) 'asche,' Fick 792.

— 78 —

14. '*Brethem no Dobeir*, judges or givers.' *Brethem* means 'a judge,' and *dobeir* is not a noun in the plural, but the 3d sg. pres. indic. act. of the verb *dobiur* 'I give.' What would be said of a Greek lexicographer who translated δίδωσι as if it was ἑωτῆρες?
15. '*Cing* .... cf. A.Sax. *cyning* .... Eng. *King*.'
16. '*Claidem Mór*, a large sword .... Welsh *Llawmawr*' (sic).
17. '*Cnairseach*, probably a sledge or large hammer,' rectè *cnairrsech* 'javelin,' a diminutive of *cnarr* 'spear,' O'Dav. 68.
18. '*Comopair na bairse*, the instrument of the manufacturing woman .... iii. 116.' This is *comopair n-abairse* 'instruments of work,' where *comopair* is an accusative sg. and *abairse* the gen. sg. of *abras*.
19. '*Comracut*, concentrated, iii. 238,' read *comracat* 'they meet.'
20. '*Corp*, until, iii. 90.' The word is doubtless *corop* (= *con-ro-p*) 'donec sit.'
21. '*Craes*, mouth.' It means 1, 'gullet;' 2, 'gluttony.'
22. '*Did*, two,' see *Adid*.
23. '*Didla*, to cut, see *Didlastais*.' *Didlastais* is the 3rd pl. reduplicated secondary s-future of a verb *dlongim*, whence *ro-dloingset*, iii. 448. *Didla* 'to cut' is a mere invention. To set down in a Greek lexicon λελει 'to leave' because the form λελείψεται is found in Homer would be a fair parallel. A similar instance of guesswork occurs in the notes to Mr. Crowe's edition of the *Siaburcharpat Conculainn*, p. 409, where *mebdatar* (for *memdatar*,[a] Corm. B. s. v. maidire, *me-mad-atar*, the 3d pl. reduplicated preterite active of *maidim* 'frango') is actually referred to "the verb *meb* 'to break.'"
24. '*D'innaigid*, towards each other, iii. 440.' *D'innaigid* (for *do innsaigid*) simply means 'insequi,' 'adire.' In iii. 440, *Tanic cách dib d'innaigid a chéile* literally means 'each of them came to approach his fellow,' *i. e.* 'towards each other.'
25. '*Domna*, base of' (sic).
26. '*Dot nimcellat*, encircled by, iii. 508.' This is *do-tn-imchellat* 'they encircle him,' the third pl. pres. indic. active of the verb *timchellaim*, with the infixed pronoun *tn*.
27. '*Duilemain*, the creator.' This is the acc. sg. of *dúlem*.
28. '*Eochraide*, gen. plu. of *each*, a steed.' The word meant is *echraide*, gen. singular of *echrad* 'cavalry,' a collective noun, Z. 856. Compare, for the knowledge of Irish declension here displayed, No. 45 infra and vol. iii. 56: "This word *coictighis* is compounded, according to the published translation, of *coic* 'a cook' and *tighis*, the plural of *tigh* 'a house.'"
29. '*Ereman*, a ploughman.' The word meant is *aireman*, which is the gen. sg. of *airem*. Like mistakes are made in vol. i., p. cii., where *caireaman* (gen. sg. of *cairem* 'a shoemaker') and *daile-*

---

[a] So *forruib* Fiacc. h. 8 is = *forruim*, Tir. 13.

man (the gen. sg. of *dailem* 'cupbearer') are quoted. What would Mr. Sullivan say to a Latin lexicographer who gave as nominatives singular *aratoris, sutoris,* and *cauponis?*

30. '*Faesam*, the right possessed by freemen of entertaining strangers for a certain time, varying with the rank of the host, without being obliged to give bail or security for the guests.' What sheer guesswork all this is appears from the fact that (under *Mac Faesma*, iii. 587) the gen. sg. of *faesam* is rendered 'of adoption.' *Faesam* (otherwise spelt *foessam* Colm. 4, 2, *fóesam* ib. 52, *fóessam* Broc. h. 106) means 'protection,' and in law-language 'the escort or protection which a guest received on his visits while passing from one house to another.' See O'Don. Supp. s. v. *faosamh*. The W. *gwaesaf* 'a pledge,' *gwaesafu* 'to insure,' may also be cognate.

31. '*Fén, Fedhen, Feadhan*, a bier or hearse.' There is no such word as *fedhen*; and *feadhan* means 'yoke' or 'team,' Corm. Tr. 79. *Fén* (gl. plaustrum) Z. 19, which Mr. Sullivan (i. ccclxxvi) says 'seems to have been the special vehicle used as the bier or hearse of kings and warriors,' he will find, in the gloss on Broccán's hymn, line 25, meaning 'a butter-cart.'

32. '*Ferbolgs*, pawns for chess-playing.' *Fer-bolg* means 'a man-bag,' the bag (sometimes made of bronze wire) in which were kept the pieces used in playing *fidchell.*

33. '*Fersad*, a club.' The word meant is *fersaid* (W. *gwerthyd*) 1, 'a spindle;' 2, 'an axis' (Mart. Don. 154); 3, 'a spit of sand at a ford or estuary.' If it really was the name of a weapon used by the Firbolg (ii. 256) it probably meant 'an arrow;' cf. the Greek ἅρπακτος 1, 'spindle;' 2, 'arrow.'

34. '*Fessir*, knoweth, iii. 510.' This (better spelt *fesser*) means 'thou shouldst know,' and is the 2d sg. deponential s-conjunctive (Z. 468) of *fetar* 'I know'; 'knoweth' is *fitir.*

35. '*Fetorloic*, patriarchal.' This word (properly spelt *fetarlaic*) is a substantive, not an adjective, and means the Old Law, the Law of the Old Testament. It is a loan from *vetus (veteris)* and *lex (legis).*

36. '*Fidu*, a tree, iii. 448.' This is the acc. pl. of *fid.* It is here treated as a nom. sg. So *gnimu* No. 42.

37. '*Fonluing*, the same as *folaing*, to endure, to suffer, to bear or support, iii. 518.' *Fo-n-luing* means 'who endures.' *Folaing* means 'endures.'

38. '*Forttrena*, brave rumped' (*sic*). *Forlethan*, broad-rumped, iii. 428.' Of these words the former is the pl. of *fortren* 'mighty,' one of the commonest of Old-Irish adjectives, the latter merely means 'very broad.'

39. '*Frepaid*, to cure, *no Frepaid*, incurable (*sic*), iii. 521.' Ir. *no* means 'or,' and is not connected (as Mr. Sullivan apparently supposes) with the English negative *no.*

40. '*Frisaicci*, are consulted, they appoint, or elect, or respond? iii. 501.' This common verb means 'expects,' 'awaits.' It is the third sg. pres. indic. act. of *frisaiccim* (gl. opperior, Z. 429, 1024).
41. '*Gena* (same as *dena*), to do.' *Gena* (leg. *géna*) the subjoined form of the 3d sg. reduplicated future act. of *gonaim*, means 'occidet;' (cf. O'Clery, s. v. *gén* : *fear do-da-géna* .i. *fear ghonfas tú*) : there is no such word as *dena*. *Dénum* means 'to do.'
42. '*Gnimu*, a deed or deeds.' The word meant is *gním̃u*, the acc. pl. of *gním* 'a deed.'
43. '*Indlach*, instigation, iii. 448.' *Indlach* means 'interruptio,' *Rev. Celt.* i. 155, or 'divisio,' Z. 855, and is cognate with *indlung* (gl. findo), Z. 877.
44. '*Inna*, these, iii. 493.' *Inna* is here the gen. pl. of the article. The blunder is as if one should confound τῶν with τούτων.
45. '*Laechraid*, a form of the gen. pl. (*sic*) of *laegh*, a calf, iii. 500.'
46. '*Maclan* [sic] *airgit*, shoes of silver, iii. 159.' Our glossarial indexer means *mdelán*, a nom. dual occurring in the following short passage from LU. 24b—25a printed (with only fifteen faults) in vol. iii., p. 153 : Isinchet*r*amad lou iar*um* dolluid in-banscál an-do-*cum*, alainn em tánaic ann. brat gel impe 7 buinne óir imm-á-moing. mong orda fu*rri*. dá-máclán argit imm-a-cossa gelchorcrai. bretnas argit *com*-brephnib óir in-a-brut 7 léne srebnaide síta *fri*-a-gelchnes.
47. '*Mbis*, when he has, iii. 490.' The passage in which this singular word occurs is : *in-tan m-bis diabol n-airech desai lais* 'when double (the property) of an Aire-desa is with him' : *bis* (recte *bís*) is the 3rd sg. relative present of *bíu* 'sum,' and the prefixed *m* is the transported *n* of the accusative *tan* 'tempus.' The phrase *intan m-bis* (cum est) occurs twice in Z. 492.
48. '*Melastar*, he grinds [*recte* thou art ground (*sic!*)] iii. 488.' This is a deponential 3rd sg. s-pret. and means 'he ground'; the '*recte*' is Mr. Sullivan's. So at p. 598 he renders *snigestar* 'stillavit' by 'thou art thrown.' One would like to see his paradigm of an Irish verb in the passive.
49. '*Memaid*, frightened to flight, iii. 450.' *Ro-memaid* (3d sg. redupl. pret. of *maidim*), simply means 'fregit.'
50. '*Miodhcuaird*, mead-circling, i. ccciii.' This word, rectè *mid-chuairt*, simply means 'mid-court.'
51. '*Nel*, a trance, iii. 452.' The word meant is *nél* 'a cloud.'
52. '*Nenaisc*, to bind, to govern, iii. 514.' This is the 3d sg. reduplicated pret. act. of *naiscim* and simply means 'nexuit.'
53. '*Nin*, "id est" that is, etc., iii. 492.' This, one of the commonest of Irish contractions, stands for *ninse*, which does not mean 'that is,' but 'not difficult' (*ni-ansa*).

54. '*N-ue*, grandsire, iii. 479.' The passage in which this occurs is *is nue o rogabh treabhadh*, where *nue* is obviously the common adjective meaning 'new,' 'recent,' referring to the time at which the *óc-aire* or 'young noble' commenced householding. Compare *ó gabais trebad* LU. 96a, rightly rendered by O'Curry, iii. 149, 'since he has taken to housekeeping.'

55. '*Ordain*, the thumb, iii. 14.' This is the dat. sg. of *ordu*, gen. *ordan*.

56. '*Pes-Bolg* a foot-bag (*sic!*) in which sorted wool is kept by carding women.' *Pes* is a loan from the Lat. *pexa*, and has nothing to do (as Mr. Sullivan supposes) with the Lat. *pes*.

57. '*Rop* is, it is.' This, one of the commonest of Irish verbal forms, means 'sit,' not 'est.' Z. 494.

58. '*Ropp*, a tuft.' The word meant is *popp* = *pamp*-inus.

59. '*Seir*, the rear, the back part.' '*Seirtiud*, [rectè *seirthid*,] 'a young man of noble race.' *Seir* means 'heel,' and *seirthid*, 'heelman,' i. e. 'one who stands at his chief's heel.' The other guards were called *rigthid* 'forearm-man' and *taebthaid* 'side-man.'

60. '*Sicc Occ, Sic Oc*, a name given to *Aires* having *Sac* and *Soke* that is to those entitled to hold the *Airecht Foleithe* or Court Leet.' It is scarcely credible, but it is a fact, that this is nothing but the Latin *sic hoc*, an expression of a surety's or guarantor's assent to the statement of his principal (*Athenæum* Jan. 31, 1874, p. 156).

61. '*Snadad, Snadha*, to traverse.' The word meant (*snádud*) means 'to protect.' The cognate verb is of constant occurrence in the Félire of Oengus. It is the Irish reflex of the W. *noddi* 'protegere,' 'defendere,' 'asylum præbere,' from *nawdd* 'protectio.'

62. '*Snegair*, is thrown.' *Snegair*, the third sg. pres. indic. pass. of *snigim* 'stillo' (misspelt *snidhim* by O'R.) means 'is dropt.'

63. '*Sonn*, a sound, from the Latin *sonus*, iii. 308.' On looking to iii. 308 we find the passage '*co cluinn a sonn fona .iiii. nimib*,' which is rendered by 'until they are heard throughout the seven heavens.' But no such gibberish ever existed. The MS. (LB. 111a) has distinctly *co cluinter fona .iiii. nimib* 'so that it—Gabriel's trumpet—is heard throughout the seven heavens.' Mr. Sullivan's *sonn* (like his *ropp* supra) is a mere misreading of the MS.

64. '*Sruith*, high.' *Sruith* (pl. *sruithi* = O.W. *strutiu* gl. antiquam gentem) means 'vetus' (*inna sruithe* gl. veterum, Ml. 55r). I know not whether to connect it with the Old-Latin *struere* 'augere' or with the Skr. *sthavira* 'old,' *sthāvira* 'old age.'

65. '*Suifi*, to return or fall back into vice, iii. 493.' The passage referred to is: *in gell nad suifi friu aither(r)ach* 'the promise that he will not return to them again.' -*Suifi* is the subjoined form of the 3d sg. b-fut. act. of a verb cognate with the Lat. *su-cula* 'windlass,' root SU 'to turn.'

66. '*Togarmand*, a title of distinction or honour.' This is the nom. or acc. plural of the neuter n-stem *togairm* 'appellatio,' Z. 268, 269, but is here treated as a nom. sg.

67. '*Tomadmmaim*, to break up the ranks of an army, &c.' Here again an oblique case is given as a nom. sg. *Tomadmainm* is the dat. sg. of *tomaidm* 'a bursting,' 'a breaking-forth,' *Chron. Scot.* 6.

68. '*T-Saland*, salted' (!)

But enough of this melancholy production. We have unfortunately here in India more than one dictionary, the authors of which have omitted to learn how to translate the commonest words, to decline the commonest nouns and to conjugate the commonest verbs of the language with which they purport to deal. But is there any country in Europe save Ireland (*penitus toto divisa orbe*) in which such a glossary as Mr. Sullivan's could be compiled and published?

ADDENDA.

p. 6, No. 7. The root LAK 'to hide' seems only a sister-form of ALK: *fo-s-ro-laich* 'hid them,' Fiacc's h., 6, 2, *oc fo-luch a lochta* 'hiding her fault,' LU. 52a :

„ No. 14. Add 'and in *aitchim* (= *aith-dichim*) 'abjuro' : *ro-aitgiset hautem ainm ṅdé* 'they abjured the name of God' LH. 32b, Goid. 172.

„ No. 29b. *celmaine* 'tidings,' 'a message,' LL. 74b. 2, dat. *celmuiniu*, ib. The original *r* seems in *cor* .i. *ceol* 'music' (*ilar cór*, Goid. 180), O'Cl., in *coirchi ceoil* 'a strain of music,' O'Don. Supp., and in *cear-t-án* 'a kind of music,' ib :

p. 7, No. 37. Ir. *géc* 'branch' = W. *cainc*, Skr. *çākhā*, is another instance of the medialisation of *c* in anlaut :

„ No. 42b. Add Ir. *coirthe* 'pillar-stone,' and *corad* 'stone-wall,' O'Don. Supp. :

p. 8, No. 47, l. 2, after *sétche* insert 'or *sétig*.' In *im-chell, t-im-chell* we have an accurate reflex of Lat. *callis*:

„ No. 53. Ir. *creim* 'gnawing' seems to belong to this :

„ No. 56. κῆπος. With Lat. *campus* we may put Ir. *cepach*. See infra at No. 108 :

p. 9, No. 64. With ἀκού(σ)ειν, ἀκουστός and Goth. *hausjan* here cited, the Ir. *cois-t-im* seems cognate : *dia coistithe frim* 'if thou wouldst listen to me,' LU. 43b, *ni choistfem-ne an-airfiteod* 'we will not hear their playing,' LB. 89, *coisteacht* .i. *eisteacht*, O'Cl. :

p. 10, No. 72. Add Ir. *cruth* 'forma' = W. *prŷd* :

p. 11, No. 89. The old form *Brech-mag* occurs in LB. 89 :

„ No. 108. Root σκαπ. To this belong several Irish words in which *p* may stand for *mp* : *cepach* (now *ceapach*) 'a plot of ground laid out for tillage,' O'Don. Supp., *ceaptha* 'shaped,' ib., and *scip* or *cip* 'hand,' Amra, ed. Crowe, 64. As *pt* becomes *ct*, we may also connect *cecht* 'plough' (*hi cecht* gl. in burim, Sg. 127b) :

p. 13, No. 128. Add *né no nei* .i. *ben* 'woman,' O'Dav. 108 :

p. 15, No. 144. That Pictet is right here is, I think, certain. Consider Benfey, *Jubeo und Seine Verwandte*, Göttingen 1871, p. 10 : " Sieht man nun, wie im Sanskrit von *yuj* das Passiv (eig. 'angebunden werden,' medial 'sich anbinden, anfügen ') die Bedeutung 'passen, zukömmlich sein, *recht* sein' annimmt, das Ptcp. Pf. Pass. *yukta* 'passend, *recht*' bedeutet, das Abstract *yukti* 'Angemessenheit, Richtigkeit, richtige Weise, Fug,' ferner wie im Deutschen mit 'fügen' das Wort 'gefüge' und das dem Begriff 'Recht' so nahe stehende, fast damit identische, 'Fug' zusammenhängt, so kann man unbedenklich annehmen, dass aus *yu* ein Wort hervorgehen konnte, welches, wie im lateinischen *jous*, die Bed. *Recht* erhielt":

p. 15, No. 153. Add Ir. *ro-rigi a laim* 'he stretched forth his hand,' LU. 111b:
,, No. 155. Add Ir. *timt[h]ach* .i. *edach* 'dress' O'Dav. 119:
,, No. 156. W. *ffel* ' callidus,' 'astutus' may be referred to the root SPAL, with which Curtius (No. 558) connects φηλός:
p. 17, No. 168. With ἔ-λεγχος put also Ir. *lang* .i. *brég no mebul*, 'a lie or disgrace' H. 3. 18. p. 71, col. 2, and see Corm. s. v. gaileng:
,, No. 174. As the Ir. reduplicated preterites *ne-naig* 'lavit' *senaig* 'stillavit' point to roots NAG, SNAGH, more primeval than Skr. *nij*, Zend *çnigh*, so the Ir. reduplicated pret. *ro-leluig*, O'Curry's Manners and Customs, iii. 158, seems to point to a primeval root LAGH more primeval than LIGH : the 3d pl. *lelgatar* occurs in LU. 57b: *lelgatar* (.i. *lomraiset*) *immurro da ech conculainn inn-úir cor-rici na-clocha indegaid ind-féuir* ' Cúchulainn's two horses, however, licked (i. e., stript off) the mould as far as the stones behind the grass' :
p. 18, No. 189, *fine* here cited is cognate with A.S. *wine* 'amicus,' *wine-scip* 'sodalitium' :
,, No. 205. With στεροπή cf. the Ir. *srab*-tine 'lightning,' O'Dav. 118, and with τέρας, gen. τέραος, the Ir. *torathor* ' monstrum' :
,, No. 215. Stem πετα. Add πετασών, Lith. *petis* 'shoulder' and Ir. *aiss* 'back' ex *pat-ti : *acroch derg fria ais* ' his red cross on (lit. 'against') his back,' LU. 17a, *dambeir ria aiss tarsinn-uisci* 'he brings it on (lit. 'against') his back over the water,' LL. 184, b. 1 :
p. 19, line 1, after τάλαντον insert ' or talentum, *indraic* = integer' :
p. 20, No. 216. With σταῖς 'dough,' gen. σταιτ-ός, here cited cf. Ir. *táis*, Ml. 140b, or *taes* (ex *stait-to-*), W. *toes* :
,, No. 226. With στιγ-μή compare Ir. *tiug* or *tig* 'end' Corm. s. v. tigradus in *tiug*-beo 'survivor,' *tiug-fhlaith, tiug-láithe, tiug-lomrad, tiug-maine*, etc.
,, No. 226b. Corn. *stefenic* (gl. palatum), Br. *staffn*, from an Old-Celtic *stamana*, are certainly cognate with στόμα and Zend *çtaman* :
,, No. 230b. Root ray. Add Ir. *tagat* in the phrase *uaim thagut* (leg. *thagat*) 7 *latrand* ' furum latronumque spelunca,' LB. 11b:
,, No. 234. Other examples of hard *m* from *ngv* are probably *amm* 'time,' *tromm* 'heavy' (W. *trwm*, O.N. *thröngr*, Rhŷs) and *uimm* .i. *talam* 'terra' O'Cl., which may be cognate with Goth. *vagg-s* :

p. 21, No. 236. Add Ir. *tuillemain*, gl. perpendiculum, O'Mulc. Gl. No. 745 :
p. 23, No. 286. Add Ir. *is meisi* (ex *med-tio) .i. *is tualaing*, H. 3, 18, p. 636, col. 4 :
„ No. 298. Add Ir. *uidheach* .i. *ceolmar* 'musical,' O'Cl., and *onnar* .i. *aisnethar* 'is declared,' ib. :
p. 24, No. 301. The dental of the root (VADH) is unassibilated in Ir. *odhar* .i. *eisci no aonta* ut est *crenar odhar airlicthar** 'is bought, is pledged, is let on hire,' O'Dav. 108. A trace of the *v* is found in W. *gwystl* ex *ved-tla:
p. 25, No. 324. The W. *gwddi* 'hedging-bill' seems cognate :
„ No. 341. Two other examples of *pp* from *mp* are apparently *cepach* = *camp-us* (v. supra Nos. 56, 108) and *capp* 'a (light?) cart,' cognate with κεμπός· κοῦφος, κεμφάς· ἔλαφος. (So *cabriolet* is cognate with *capriole* and *caper* :)
„ No. 326. Add to the unnasalised forms *aidbse* (=*ad-bid-tia) 'a *yodling* chorus,' Corm. s. v. Adann, and to the nasalised *ad-bond* (gl. oda) LB. 89.
p. 27, No. 385. If, as I suspect, the Ir. *uathad* (*uathid?*) 'lunar month' [*hicoicid huathid* (gl. quinta luna) Z. 310, *in ochtmad uath*aid *rogenair Brigit*, LB. 62b : *in ochtmaid uath*aid *rogenair*, LB. 64a] has lost initial *p*, we may also connect it, as well as *úr*, with the root PŪ : cf. Skr. *pavamăna:*
p. 28, No. 387. Mr. Brash (*Journal of the Royal Historical and Archæological Association of Ireland*, July 1874, p. 170), states, as the result of a personal examination of the stone, that the marks hitherto read D and T do not belong to the Ogham part of the Killeen Cormac inscription, that they are in fact spurious. I would therefore now read this bilingual thus—

IVVENE[S] DRVVIDES
UVANOS AVEI SAHATTOS

and render the Celtic part of it ' (lapis) juvenis nepotis sapientiæ.' The gen. sg. *uvanos* is exactly the Skr. *yūnoḥ* or Indo-European *yuvanas*, gen. sg. of the *n*-stem *yuvan*. *Avei* is the gen. sg. of *aveos* 'nepos,' in Old-Irish *h-aue*. *Sahattos* is the gen. sg. of a stem in *nt*, cognate with Lat. *sapiens*. The expression *aveos sahattos* 'nepos sapientiæ ' (the gen. sg. of which here corresponds with that of *druis* ' soothsayer ') is comparable with *mac légind* ' filius legendi,' ' a student,' the Corn. *mab lyen* :
p. 29, No. 417. The Ir. verb substantive *bíu* Windisch here refers to the root *bhū*. But the older form *biuu* (leg. *bíuu*) Z. 491 seems = *jīvāmi*, βιόω, *vīvo* (No. 640), just as the adj. *bíu* = *jīva-s*, *vīvus*. Compare the frequent use in Plautus of *vivere* for *esse* (*Aulularia* ed. Wagner, v. 417). The 3d sg. future *bía* (= *vivet?*) is a dissyllable in Fél. Ep. 168 : so are its relative form *bías* ib. Mar. 13, Ep. 289, and its plural *bíait* Prol. 308. The 3d sg. conjunctive *bía* is also dissyllabic ib. Jan. 13. All this points to the loss of either *v* or *s* between vowels.

---
* See SM, iii. 492.

p. 31, No. 439. *nocht* .i. *nighi* 'washing,' O'Dav. 108:

p. 31, No. 454. ἡ-ρέμα. Add the Ir. root *REM* which occurs in the *ia*-stem *fuirmim* (ex **vo-rim-im*) : 3d sg. pres. *ni fuirmi nech dimiccim foir* 'no one contemns him,' lit. 'puts contempt on him,' 'causes contempt to rest on him' Z. 630, 1st sg. s-pret. *fo-rui-RM-i-us láim fair* 'I put a hand on him,' LU. 114b, 3d sg. *fo-rui-rim* 'posuit,' Ml. col. 1 (Goid². 32) = *fo-r-ruim*, Tir. 13, and (with substitution of infected *b* for infected *m*) *forruib*, Fiacc's h. 8: passive: *sén fuirmither dichmairc* 'a birdnet that is set without asking (leave),' O'Dav. 89, *do-fuirmheadh támh forra* 'a plague was inflicted upon them,' O'Cl. s. v. *fuirmeadh* :

,, No. 462. Add *mogh* .i. *mor* 'great' O'Dav. 106. The gen. pl. of *maglorg* 'a great club' ocurs in LU. 86a, *tri .lll. maglorg co fethnib iarind inalamaib* :

p. 32, No. 469. Add *mid-guallib*, *mid-lisi*, LU. 79, 108b:

,, No. 476. Add Ir. *maistred* 'churning,' gen. *maisterda*, LB. 63a, ex **MAT-t-red*, and cf. the Skr. *mathana-m* 'butterbereitung':

p. 32, No. 478. Add Ir. *mothar* .i. *dorcha* 'dark' O'Dav. 105:

p. 34, No. 502. Add Ir. *coisle* (= **con-selia*) 'trampling,' 'walking':

,, No. 529. With ἔριφος here cited, cf. Ir. *erb* 'roebuck' Corm. Tr. 68, *erboc*, *heirp* (gl. capra, gl. damma) Z. 67 :

p. 38, after line 6 insert *icht* 'proles' Corm. Tr. 98, ex **vip-ti*, **viptu?* Skr. VAP 'to sow,' perhaps ὀπυίω.

p. 40, No. 630. Add Ir. *cucan* (gl. penus) Z. 69, if it is not merely misspelt for *cucann*, *cucenn* :

,, No. 634. With *vadan* I would put the Irish law-terms *fuidir* (ex *VAD-ari-*) 'a stranger tenant, a fugitive or migratory husbandman,' (Cf. A.S. *wædla* 'vagabundus,' 'mendicus,' 'pauper'), and *fuidhrecht* 'desertion,' O'Don. Supp. :

,, No. 654. Ir. *fainnel* 'evagatio' may also come from *VAG*:

p 46, add the following:

> *donn* 'theft' (gen. *duinn*) O'Don. Supp., ex **dogno*, AS. *tacan*.
> *drenn* 'sorrow' ex **dreg-no*, Skr. *drāgh*, Goth. *trigon*.
> *tonn* 'skin' ex **(s)togno*, root STAG.

p. 58, l. 19. Add 'It may mean 'dashes' and be the 3d sg. pres. indic. act. of the verb of which *adcomcisset* (gl. offenderunt) Z. 269 is the 3d pl. s-preterite.'

p. 68. Add 'In para. 10 the verbs are historical presents, and would be more literally rendered by 'offers', 'kneels' and 'gives.''

p. 70, l. 7, after 'was' insert *for* 'a sealskin' read 'Ronchenn's' (Ronchenn was Brigit's subdeacon); l. 12 *add* 'l. 5 from bottom, *for* comna read co[e]mna 'protection.'

p. 74, note 6, *add* 'See M. Maspero's review of Lenormant's *Études accadiennes*, in the *Rev. Archéologique*, Septembre 1874, pp. 213—216, and Sayce's *Principles* of *Comparative Philology* (London 1874) pp. 22, 140, 141.

INDEX.

	Page.
accent, its effect on liquids	19n
accusative of time	26
Aided Echach maic Máireda, Mr. Crowe's edition of,	55
Amra Choluimbchille 10, 23, 35, 37, 39; Mr. Crowe's edition of, 35, 60,	61
Amra Chonroi	39
ant-stems	5
Archæologia Cambrensis	62
article, Irish	48, 80
Ascoli, prof., his *Corsi* cited, 21; his *Archivio glottologico*	36
assibilation	24
assimilation of *t* to *l*, 19, of *s* to *r*, 33, 34, of *s* to *t*, 30; of *g* to *n*, 2, 40, 46, 85; of *n* to *m*	42
Aufrecht, prof., cited	15
augury	7
Aulularia	84
Auxilius	73
aw from *ag*, 17; from *ám*	33
b written for *v*, 5; from *p*, 12; from *g*, 43; from *gv*, 40; perhaps from *sm*, 32; provected to *p*, 29; lost before a liquid	31
Badb	22, 67
Benfey, prof.	39, 82, 83
Benna Boirche	69
birds' names	16
bl from *ml*, 49; from *vl*	34
Book of Kells, charter in, cited	68
Book of Leinster cited	41, 66
Book of St. Chad	62
Bopp	27n, 47
br from *vr*	11, 14, 15, 17, 33, 41
Bradshaw, Mr.,	19, 62n, 72, 73
Bréal, M.	46n
Brigit, St.	84
British languages	1
Broccán's hymn	6
Bruden da Derga cited	66
Bühler, dr.	3n

	Page.
c from *p* in loanwords, 7; from *ng*	16, 17
causatives in *igim*	53
ch in Welsh from *nc*, 9; from *cc*	49
Christ, the four quarters of the earth cleansed by parts of body of, 67; born twice	71
Chronicon Scotorum	82
civilisation, false theories of Irish,	74
collectives in *iá*, 43; in *-rad*	78
Columba	61
Connaught	66
Conn's part	61
consonantal stems,	47
contractions, expansions of, 61, 62,	80
Cooper, C. P., his *Report on the Foedera*	62
Cormac	45n, 47, 6
Corssen, prof., cited	3n, 16
cranes	3
Crith Gablach	5n, 58
Crowe, Mr.,	1, 2, 3, 9, 35n, 54 to 62, 60, 78
ct, *cht*, from *gt*, 15; from *pt*	28, 82
Cúchulainn,	3, 28, 41n, 57, 66, 75
Curtius, professor	20, 45
Cynddelw	45n
d between vowels in Mod. Welsh,	1
d from *j* in Welsh	43
Daghda, the,	66
Davies, *Dictionarium* (1632)	29
dd in Mod. Welsh	1
Devil's knees	71
Diefenbach, *Origg. Eur.* cited 3n, 6, 8, 27n, 32,	38
diminutives in *-án*, 38; in *-natan*, 59; in *-sech*	78
dissimilation	24
dittography	57
dotted *f*	19
druids	43, 52, 84

	Page.
Ducange cited ... 7, 12,	19
dunghill in doorway of palace ...	74
Ebel, prof., referred to, 4, 7, 17, 18, 19, 21n,	46
Echtra Condla Cáin, Mr. Crowe's edition of, ...	58
Elene cited	67
Esus	39
eu from *ag*	17
f prosthetic, 6, 34; from *sp*, 16, 40; dotted	19
facsimiles of Celtic texts ...	62
Félire Oengusso cited, 4, 9, 10, 16, 23,	37
Fiacc's hymn, ... 5, 7, 35,	78n
Fick cited, 3, 4, 6, 8, 10, 17, 18, 23, 24, 32, 38, 39,	44
fidchell	79
Firbolg	79
Fomoire ... 66,	67
future, reduplicated, 65, 80; in *b*, 81, in *s*, 58,	78
g for *c* in anlaut, 7, 82; lost between vowels, 13; vocalised, 13; lost before *l*, 14; lost before *r*, 16; lost before *n*, 14; lost from *gl* ...	14
gh for *ch*	53
glosses, Old-British, 72; Old-Irish	73
glossographers, Irish ...	96n
Glück, C. W., cited 6, 9, 10, 16, 17, 81, 24,	32
Goidelica, 2nd ed., corrected 2,	67
Góidil	66
Græco-italo-celtic unity ...	49
grain, names for, ...	33
Grassmann, *Wörterbuch*, cited ...	13
Grein	10
Grimm, J. ... 9n,	36
guards of chiefs	81
gv from *g*	43
h after fem. possessive pronoun...	51
Hennessy, Mr. ... 65,	66
Hesychius cited ... 9,	13
Homeric forms ... 15,	78
Horace quoted	29

	Page.
i from *a* before a liquid and another consonant ...	14
infixed pronouns 76, 77,	78
irrational vowels	10
Isserninus	73
jargon of Vul-Soana ...	36
Keating cited	49
Kemble, J.M.	67
Kern	43
Killeen Cormac inscription ...	84
knees, Devil's	71
l from *tl*, 21; vocalised before *t* in Breton	27n
lch from *lg* in Breton ...	28
Lebar Brecc cited, 58, 84; facsimile of	64
Lebar na huidre cited, 4, 16, 50, 68, 80; facsimile of, ...	64
Legal terms, *adh*, 23; *aicc, aicce*, 26; *band*, 25; *cin*, 10; *dir, dire*, 25; *faesam*, 79; *fine*, 83; *fuidir*, 85; *geilfine*, 18; *iúgshuide*, 15, 82; *locht*, 17; *oin*, 31; *odhar*, 84, *óis*, 42; *recht*, 15; *serbh*, 20; *taile*, 21; *uain*	31
leviathan	58
Lhuyd, *Archæologia Britannica* ...	8
Liber Armachanus cited 4, 5, 36n,	42
liquids in position doubled ...	13n
ll from *tl*	19
loanwords in Irish ... 7, 26,	19
locative of *sa*	38
louse	35
Lucretius ... 3,	38
m from *n* before *m*, 42; lost before *t*	21
Mac Lonán cited	22
Magonius	36n
male, parturition by a ...	71
Manx, loss of initial *n* in ...	31n
Mars, pigs sacrificed to ...	36
Matóc	72
mb, mm from *ngv* ... 20, 21,	83
medials hardened by a following spiritus asper	2

	Page.
Mesca Ulad	4
metathesis of r ... 11,	41
Molling, St.	70
moon	84
Mór-Rigan, wife of Daghda ...	66
music and musical instruments, aidbse, 84; trirech, 15; fonn, 23; odh, 27; cor, ceartán, 82; timpán	23
mythology (see Esus Succetus) ...	5
ṇ (lingual) in Sanskrit ...	3
n lost before l, 3; lost before t, 30; transported, 9; in anlaut lost...	31
nasalisation	15
Nemaind	67
nd from nt in loanwords ...	19
nh = nn	27
Nigra, Chevalier, cited or referred to, 7, 11, 14n, 36, 41,	70
nn from gn ... 9, 10, 46,	85
nt, treatment of, 18, 19; from nst	44
O'Clery's Glossary, 6, 7, 14, 31, 33, 34n, 38, 39, 68,	69
O'Curry, his Manners and Customs cited, 8, 14, 25, 41, 73, 74, 75, 81,	83
O'Davoren, cited 5, 7, 20, 44, 49, 82,	84
O'Donovan cited ... 7, 11,	47
ogham inscriptions 28, 38n, 53,	84
O'Grady, Mr.	65
Old British glosses ... 31, 40, 72,	73
O'Mahony, Professor ...	65
O'Mulconry's Glossary ...	16
Oscan words ... 48,	65n
O'Reilly's Dictionary 2, 47, 48, 49, 73,	81
oven	45
p in Celtic, 2: in Irish, (paisiu, popp,) 25n, 82, 84; in loanwords sunk to b, 12; lost in anlaut, 12, 26, 84; from b, 29; from mb, 34, 35; from mp, 82; from kv, 40, 42; from sv	50
pallium 'veil'	7
parasitic sounds	42
Parker Collection No. 279, 24,	73
parturition by a male ...	71

	Page.
Patrick, St. ... 35, 36,	73
patronymics	16
Philippe de Thaun	71
Pictet, M., cited ... 15, 34, 39,	82
pigs sacrificed to Mars ...	36
pillar-stone	66
Pliny, Hist. Nat., emendation of,	33
polysynthesis	74n
Pott, professor, cited ...	44
pp from mb, 25; from mp, 25,	84
Preller, Römische Mythologie ...	36
preterites formed by prefixing ro	3
pronouns, infixed 76, 77, 78, suffixed, ...	55
provection of b to p	29
proverb	41n
pt becomes ct ... 28,	85
πτ from σπ	28
Pughe	45n
r not lost in Celtic, 49; metathesis of ... 11,	41
rc from rg	14
rch from rg	28
reduplicated future, 65, 80; s-future, 78; preterite 80,	83
Reeves, Dr., his Columba 5, 8, his Codex Maelbrigte	44n
Rhŷs, Mr., cited 6, 8, 10, 17, 23, 28, 34, 38,	43
river-names, Celtic ... 19, 32, 34,	39
ropes of slaughter	67
Royal Irish Academy, Proceedings of, 58, facsimiles published by, 63,	64
rr from rs ... 33,	34
Rumann cited	14n
s a determinative, 22; from dt, 23; from t-t 83; lost in anlaut, 23, 24; prosthetic, 26; assimilated to r, 33, 34; assimilated to t, 30; loss of, 42; loss of final, 48; lost between vowels	49
Salamon and Saturn cited ...	67
Sanctáin	72
satirist	7
sc for cs, 15: ex dc ... 24,	45

	Page.
Scéla na Esérge, Mr. Crowe's edition of,	54
Schmidt, Johannes	8, 43, 45
Senchas Mór cited	13, 14n
Shaw	47
Siaburcharpat Conculainn, Mr. Crowe's edition of,	55, 56, 57, 78
Siegfried cited	6, 18, 19, 45
sneezing	20
sp sometimes loses initial *s* in Welsh, 12; becomes *f*	16
spear	78
spindle	79
ss from *st*	ib.
St. Gall verses	14, 15
st loses *t*, 20: in inlaut sometimes becomes *tt*, 30; in anlaut	50
stems in *-men*, 5, 45; in *-ant*, 5; in *t*	62
str in inlaut loses *s* in Irish, *st* in Welsh	12
Succetus	36
suffix *-maoid*	52
suffixed pronouns	55
Sullivan, Dr., his translation of part of the Táin, 75, 76; his glossarial index	76 to 81

	Page.
sv how treated in Irish	28
Synodus Patricii, etc.	73
Táin bó Cualnge	75, 76
Táin bó Fráich, 9, 10, 13, 41; Mr. Crowe's edition of,	58, 59
tenues weakened	42
Tethra	66n
th (W. *t*) from *nd*	51
Thorpe, *Anglo-Saxon Homilies*	67
Tírechán's annotations	19, 78n
Tochmarc Becc-fola	15
tr in Mod.-Welsh from *dr*	4n
transported *n*	9, 80
Tripartite Life of S. Patrick, cited	30n
tt (W. *th*) from *st*	30
ua from *ue*, 5; from *uo*	8
v lost in anlaut, 37, 38; *b* written for,	5
Whiterne	72
Windisch, prof.,	1, 7, 20, 23, 36, 52, 67, 70, 71n
y sometimes preserved in Irish	39
Zeuss, 46, his *Grammatica Celtica* corrected	3, 62, 72, 73
zl, *zr* in Middle-Breton	4n

GREEK INDEX.

	Page.		Page.		Page.
r. ἀγκ, ἀγκών	6	ἅρπη	3n	r. δεμ, δέμω	22
ἄγνυμι	40, 46	ἀρχός	16	δείξει	1
ἄγος	12, 13	ἄστυ	19	δεξιός	22
ἀγών	12	ἄτρακτος	79	r. δερ, δίρω	ib.
ἄεθλον	24	ἄτρεγκτος	9	δίεμαι	8
ἀϊές	37	αὔξω	37	δίεσθαι	23
ἀΐθω	24	rr. ἀχ, ἀγχ, ἄχομαι,		r. δικ	6
αἴξ	13	ἄγχω	16	δῖος	23
ἀκούειν, ἀκουστός	82	ἄω	37	διπλοῦς	45
r. ἀκ, ἄκρος, ἄκρις		r. βα, ἔβην	40	r. δο, δίδωμι	23
	6, 57	βαμβαλίζω	35	δοκέω	6
ἄκχος	6	βδέσμα	30	δρῦς	52
r. ἀλ, ἄναλτος	34	βδόλος	ib.	δύνω, δύω	24
r. ἀλθ, ἄλθομαι	24	βιόω	84	ἔαρ	37
ἀλίη	34	βίοτος	40	ἔγχελυς	17
r. ἀλκ, ἀρκ, ἀλκή,		βλάστη	41	r. ἐξ, εἴω	23
ἀρκέω	6	βοή, βοάω	40	r. ἐδ, ἕδος	ib.
ἄλληκτος	15	βόμβος	35	εἴλω	41
ἅλλομαι	41	βομβυλίς	28	εἴργνυμι	14
ἄλλος	34	r. βορ, βορά	40	εἶρος	33
ἅλς	41	βραδύς	67	ἐκεῖ	40
ἅμα	31	βρέχω	17	ἔλαφος	34
ἀμάω	ib.	βρόγχος	43	ἐλέγχω, ἔλεγχος 17, 83
ἀμέλγω	49	γάλα	13	Ἕλλη	41
ἀμνός	38	γένυς	29	ἐλύω	34
ἀμφήρης	33	γέρανος	3, 13	r. ἐνεκ, ἠνέχθην	29
ἀμφί	28	γέρων	13	ἐνί	ib.
ἀνά	29	γέστρα	12	ἔνος	ib.
ἀνεμός	ib.	γῆρυς	13, 50	ἐνώπια	43n
ἀνήρ	ib.	γλαυκύς	14	ἐξ	49
ἄνθος	42	γλύφω	ib.	ἔξ	37
ἀντί	18	γνωτός	ib.	r. ἐπ, ἔπος	39
ἄξων	37	γοργών	43	ἐπισμυγερός	42
ἀπλόος	45	γῦρος	ib.	ἔπω	39
ἀπολλῆξαι	15	r. δα, δέδαεν	22	r. ἐρ	33
ἄρακος	33	δάκρω	51	ἔργον	14
ἅρις	43	δαρθάνω	22	ἐρείκη	43

— 91 —

	Page.		Page.		Page.
ἐρείκω	.. 43	καινός	... 9	κρύκη	... 7
ἐρεύγω	... 15	καίνω	... 10	κρόμυον	... 44
ἔριφος	... 85	κάκκη	... 6	κρύος	... 10
ἕρπω	25	r. καλ, καλιά	7	κτείνω	... ib.
r. ἐρυθ, ἐρεύθω	... 24	καλέω	... 6	κύαθος	... ib.
ἐτεός	... 19	κάμινος	... 45	κύκνος	... 16
ἔτι	... ib.	κάπρος	... 7	κυλίω	... 11
εὐπλεκής	... 12	καρπάλιμος	.. ib.	r. κυρ, κυρτός	... 10
εὗρον	... 43	κείρω	... 8	κῶνος	... 11
εὐρύς	... 33	κείω	... ib.	κώπη	... 7
ἔχις	17	κέκαδον	... 23	λάγνος	... 46
ζειά	... 43	κέλευθος	... 8	r. λακ, ἔλακον	... 11
r. ζυγ	... 15	κέλης	... ib.	λάκος	... ib.
ἥδομαι	... 3	κεμπός	... 84	λαμβάνω	25, 35
ἡδύς	... 22	κεμφάς	... ib.	λάστη	... 30
ἠίθεος	43	κενεός	8	λαχαίνω	... 44
ἡμι-	... 31	κεντέω	... 44	λείπω	... 34
ἥν	.. 43	κέντρον	... ib.	r. λεχ, λέχος	... 17
ἠρέμα	... 84	κέρας	... 8	λήγω	... 15
θάλος	.. 49	κέρκος	... 44	λιμός	... 35
r. θε, τίθημι	24, 52	κήδω	... 23	r. λιχ, λείχω	... 17
r. θερ, θέρος	27, 40	κῆλον	8	λόγχη	... 44
θέω	... 24	κῆπος	... 82	λοξός	15, 35
θήγω	... ib.	Κήρ, κηραίνω	... 8	λούω	... ib.
θίς	... ib.	κίρκος	... 11	λύγξ	... ib.
θολός, θολερός	... 44	κίω	... 8	λύκος	... 11
θοός	... 24	κλάδος	... 44	λῦμα	... 35
θρασύς	24, 30, 49	κλίνω	... 9	r. λυπ, λυπρός	... 25
r. θρε, θρέομαι	... 25	r. κλυ, κλύω	... 51	λύω	... 35
θρήσασθαι	... ib.	κλύζω	... 9	r. ᾿μαθ, ἔμαθον	... 30
r. θυ, θύω	... ib.	κλυτός	... ib.	μακρός	... 11
θυγατήρ	... 49	κνήμη	... 44	r. μαρ, μάρτυρ	... 32
θύρα	... 25	κόα	... 9	μαστός	... 44
r. ἰ, ἱμάς	... 38	κόγκος	... ib.	μάταιος	... ib.
ἰάομαι	... 38	κοίτη	... 8	r. μαχ, μάχομαι	... 31
r. ἰς, ἰότης	... 39	κόκκυξ	... 9	r. με, μέτρον	... ib.
ἴσος	... 36	κοννέω	... ib.	μέγας	... ib.
ἵστημι	... 20	κόραξ	... ib.	μέλας	... 35
ἰσχνός	... 44	κόρδαξ	.. 10	r. μελγ	... 15
ἰταλός	19	κρέας	... ib.	μέμφομαι	... 44
ἰτέα	... 38	κρίνω	... ib.	r. μερ, μέρμηρα	32

	Page.		Page.		Page.
μέσσος	... ib.	ὀφρύς	... 28	πτάρνυμαι	.. 28
μήδεα	... 3	ὄχος	... 17	πτύρω	... ib.
μήτηρ	... 32	πιίω	... 2	πύθω	... 27
μῆχος	... ib.	πιωνία	... 16	πῦρ	... ib.
μίσγω	... 4	παλάμη	... 26	πυρός	... ib.
μόθος	... 32	πάσσαλος	ib.	r. πω, πῶμα	... ib.
μόρον	... 44	πατέομαι	... ib.	πῶλος	... ib.
μῦθος	... 32	r. παν, παύω	ib.	ῥάκος	... 11
μυκτήρ	... 11	πέλας, πελάζω	... 27	ῥηγεύς	... 15
μύρμος	... 32	πέλεκκον	2, 12	ῥήγνυμι	38, 41
ναίω	... 30	πελιτνός	... 26	ῥῆμα	... 49
ναῦς	... ib.	πέλλα	... ib.	ῥήτρα	11, 33
νέκυς	... 11	πελός	... ib.	ῥοφέω	... 29
r. νεμ, νέμω	... 30	r. πενθ, πενθερός,		ῥύμα	... 45
νεφρός	... 31	πεῖσμα	4, 25	r. σα, σάω	... 36
r. νυ, νέω	... ib.	πέος	... 26	σέλας	... 41
ὀδούς	51	πεπτός	... 40	σεμνός	... 38
ὄζος	... 30	περαῖος	... 42	r. σεπ, ἕσπετε	... 40
r. ὀθ, ὠθέω	... 25	περάω, περήσω	... 26	σιωπή	... 28
ὀθόνη	... 44	πέρκος	... ib.	σκάλλω	... 42
ὄις	... 38	πέρυσι	... ib.	σκαμβός	... 45
ὀλιβρός	35	πετασών	... 83	σκαπ, σκάπυω	... 82
ὄμβρος	... 32	πέτομαι	... 19	st. σκαρτ (σκώρ)	... 12
ὀμός	... 53	πέτρα	... 45	r. σκεπ, σκέπτομαι	ib.
ὀμφαλός	... 49	πεύκη	... 12	σκόλοψ	4
ὀνίνημι	... 31	πήγνυμι	... 26	σκομβρίσαι	... 35
ὄνυξ	... ib.	r. πι, πίνω	... 27	σκύρδαξ	... 10
ὀπ, ὄμμα	... 39	r. πικ, πικρός	... 12	σμαρκόν	... 32
ὀπός	... ib.	πίπτω	... 19	σμικρός	... ib.
r. ὀρ, ὄρνυμι	... 33	πίων	... 27	σμινύη	... 42
ὁράω	... ib.	r. πλα, πίμπλημι	... ib.	σμύχω	... ib.
ὀργή	... 15	r. πλακ	... 12	r. συ, νέω, νάω	... 31
ὀρέγω	... ib.	πλέκτη	... ib.	σόβη	... 36
ὀρμή	... 34	πλίνθος	... 51	r. σπαρ, σπαίρω	... 28
ὄρνις	... ib.	πλοῦτος	... 27	σπαργή	... 45
ὄῤῥος	... ib.	r. πο, πότος	... ib.	σπέρχομαι	... 17
ὀρφανός	... 28	πολλός	.. 45	σπλήν	... 16
ὄρχις	... 45	πολύς	... 4	σταῖς	... 83
οὐλή	36	πορθμός	... 26	r. στεγ, στεγνόω	... 15
οὖρον	34	r. πρη, πίμπρημι	... 27	στείχω	... 50
οὐτάω	... 45	προτί	... ib.	στερεύς	... 20

		Page.			Page.			Page.
στερέω	..	ib.	τῖλος	...	45	φηλός	...	83
σ:εροπή	...	83	τίτθος	...	24	φημί	...	29
στίγμα	...	20	τλητός	...	21	r. φλα, ἐκφλαίνω	...	ib.
στιγμή		83	τολμάω	...	ib.	φλάω	...	41
στόμα	...	ib.	τονθορυγέω	...	25	φρακ	...	29
r. συ, κασπύω	...	36	τόξον	...	21	φράτηρ	...	ib.
σῦς	...	ib.	τρέπω	...	40	φρέαρ	...	ib.
r. σφαλ, σφάλλω	...	ib.	r. τρεχ, τρέχω	...	17	r. φυ, φύω	...	ib.
σφάραγος	...	16	Τριτογένεια	...	46	φῦσα	...	40
σφίγγω		ib.	τρόχος	...	17			
r. ταγ, τεταγών	..	83	τύλη, τύλος	...	21	χάλιξ	...	45
ταχύς	...	18	τυφλός	..	22	χαλκός	...	18
τέγος	...	1	ὑγρύς	...	16	χείρ	...	ib.
τείρω	...	21	ὕδω	...	23	χλωρός	...	ib.
τεῖχος	...	46	ὕδωρ	...	24	χρεμίζω	...	bi.
r. τελ, ταλ, τλῆναι,			ὕει, ὑετός	...	39	χρέμπτομαι	...	45
τάλας	...	21	υἱός	...	ib.	χρέμψις		ib.
τέλος	...	ib.	ὑπαί	...	28	χρίω, χρῖμα	...	18
τέμνω	...	ib.	ὑπηρετεῖν	...	33	χρόμη	...	ib.
τέρας	...	83	ὑπό	28,	33	χρόνος	...	ib.
τέτραξ	...	21	ὑποχείριος	...	18			
τέττα	...	ib.	ὑσμῖν	..	39	ὠθέω	..	25
τητάω	...	45	φαλλός	...	45	ὦνος	...	31
τίκτω	...	21	r. φεν, ἔπεφνον		29	ὠτειλή	...	45

LATIN INDEX.

[*Low Latin in brackets.*]

	Page.		Page.		Page.
adspectus	... 12	conspectus	... 12	grandis	... 3n
agmen	... 13	consternare	... 28	grando	... 51
agnus	... 38	convicium	... 39	grus	... 3
alius	... 52	corvus	... 9	helvus	... 18
amita	... 65	coquus	... 40	heri	... ib.
anguis	... 17	cuculus	... 9	hir	... ib.
augustia	... 16	culex	... 8	hirudo	... ib.
ante	18, 19	cuneus	... 11		
antiæ	... ib.	curtus	... 8	idus	... 24
ănus	... 6	[curuca]	... ib.	imber	... 32
aqua	... 40	decem	... 49	ind-	... 19
arduus	... 24	dens	... 51	indago	... 12
argentum	... 13	descisco	... 8	integer	... 83
audio	37	donum	... 23	inter	... 29
avidus	ib.	dormio	... 22	interpretor	... 2
				iuvitare	... 39
[besco]	72	edo	23	jous, jus	... 83
caco	... 49	en	... 43	lacero	... 51
cado	... 23	esca	... 24	lacryma	... 6
callis	8, 82	examen	... 13	[lacto]	... 72
camisia	... 21-	fama	... 33n	lancea	... 44
campus	82, 84	fascis	... 25	languidus	... 15
cano	... 7	femina	... 29	larva	... 6
caper	7, 84	fides	... 26	laurus	... ib.
caro	... 10	flavus	... 18	laxus	15, 35
castrum	... 12	foretus	... 21	lex	... 25n
caucus	... 10	forma	... 25	liber, libet	... 35
[cayum]	... 8	formus	27	ligo	... 44
cedo	... 23	frango	... 41	ligula, lingula	... 17
celer	... 8	frendo	... 18	linguo	... 34
cella	... 7	futuo	... 29	liqueo	... 34
celo	... ib.	gallus	... 16	liquor	... ib.
censeo, censor	... 44	genista	... 30	loquor	... 11
ciconia	... 16	genitor	... 52	lumbricus	... 35
cio	... 8	glabro	... 14	lumen, luna	... 19n
cis, citra	... 40	gladius	... 10	luscinia	... 16
clavis	... 8	glis	14. 35	luxus	... 35
clino	... 9	glubo	... 14	macte	... 11
cluo	... 51	gnavus	... ib.	magnus	... 46
colo	... 8	graculus	... 16		

	Page.		Page.		Page.
mando	... 44	prudens	... 25	sucula	... 81
manuor	... 30	pusio, pusiola	... 27n	sucus	... 39
manus	... 31	pustula	16, 40	tabes	... 20
metior	... 3	quæro	... 51	talentum	19, 83
mille	... 50	quies	8	/tata/	... 22
minor	... 53	quisquiliae	4	templum	... 20
mollis	... 67	rapio	... 3	tempus	... ib.
morum	... 44	rigo	11, 17	terebrum	... 21
mungo	... 11	rota	... 33	tergo	... 36
mutire	... 32	ructo	15	tinguo	... 21
natrix	... 31	rumen, Rumo	5	tintino	... 7
nefrones	... ib.	sapiens	... 84	tollo	... 21
nidus	... 30	satis, satur	... 37	torqueo	... 40
no	... 31	scio	... 8	trans	... 53
notus	... 14	scrutinium	... 27	truncus	... 9
oculus	... 39	sedeo	23	tuli	... 21
offendimentum	... 25	sedulus	... ib.	turgeo	... 44
offendix	... ib.	semen	... 36	umbilicus	... 49
ovis	... 38	serenus	... 41	unguen	... 21
palma	... 26	sericus, sericeus	... 57	unguis	... 49
pallium	... 7	serpens	... 25	uxor	... 17
pampinus	... 25	sic	... 38	vacillo	... 40
pastinum	... 40	similis	... 53	vado	... ib.
pastio	... 26	simitu, simul	... 21	vas	... 24
pax	... 12	sisto	... 20	[vassus]	... 19
penis	... 26	sopio	... 28	vastus	... 30
pexa	... 81	sorbeo	... 29	vellus	33, 38
piper	... 26	spargo	... 28	ventus	... 37
pirum	... 2	sparus	... 12	vernum	... 38
pix	... 12	sphæra	... 50	versus	... 4n
planca	... 9	splen	... 16	vesica	... 3
plico	... 12	splendens	... 25	vesper	... 38
polleo, pollex	... 45	stamen	... 20	vestitus	30, 38
pollen	... 12	stella	... 3	vir	... 52
poto	... 27	sternuo	... 28	vivax	... 40
præda	... 26	sto	... 20	vivo, vivus	... 84
prologus	... 12	stıuo	... 81	volnus	... 36
prospectus	... ib.	suavis	... 22	voxor	... 17

SANSCRIT INDEX.

	Page.		Page.		Page.
aja	13	tapu	68	ratha	33
anila	48	tul	21	rāj	48
anti	18	tṛtīya	43n	ruh	48, 50
andbas	42	tolayāmi	21	langh	17
ap	40	darh	28n	liṅga	35
abhra	32	dahā ni	52	vaksh	37, 52
abhyava	72	dīyate, dedīya	8	vadāmi	23, 50, 52
amasa	48	debī	46	vadhu	43
ambhṛṇa	32	dvāra, dvāraka	25	vande	23
açmanta	45	dhariman	ib.	var	41
astā	30	dharma	ib.	varīyas	26, 33
asya	51	dhṛsh, dhṛshṭa, 24, 30,	49	valg	11, 17, 21
āvasāmi	48	nad	51	vasta	16, 38
āvis	ib.	nānad	ib.	vastra	12, 67
āçu	6	nij	83	vāñchā	37
āsad	23	pac	26	vāta	ib.
icha	46	para	2	vāri	34
indu	24	paraçu	ib.	vishu	36
ish, ishṭa	39	palita	26	vraṇa	ib.
ulkā	38n	pasas	ib.	çaṅkha	9
kaṭu	7	prach	49	çākhā	82
kara 'hand'	10	prati	27	çūnya	8
karaka 'water-pot'	8	prīṇāmi	2	çru	51
kūrd	10	prush, plush	27	çvas	44
koça	10	brū	33, 49	satya	19
kravya	52	bhanajmi	41	sud	23, 53
krī	ib.	bhavishyati	49	saduṇan	23
gaṇḍa	3	bhās	47	sabhā	31
gavyā	43n	maṅh	58	sama	53
grāvan	13	maghavan	36	sarpa	25
ghur (ghṛ)	18	mathana	85	sasya	33
gharma	52	mathāmi	32	sāti	53
ghṛta	18	mah	53	sthā	50
cetar	19	mṛd	67	sphurj	16, 45
ceshṭ	51	yava	43	smayati	50
jambha	35	yukta, yukti	83	svar	ib.
jala	13	yuj	15, 83	hari	18
jīvaka	48	yudhma	39	hasta	30
jīvāni	84	yuvan	84	hrād	50, 51
takn	18	yūsh	ib.		

— 97 —

GERMANIC INDEX.

	Page.		Page.		Page.
ahva	... 40	heáwan	... 98	skin	... 9
ammâ, amme	... 65	heiva	... 8	slac	... 15
arjan	... 43n	hëlan	... 7	slahan	... 8
ars	... 34	hell	... 6	smart	... 32
auhsa	17, 38	hjal	... ib.	smeleu, smell	... ib.
banna, bannan	... 29	hlaunasverdh	... 28n	smëru	... ib.
beschlafen	... 22	hlutrs	... 9	smîtan	... ib.
blâr	... 18	hnjôdha	... 44	smoulder	... ib.
brâwa	... 29	holt	... 44	smugall	... ib.
brikan	... 41	hraiv	... 10	sôth	... 19
brunna	... 29	hrêdher	... 98	spalt	... 27n
darn	... 22	hugs	... 9	spalten	... 16
daubs	... ib.	hvan	... 40	spër	... 12
denegan	... 24	hvôsta	... 42n	spjôt	... 16
dengja	... ib.	kehren	... 38	sprauto	12, 16
digju	... 21	kelikn	... 7	sprëcan	... 16
dökkr	... 22	cild	... 98	spýta	... ib.
dûmo	... 38n	kirru	... 50	stæger	... 50
dvals	... 44	cordhor	... 38	strand	... 51
egala	... 18	kus	... 53	strauja	... 20
endi	... 19	limber	... 34	svistar	... 12
fàh	... 12	magath	... 53	tacan	... 85
fairnis	... 26	mâgr	... 32	tahja	... 51
fal	... 2	magus	... 53	taihsva	... 22
fallan	... 36	mast	... 30	thairh	... 53
falo	... 77n	mastiff	... ib.	thömb	... 20
far	... 34	mavei	... 53	thumb	... 38n
filu	... 4	megs	... 32	tîd	... 8
fintha	... 19	minna	... 30	tîmi, tîma	... ib.
flint	... 51	missa	... 10n	trauan	... 43n
fraliusan	... 35	naut	... 39n	triggvs	... 52
frathi	... 2	nicro	... 31	trigon	... 85
frijôn	... ib.	oddr	... 30	tunthus	... 51
fug	... 83	ord	... ib.	vadi	... 24
fûls	... 27	ort	... ib.	vaggs	... 83
gairnja	... 52	paltry, palt	... 27n	vanta	... 38n
gandra	... 3n	riemen	... 45	varmjan	... 27
gannet	... ib.	rodjan	... 50	verlieren	... 35
ganta	... 3	rögn	... 23	wædla	... 65
ganzo	... 3n	rust	... 30	walahraban	... 9n
gimahhâ	... 32	sceadhan	... 26	wara	... 37
glaggvus	... 14	schaden	... ib.	wine, winescip	... 83
gleáw	... ib.	scinno	... 10	wreck	... 14
greát	... 3n	seths	... 53	wunsc, wish	37, 47
grêtan	50, 51	sibja	... 31	yester-day	... 18
hamo, hemidi	... 21	skarpr, skarph	... 12	zeit	... 8
hausjan	... 82	skathjan	... 26	zûwen	... 24

CORRIGENDA.

p. 2, lines 11 and 14 : it is right to say that W. *prid* may be just as well referred to the root *KR1* (Beitr. viii. 38) that *pryder* may be = A. S. *hrê-dher* 'animus,' 'pectus,' 'gremium,' Ettm. 507, and that *pwyo* (like Ir. *coach* 'skirmish' Corm. Tr. 46, *neph- choachtae* gl. imbellem, Ml. 126c) may come from a root *RU*, whence the Lith. *kovā* 'kampf,' Fick[2] 351, AS. *heáwan*, Mod. Eng. *hew*:

ll. 31 and 32. This sheet was unfortunately printed off before I received Windisch's paper *Die Celtischen vergleichungen in den Grundzügen der Griechischen Etymologie*. He is not guilty of introducing into Curtius' book *capat*, *aidhe* and *bar*, which, it appears, were in its third edition ; and with admirable candour and temper he admits the justice of most of my corrections :

p. 7, W. *pall* is rather from *palla* :

p. 11, No. 86, l. 1, *omit* 'From' and 'a reduplicated form'; *omit* l. 2. In l. 3 *omit* 'With the same root':

p. 15, l. 6, for [*n-óibda*] read [*nar-ross*] :

„ ll. 7, 8, *read* vere, propter meum Dominum epuli, bene scribo ad symphoniam silvularum :

p. 18, l. 5. As the primary meaning of *gillae* is 'lad,' I would now connect it with AS. *cild* 'puer' :

p. 25, No. 338, l. 3, read *prud(ens)* ; note *b*, *for* 'is probably,' *read* 'can hardly be' :

p. 30, l. 27, for *dṛshta* read *dhṛshṭa* :

p. 32, last line, *read* ambhṛṇa :

p. 37, l. 3 from bottom, for *vañcha* read *vāñchā* :

p. 39, l. 16, for *idnu* read *idnae* :

p. 42, l. 8 from bottom, for *sód* read *imb-sód* :

p. 43, l. 3 from bottom, *read* Verwantschaftsverhältnisse :

p. 44, l. 12, for *sva-n-sta* read *sva-n-s-ta* ; l. 13, *for* Gründz. *read* Grundz. ; l. 33, *for* '58' *read* '5b' :

p. 46, l. 17, for **ligno* read **ligni* :

p. 47, l. 8 from bottom, for *vañchā* read *vāñchā* :

p. 48, l. 8, for *lochet* read *lóchet* :

p. 51, l. 3, for *chesht* read '*cesht* :

p. 56, last line but one, *for* 'accurary' *read* 'accuracy' :

p. 70, l. 7, *for* 'l. 9,' *read* 'l. 91' :

p. 74, l. 19, *for* 'with' *read* 'and' :

p. 77, No. 8, *as-at-lṭé* may also be regarded as a verb compounded with two prepositions (Z. 882), *as* and *at* (Z. 869). If so, it should be rendered 'flees forth' :

„ l. 2 from bottom, *for* '58' '67' '68' *read* '55' '66' '67' :

p. 96, col. 2, *for* jnij *read* nij.

www.ingramcontent.com/pod-product-compliance
Lightning Source LLC
Chambersburg PA
CBHW020154170426
43199CB00010B/1040